The Comp
of Insuran

The Consumer' Guide to
Insuring Your Life, Health,
Property, and Income

Revised Edition

The Complete Book of Insurance

The Consumer's Guide to Insuring Your Life, Health, Property, and Income

BEN G. BALDWIN

IRWIN
Professional Publishing®
Chicago • London • Singapore

Times Mirror
Higher Education Group

Library of Congress Cataloging-in-Publication Data

Baldwin, Ben G.
    The complete book of insurance: the consumer's guide
to insuring your life, health, property, and income/Ben G.
Baldwin.—Rev.
ed.
        p.   cm.
    Includes index.
    ISBN 1–55738–880–6
    1. Insurance.   I. Title.
    HG8051.B325   1996
    368—dc20   95–50817

Printed in the United States of America
1 2 3 4 5 6 7 8 9 0 BS 3 2 1 0 9 8 7 6

A major portion of everyone's budget goes to paying for various forms of insurance. Some of those dollars are spent wisely, some are wasted—the trick is in knowing which is which. The purpose of this book is to eliminate the mystique that surrounds insurance that makes it seem incomprehensible. I hope to make the insurance decisions you face in your daily life not only comprehensible but actually easy.

The world of insurance and financial products is filled with salespeople who want to sell the latest "hot product" for one reason: to make the sale. Unfortunately, consumers often let them. This book will help you match your insurance needs with products that satisfy them.

A major milestone in the development of this book occurred when a Chicago investor by the name of Angelo Geocaris visited me in 1981 and said that he wanted to build the "McDonalds" of personal financial planning, a free-standing financial planning center where people could obtain a quality, objective, financial plan at a reasonable cost. While the Financial Security Centre was in full operation, manufacturing financial plans, I would find myself with half a dozen plans all opened to the risk management and insurance section. With cassette recorder in hand, I would go from plan to plan dictating recommendations for each client for disability insurance, medical insurance, home, auto and liability insurance, life insurance, and annuities . . . repeating myself time after time: In effect, I was writing a book on insurance for each individual. Each "book" had a great many details in common. I found that much of what I wanted for each client was what I wanted for myself and what I want for you.

The next step in the development of this book was to begin teaching financial planners how to build the personal risk management section—the defensive section—of a financial plan. This culminated in a course written for the American Institute of Certified Public Accountants (AICPA). The course, "Risk Management and Insurance in Personal Financial Planning," was used as part of the Certificate of Educational Achievement Program in Personal Financial Planning. Since it was published in 1988, it has been taught to hundreds of CPAs around the country. While I was teaching the course, CPAs asked the me to present the course in book form for their clients. The idea was that professionals can do a better job and charge less when working with well-informed clients. The book for clients is this, *The Complete Book of Insurance.*

ACKNOWLEDGMENTS

No one walks alone. I am blessed with finding help from a great many people, not the least of which is my family. First is my wife, Moses, who is not only my teammate, but also my facilitator, chief editor, and critic, without whom I would get nothing done. In fact, without her I would not have the rest of my support group, business associates, editors, and critics—son and business associate, B.G. (and his wife, Rosemary Martin Baldwin), Peter (and his wife Susan Gough Baldwin), daughter and business associate, Katie (and her husband, Doug Leipprandt), and Michael (and his wife, Karen Barg Baldwin). They all work diligently to keep me on track.

Moses keeps the office going, and Kaye Burton makes the word processor hum while at the same time editing and offering helpful suggestions.

Of course, none of this would have come about had not William A. Kahn, Jr., CPA, invited me to speak before the American Institute of Certified Public Accountants' first Personal Financial Planning Conference in 1984. Jim Wilson, CPA, the conference chairman, became my mentor, thereafter. Andrew R. Gioseffi, CPA, of the American Institute of Certified Public Accountants (AICPA) worked through many updates of the Risk Management and Insurance course, Howard Robinson of the American Bankers Association worked so diligently with me to develop a quality product for the insurance section of the Certified Trust Financial Advisor (CTFA) Study Guide, and David A. Bridewell of the Senior Lawyers Division of the American Bar Association convinced me to go to work on *The Lawyers Guide to Insurance.*

I also must thank my personal insurance and financial planning clients, who have been forced to be patient with me from time to time and have served over the years as sounding boards for the concepts presented in this book.

And finally my thanks to the folks at Irwin for their unending patience and assistance: Amy Ost for taking it upon herself to make sure the buyers of our books get first class treatment, Kevin Thornton for his perseverence, and Carrie Sestak, Lara Feinberg, and Jon Christopher for working so hard to make this book the best it can be.

Ben G. Baldwin

CONTENTS

CHAPTER ONE

To Insure... or Not to Insure?

How does one decide *when* to insure, *what* to insure, and *how much* to pay for insurance? How can you make insurance decisions without spending an inordinate amount of money and time on them? These are important questions. Consider how much of your income goes to pay for insurance. You pay for social security. If you are employed, your employer pays an amount equal to what you pay for your social security. You pay for homeowner's policies, condominium policies, or renter's policies. You pay for insurance on the vehicles you drive. You pay for liability insurances. You pay for disability and long-term care insurance because incurring a disability would not only prevent you from earning a living but also leave you dependent on others. You pay for health insurance to protect against medical bankruptcy.

Your employer or the government assists you in paying for some of these coverages, but bear in mind that if your employer helps, it is as part of your compensation package and a result of your personal efforts for that employer. *You* really are paying. The government's assistance is paid for with *your* tax dollars. The government has no other way to come up with money. Fellow taxpayers may also be helping but don't ever think that the money isn't coming out of your pocket.

What this book tries to do is to make it easy for you to compare the coverage that you *need* to the insurance coverage you *have*. If this book can help you buy insurance when you should, not buy insurance when you shouldn't, and have cost-effective benefits in force when you need them, it will have accomplished its objective.

This book is designed not to circumvent the insurance professionals who earn commissions selling insurance products but to make sure they earn those commissions by giving you valuable assistance and quality products. It is designed to help you select competent insurance advisors and to use them well in helping you to save time and money.

Two tools will assist you in developing a personal risk management program. The first are insurance inventory forms. Inventory forms help you gather the important information from existing insurances so you can evaluate the benefits presently in effect and what they cost. The second tool is the "Action Letter." Action Letters are rough drafts of letters from you to your insurance providers, specifying what you want and need to know in order to make your insurance decisions.

Personal risk management means dealing with uncertainty. This uncertainty exists because we constantly are exposed to the possibility of loss, injury, disadvantage or destruction. To win the battle of living in an uncertain world is to experience *no loss*. No one can assure you that you will experience no loss if insurance is the only tool you use in dealing with risk.

Take a look at the risk management diagram in Figure 1–1. The diagram begins with the risk identification phase of a personal risk management program. We are all concerned with the risks to which we personally are exposed and those to which our family members are exposed for which we are responsible.

RISK MANAGEMENT

What you do to earn a living and what you do for fun and recreation determine many of the risks to which you are exposed daily. Family relationships and responsibilities produce additional risks. What you own and what you owe, sources of support, and spending habits all reveal additional risks. As you complete the policy inventory forms in the following chapters, you will find that you have identified and managed many risks and that you may have overlooked others that are not adequately provided for under existing policies. Your concern for others, be they family members or not, may also expose you to economic loss because they are, in effect, an important part

FIGURE 1-1

Risk Management Diagram

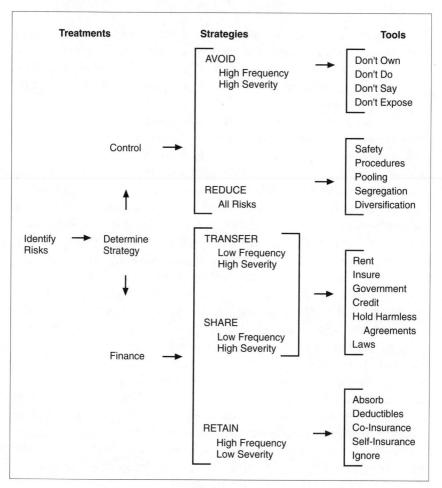

of someone else's economic security. If a risk in the lives of others would jeopardize your economic security, it's an area of potential loss that requires management.

Risk Treatment

As you identify each risk, you will have to determine how to treat it. Basically you have two choices. You can seek to "control" the uncertainty or to "finance" it. First we will discuss control.

Risk Control

Your mother's advice on how to handle risk (and you still hear it today no matter what your age) was "Be careful." Her method of handling risks was to reduce them by practicing caution. She encouraged safety procedures that we all observe to one degree or another.

However, the reduction and caution strategy is not sufficient for certain risks. Some risks are of such high severity and, under certain circumstances, of such high frequency that the best strategy is to avoid them entirely. For example, if your child owns a three-wheel, all-terrain vehicle that 13-year-olds drive recklessly at high speed over unfamiliar territory, the consequences of its use are so severe and will happen with such high frequency that the primary recommendation would be to sell the vehicle. If you reject that advice, the next suggestion would be to institute mother's method of handling this exposure to risk—control it. Fix the all-terrain vehicle so it cannot go too fast, make sure the vehicle is driven only over familiar territory, and make sure that proper safety equipment is used at all times the vehicle is in operation. You might also trade it in for the four-wheeled variety as another way of controlling your exposure to risk. To handle those high-severity, high-frequency risks, remember the "don'ts." *Don't* own, *don't* do, *don't* say, *don't* expose yourself to that particular risk. Once these control strategies have been implemented to the maximum degree possible, you will have avoided the risks that can be avoided and reduced to the greatest extent possible those risks that cannot be avoided.

Risk Financing

The next strategies dealing with risk are financing strategies. People need others to assist them in financing risks that happen infrequently and are so severe that they threaten people's economic security.

In most cases, when you seek to finance your exposure to risk you turn to insurance companies, and you find that most companies will accept the obligation to "share" your exposure to risk rather than accepting 100 percent of the responsibility for the loss if it should occur. The reason for this sharing is that if you have arranged to finance a risk by paying a small amount (accepting a small personal loss in the way of a premium payment), so that an insurance company or governmental agency picks up 100 percent of the loss if some contingency occurs, you might become less careful than you should be. The Federal Deposit Insurance Corporation for banks and savings and loans is a good example of this. Because depositors theoretically cannot lose, they do not think about the economic strength of the organization to which they send their deposits. Depositors merely concern themselves with the amount of interest they earn. Managers of these organizations pay a higher rate of interest to those depositors if they routinely make high-interest loans to less creditworthy borrowers. When bank and savings & loan managers are in a situation where they feel they cannot lose, nothing holds them back. They have proven not to be careful, and losses have been inevitable. We as taxpayers have had to pay for cleaning up the savings and loan mess. It has happened and it can happen again.

Sharing risks, on the other hand, seems to make everyone involved more careful. Insurance companies, the government, and government agencies are much more willing to pick up the major economic loss of risks that you are exposed to if you will share with them in those losses via deductibles and co-insurances. The risk sharing takes the form of your deductible—say paying the first $250, after which an insurance provider will pay 80 percent of the loss if you pay 20 percent.

There are certain risks that you just have to live with. They happen with such high frequency and/or cause losses of such low severity that they cannot be shared economically with others.

You can provide financing for them through your personal budget and manage them by being as careful as possible. Many people have difficulty recognizing these risks and they try to insure them. As a result, they pay premiums for unneeded insurances that have little prospect of paying meaningful benefits. They have, in effect, taken a potential opportunity for loss and turned it into a certain loss by paying premiums to the insurance company.

This book, then, is just as much about when *not* to insure as it is about when and how to insure. Following chapters will identify risk exposure and determine how to treat those risks—whether to control them or to finance them. When you have learned to evaluate the opportunities to avoid, reduce, transfer, share, or retain risk, you can implement the appropriate strategies for managing risk. But, first, you ask, what is insurance?

WHAT IS INSURANCE?

insurance

A device for the elimination of an economic risk, to all members of a large group by employing a system of equitable contributions out of which losses are paid.

Webster's Third International Dictionary

A plan by which large numbers of people associate themselves and transfer risks that attach to individuals to the shoulders of all.

General Insurance, David L. Bizkelhaupt, 1979, page 28.

These two definitions of *insurance* reveal two fundamental characteristics of insurance. First, insurance is a method of shifting risk from you (one individual) to a group. As people join this group in ever-increasing numbers in order to avoid a particular type of risk to which all are exposed, the risk for the group becomes more and more certain. To you, the loss *might* occur; to the total group, the loss *will* occur, at some statistical rate. The accuracy with which this rate of occurrence can be predicted determines how much each member of the group must pay in order to provide funds to cover the losses experienced by that small statistical portion of the total group. The second fundamental characteristic is that insurance is an arrangement for paying for inevitable losses and thus is a risk-financing method.

You can join any of a number of groups in order to pool your potential risks so that, should you become part of the statistic, the group will assist you in minimizing the economic loss to which you are exposed. There may be a "pass the hat" type of benefit, so that if some unfortunate occurrence should befall a member, the other members come to that person's aid.

Social Insurance

As a result of being a citizen of the United States and paying your federal income and social security taxes, you are involved in social insurance that is required by law and administered by the government. Social insurance programs are concerned with the "social adequacy" of the benefits provided and are usually designed to provide at least *minimum* economic security. Examples of these social insurances are social security, Medicare, state worker's compensation laws, unemployment compensation, some state-sponsored disability and compulsory automobile insurance programs, and the railroad retirement and unemployment and disability systems. The benefits and costs of these various programs are determined by the laws that brought them into existence. Keep in mind that "minimum economic security" is the basic concept from which social security springs. We all are aware that social security pays benefits to many who do not need it for "minimum economic security." Apparently, because taxpayers will not be able to support everyone, the social security system will have to institute a "needs test" that may affect your benefits in the future.

You participate in certain government or society programs for which you do not pay directly but which are paid for out of your federal and/or state income taxes, such as old age assistance, aid to the blind, aid to dependent children, and Medicaid. Society—that is, you, the taxpayer—pays for these programs; the recipients do not.

The government also provides various public insurance programs that, although not mandatory, have been established to benefit the entire community. Those who wish to avail themselves of the benefits join these public insurance programs by voluntarily paying the costs. The government makes available to you FHA mortgage insurance, crop insurance, government military life insurance programs, Federal Deposit Insurance Corporation Coverage, flood insurance, Securities Investors Protection Insurance (SIPC), pension benefit guarantee insurance, supplemental insurance for the aged, and sometimes riot insurance and even surety bonds for minority contractors.

Insurance as an "Economic Lubricant"

Through such insurance programs, society is fulfilling its obligation to provide a basic economic lubricant—insurance—where the private insurance companies have been unable to provide it.

It's easy to imagine that under certain circumstances the presence of risk could paralyze you into action. If the only way to avoid risk was not to do, say, own, and basically not to expose yourself to risk, you would be extremely limited in what you could do. Would a lender lend you a substantial amount of money for a mortgage on your house if you didn't cover it with fire insurance? Can you envision a society without medical insurance? Would you take a chance of driving a vehicle without insurance?

The functions of insurance are to provide you with peace of mind, assistance in economic survival, a basis for credit, indemnification in case of loss, solutions to social problems and a means of increasing your ability to use your assets. It also serves society by stimulating savings and providing investment capital. As a necessity of life, one of the most important of the insurances to have is the subject of Chapter 2.

CHAPTER TWO

Disability Insurance

disability

1. The inability to pursue an occupation or perform services for wages because of physical or mental impairment.
2. A physical or mental illness, injury, or condition that incapacitates in any way.

Webster's Third New International Dictionary

Injury or sickness restricts your ability to perform the material and substantial duties of your regular occupation to an extent that prevents you from engaging in your regular occupation. You are receiving medical care from someone other than yourself which is appropriate for the injury or sickness.

Equitable Life Assurance

You may feel that disability income insurance is not necessary for you if you do not work for wages. You may be retired or able to live on investment income. If the first definition of disability just given—"The inability to pursue an occupation or perform services for wages because of physical or mental impairment"—were the only definition of disability, you might be right. However, we also must deal with what insurers refer to as "functional disability," which is better described by the second of the three definitions—"A physical or mental illness, injury, or condition that incapacitates in any way."

To be unable to work for wages brings earning ability down to zero; to be functionally disabled brings earnings *below* zero. You can become an economic burden to others who must provide for your needs. As a result, disability insurance and long-term care insurance are essential for many people.

If you lack disability coverage, you're ignoring your risk of being disabled. Seventy percent of you reading these words have no disability coverage at all! Statistically speaking, fewer than one in six of you owns enough disability income insurance protection to provide for a disability lasting for more than 90 days. You can expect the average duration of a disability of more than 90 days to be at least 5 years. Disability not only terminates your income but increases your costs for medicine, medical care, and associated care expenses. This is the "double whammy" of disability: having no income and high medical bills. Disability in its most difficult form is referred to as the "living death." For some of the functionally disabled and those who care for them, the concept that there is something worse than death is very real.

Many people own life insurance and are concerned with the risk of dying, but ignore the risk of disability. A look at the statistics in Table 2–1 shows that the chances of becoming disabled are more than twice as great as the chances of dying.

If you have trouble visualizing yourself as disabled, congratulations. Be happy you are so healthy now. But as you look around you, notice the beveled curbs in the sidewalks. Who are they for? What about the larger stalls in the rest rooms and the

TABLE 2–1

Chances of Being Disabled for Three Months or Longer Prior to Age 65

Age	Chance of Being Disabled (%)	Average Duration	Disability vs. Death
25	58%	2.1 years	2.7 to 1
30	54%	2.5 years	2.9 to 1
35	50%	2.8 years	2.1 to 1
40	45%	3.1 years	3.4 to 1
45	40%	3.2 years	3.0 to 1
50	33%	3.1 years	2.5 to 1
55	23%	2.6 years	2.0 to 1

Sources: 1985 Commissioners Individual Disability A Table and 1985 Society of Actuaries DTS.

reserved parking spaces? The people using them probably were just like you at one time.

Most of us can't visualize ourselves as being disabled nor imagine the economic results of disability. If that is your problem, talk to a disabled friend. Consider what would happen if you took a six-month vacation or a year off without pay. If it would have no economic effect on you or your family, why don't you do it? If it would . . . you need disability income insurance. The next question is, where should you obtain it?

ALTERNATIVES FOR DISABILITY COVERAGE

Federal Programs

Social security does provide benefits for disabled workers deemed truly disabled. However, from October 1981 to July 1983, during a period of intense budget cuts, social security reported reviewing 314,000 existing disability cases and 45% (142,000) of those cases were terminated. Any ability to do any daily work activities can result in your claim for disability benefits being declined. Social Security defines disability as "an inability to engage in any substantial gainful activity by reason of any medically determinable physical or mental impairment that can be expected to result in death or which has lasted or can be expected to last for a continuous period of not less than 12 months." The 75 percent rate for rejecting claims combined with the tough definition of disability, as well as the fact that so many government programs are enduring severe cutbacks indicate that you should *not* depend on the government to provide for your disability income needs.

State Programs

What about state-mandated worker's compensation laws that impose absolute liability on an employer for certain injuries suffered by employees in the course of their work? Won't those laws provide for you? They won't if you are *not* disabled on the job! Also, consider the adequacy of amount and duration of worker's compensation payments. You likely will find that the benefits provided by your state are inadequate in amount and are payable for too short a time to provide for your real needs.

If you live in California, Hawaii, New Jersey, New York, Rhode Island, or Puerto Rico, you probably have access to a state-sponsored, compulsory, temporary disability plan that is designed to provide income to disabled workers from "nonoccupational" causes. These programs provide a *base* of benefits on which you can build; however, they are insufficient as a total provider for your personal disability income needs.

Association Disability Insurance

You may be a member of an organization or association that offers group disability income benefits to its membership. Some of these plans are enticing because of their low cost, but beware! These plans are often inadequate. They may have impossible-to-meet definitions of disability. You would not be considered disabled even if your only remaining means of self-support were selling pencils on the street corner. Many association plans offer benefits only in the event of accident and/or only for a limited period of time.

Look for the following limitations in Association Group Long-Term Disability Plans.

- Contracts can be canceled by insurance company or association.
- Rates typically increase as you get older or benefits are reduced as you get older.
- Insurance company can increase rates.
- Restrictive definitions of disability.
- No, or limited, coverage for partial losses.
- Limited or no protection ensuring your future insurability.
- Limited benefits for mental, nervous, and emotional disorders.
- Integration with other sources of compensation. (That is, if other sources like your employer plan or Social Security pay, your association plan reduces or eliminates the payment of benefits.)

You do not control what happens with an association plan. It may be canceled! If the insurance provider decides to terminate the plan, you may find yourself trying to replace the benefits at what could be an inopportune time. You may be disabled or in ill health—in which case no other carrier will insure you, and you will not be able to replace the benefits. For the moment, imagine yourself an attorney in the State of Illinois insured within your state association plan. In 1989 the association insurance programs were terminated. Some of the members who had availed themselves of these plans were already disabled or too sick to replace this coverage and, although they had enjoyed the relatively low rates the plan offered while they were insured, they were left without insurance.

Similar problems have occurred in the following associations, in which benefits have been reduced or terminated:

American Medical Association

New York State Society, CPAs

Chicago Dental Society

Texas Medical Society

American Dental Association

Fresno Medical Society

American College of Surgeons

Chicago Medical Society

Rhode Island Pharmaceutical Association

New York State Bar Association

The moral to the story is that you should not depend upon association group insurance for your primary disability insurance needs.

Group Disability Insurance

Employers also often offer group disability income insurance plans. A default recommendation to you is, if you are offered an employer-provided disability plan, take it. Accept it, and then do your evaluation while the insurance is in force. Just as in the association plans, it's important for you to check the benefits provided by the plan both for duration and quality.

The advantage of employer-provided group disability income insurance is its low cost. With employer-provided plans, your employer serves as an advocate in dealing with the insurance company. However, neither you nor your employer control the insurance company. It is that company's decision whether to continue to offer the coverage. If the insurance company finds that providing benefits for your employer is no longer economically feasible, that insurance carrier may decide to cancel that coverage. This lack of personal control is the primary disadvantage of employer-provided group disability income insurance, but the relatively low cost usually dictates that you should take it if it is available.

Group disability insurance generally discriminates against the highest paid employees because the maximum benefit is limited based upon the number of employees in the group. If you have a maximum benefit of $5,000 per month, this might be a full 60 percent of some employees' salary but only a 30 percent benefit for someone in the highest paid group. The solution is supplemental individual policies purchased on a group basis.

Employer coverages usually have restrictions regarding the amounts and durations of benefits, the definition of disability, and the integration of the benefits provided by the plan with those provided by Social Security and/or any other sources of disability income benefits. There also may be restrictions on your ability to continue the coverage should you terminate employment.

Business Overhead Expense Insurance

Personal service business owners may have purchased sufficient disability insurance to replace their earned income, but what about their office overhead? Who is going to pay the rent, payroll expenses, and other costs of doing business that continue. Business overhead expense insurance is designed to fill this need. This type of policy is unique because it *is* deductible to the business and the benefits when received are taxable; however, this is offset by the deduction the business gets when it pays the bills with the policy proceeds.

These policies are reasonably inexpensive. A 40-year-old with a $5,000 per month benefit payable after a 30-day waiting period would pay only about $800 per year for the policy. They are underwritten according to the list of business expenses that you give to the insurance company. The insurance company then will write a policy covering those bills usually for about a 2-year period. The theory is that if you're not back to work in 2 years, you might as well close the office.

The firm that is dependent upon one or two "rainmakers" (the ones who bring in the business) should certainly have this type of coverage.

Buyout Disability Insurance

Many business buy/sell agreements have been adopted that spell out what is to happen in the event of the death of a business owner. Life insurance is purchased to make sure the person or entity that is obligated to buy the interest of the deceased owner has the money to make the purchase. The death that necessitates the buyout also makes available the money to complete the buyout.

However, what can you do in the event of the disability of an operator/owner? How long can a small business continue to pay someone who can no longer produce and someone whose business interest may be being managed by the "legal represen-tative" of that disabled owner?

The buyout disability contract was created to fill this need. Underwriting for this type of policy is strict. It seems to make more sense to buy a lower cost policy, one with a 2-year waiting period prior to benefits being payable, rather than the more expensive variety with just a 1-year wait. If you are dis-abled, would you be willing to have your business ownership purchased away from you by contract after 12 months or would you be more comfortable with that idea after you had been disabled for a full 2 years?

The disability buyout policy is particularly appropriate for partnerships and professional corporations composed of five or fewer principals. It can be used with stable businesses employ-ing up to 50 people and is used most effectively for law and accounting firms, advertising agencies, architectural and engi-neering firms, computer firms, medical and dental practices, and employment agencies.

For larger businesses, with substantial tangible assets such as real estate and/or capital equipment whose net worth requires higher amounts of coverage, "excess buy-out" policies are available that are written on a five-year term basis that can provide benefits of up to $10 million.

Key Employee Disability Insurance

Key employee disability insurance provides disability benefits payable to an employer to offset losses as a result of a key employee being disabled. The employee has no part in the arrangement other than as the insured. The employer's premium payments are not tax-deductible but the benefits are tax-free when received.

Individually Owned Disability Insurance

The most desirable personal disability income insurance policy is an individually owned disability income policy issued by an insurance company that states that the contract may not be canceled (noncancelable) during your entire working life. The policy also should stipulate that the insurance company may never, during that period of time, charge you any more than is specified in the policy on the date the policy is issued (guaranteed renewable). This is referred to as noncancelable *and* guaranteed renewable coverage. The policy owner, not the insurance company, has control with this type of policy.

If You Want it, Act Now!

If you want noncancelable, guaranteed renewable disability insurance you had better act quickly. Many major disability companies no longer offer this type of coverage. Replacing this product are disability insurance policies referred to as "guaranteed renewable." In a policy that is only guaranteed renewable, the insurer retains the right to charge more in the future if claims and expenses cause the product to become unprofitable to the insurer at the current rates. This right to change rates is tempered by the fact that the primary regulator of the insurance industry, your state insurance commissioner's office, must be consulted (and approval received) prior to any increase in rates.

DEFINING DISABILITY

The strongest definition of disability you are likely to find is referred to as the "own occ" definition. The own occ definition defines *disability* as you being unable to perform the duties required by your "own occupation." That definition of disability should insure you within your own occupation for as long as possible, preferably for life.

It will be to your advantage to get today's insurance prices locked in for a lifetime (noncancelable). Prices are increasing because claims have been going up faster than expected. The risk of disability is increasing substantially today because the killer diseases no longer kill quickly; they disable. AIDS-related claims are up, and disability claims by women are higher than the insurance industry had anticipated. Claims for mental, nervous, and drug and alcohol situations are up. The medical profession is increasingly capable of extending the dying process. All of this will continue to increase the cost of disability insurance and restrict supply. No one knows the importance of disability insurance as well as someone who cannot buy it at any price—ask your disabled friends. The various definitions of *disability* (going from the strongest definition of disability providing you with the best protection, to the weakest providing you with the least protection) offered by insurance companies are as follows:

- Inability to perform all duties of the insured's own occupation. Simply, if you cannot work in your own occupation you receive benefits even if you can work in another occupation.

- Disabled in "own occ" and *not* working in another is one of the new, more limited definitions the industry is beginning to see.

- Inability to perform the substantial and material duties of insured's own occupation. You will receive benefits even if you can perform some but not all duties of your occupation.

- Inability to perform any occupation the insured is reasonably qualified for by education, training, or experience.

♦ Inability to perform the duties of any occupation. If you can perform *any* occupation no matter how menial, you would not be considered disabled.

You may also find extenders on these definitions that may limit your ability to make a claim. Although you may be disabled under one of these definitions, your policy may say that in order to make a claim you also must show that the disability has resulted in at least a 20 percent loss of income. Read any extenders very carefully.

As you consider the benefits of residual disability, think of those who do a good job of managing their taxable income and, although disability may indeed harm them economically, they may have a difficult time proving "loss of income" with their income tax returns. Check on what would be required to prove a claim (expect an insurer to ask for business and personal financial information and tax returns), then determine whether you would be willing to provide it to an insurance company to prove a claim.

COMMONLY RAISED ISSUES ABOUT DISABILITY INSURANCE

How Much Disability Insurance Should You Have?

This discussion could get very scientific about "how much is enough" by dissecting your budget to determine what expenses would terminate, what expenses would remain, and what expenses would increase if you were disabled. You could use a great deal of care in estimating such expenses in order to determine as accurately as possible the amount of disability income insurance you should have, or you could say to the insurance company, "Make me an offer. How much disability income insurance will you issue to me?" That's a frightening prospect, because it obviously is in the interest of the insurance company to issue you as much insurance as it can, and to sell as much of their product as it can. What's to keep this situation under control?

Actually, the insurance company tries hard not to "overinsure" you for disability. As you recall, you are going to ask the insurance company to pay these benefits for as long as possible—preferably for the rest of your life—if you should be disabled that long. What would encourage you to go back to work? Insurance companies feel that you will be encouraged to go back to work (thus relieving them of their obligation of continuing to pay benefits) if you have some economic incentive, that is, if you can make more money by going back to work than you can by continuing to receive the benefits of your disability income policy. The insurance company will not offer you 100 percent of your regular earnings because you then would have no incentive to go back to work. The insurer will offer you coverage for only about 60 percent to 70 percent of your income. The clue to purchasing insurance to replace your wages is to ask for as much as the insurer will give you and buy as much as you can afford. If you are ever disabled, it is unlikely you will feel that you have too much income!

If you counsel someone about purchasing disability insurance, your errors and omissions insurance carrier would want you to advise people to buy as much as the insurance company will sell them. If you advise a lower coverage and that person is ever disabled, you could find yourself under the litigation gun with your peers asking why you advised your client that this paltry amount of insurance was adequate when it is obvious that now, since the person has become disabled, you were wrong and thus caused harm to the disabled person. This has happened.

Disability Income without Taxation
Uncle Sam encourages *you* to buy and pay for your own disability income insurance through a tax law that states that if you have purchased and paid the premiums for your own disability income insurance policies, the benefits paid to you as the result of a disability are to be delivered *without* being subject to income tax (IRC Sec. 104 (a) (3). Suppose your policy states that in the event of your disability, your benefits will be $1,000 per month. If you have paid for that policy with your after-tax earnings, that $1,000 is delivered month after month without any taxation whatsoever. However, if you have paid that premium with pretax dollars through some employer plan or your employer paid those

premiums for you and did not add the cost of those benefits to your W-2 compensation, then those benefits would be subject to ordinary income taxation. Thirty percent or more of your disability benefit, depending upon your state and federal income tax brackets, could go to the government. To be disabled and pay part of your benefits to the government is not an optional arrangement. Avoid it. Pay the premium for your own disability insurance with after-tax dollars.

Employers Can Help

Employers can help you buy an individually owned, noncancelable, guaranteed renewable disability income insurance policy (the kind recommended earlier in this discussion) that is entirely portable. Despite the fact that, in most cases, you personally must pay the entire premium on that policy, it still is less expensive than your premiums for the identical policy purchased on your own. Insurance companies frequently discount rates 15 percent to 20 percent for policies that they can bill through employers. In some cases, they even make it easier for you to qualify for coverage. This is a great way for your employer to help you without cost other than that of paperwork for deducting the premiums from your paycheck.

Split-Dollar Disability Income Insurance

Employers also can help by paying for part of the coverage. This is an efficient arrangement because employer generally can pay for (and deduct) the cost of benefits without adding it to an employee's income. However, when benefits become payable, the benefits paid for by the employers are taxable income to the employee. A solution is to have the employee pay for the long-term income benefits and have the employers pay for the riders on the policy and possibly the premium allocable to the first year or so of benefits. In this way employer and employee split the costs but the important long-term income benefits, paid for by the employee, remain income-tax free.

Accident and/or Sickness Benefits

Some policies stipulate that benefits will be payable for life if the insured is disabled as a result of an accident, yet pay benefits for only two years if the disability is caused by sickness. These policies are inadequate and should not be accepted unless you cannot obtain anything more advantageous to the insured. Your policy should stipulate that benefits will be payable for as long as possible, regardless of what has caused your disability.

How Long Should Benefits Be Payable?

You may not be able to obtain a policy that will guarantee disability benefits for the rest of your life in the event of your disability. Insurance companies require many qualifications in order to issue such contracts. Nevertheless, you will want to find out whether such a policy is practical (possible, and affordable) for you. If the insurance company is unable to issue a policy that provides benefit payments for life, you will want to have the insurer offer you the closest thing to it.

The bottom line is that you want benefits payable for as long as you can to get them. You do not want your benefits to terminate during the course of a disability!

How Soon Should Benefits Begin?

Insurance companies can issue policies that will begin your disability benefits the moment you are disabled, but such policies can be expensive. To reduce the cost of your policy, have the insurance company defer benefit payment until a period of time after your disability occurs. If you can wait 30, 60, or 90 days—referred to as an "elimination" or a "waiting period"—there is a substantial reduction in premium. The 90-day wait is often the most cost-effective choice. Remember that the insurance company pays the benefit at the end of the month in which it is due, so with a 90-day waiting period you would receive your first benefit payment 120 days after the start of the disability.

OPTIONAL AT EXTRA COST: COVERAGE FOR PARTIAL AND RESIDUAL DISABILITY AND INDEXED BENEFITS

Numerous riders may be added to disability income policies in order to provide additional benefits under various circumstances. The following are a number of the more popular options.

Benefits for Partial and Residual Disability

Following a period of disability, there frequently is a time during which you can perform some tasks and cannot perform others—a partial disability, so to speak. You would prefer not to have the benefits of your disability income policy stop immediately as you go through a period of trying to go back to work on less than a full-time basis. Insurance companies have two phrases to define this set of circumstances, *partial disability and residual disability.*

Partial disability relates to what you are able to do. You suffer a partial disability if you can do only part of the material and substantial duties of your occupation. Therefore, to the extent that you are partially disabled, at least part of your benefits should be payable.

Residual disability on the other hand, relates to your earning power. You suffer a residual disability if you are not able to *earn* what you used to earn. Coverage for this provides benefits proportionate to the loss of your earning power, regardless of the type of work you do and how you are compensated. This provision allows you to receive a portion of the total disability payment if you can show "disability" has caused a reduction in income. Most policies require a minimum 20 percent loss of earnings, inability to perform the substantial duties of your occupation, and the continued supervision of your condition by a physician. The physician's care provision can be waived in some policies if it's proven that, as a result of the nature of your disability, continuing care would not benefit you.

CPI Cost-of-Living Adjustments

Another policy option guarantees that after a year of continuous disability, the amount of total or residual benefits will increase in some proportion to the increase in the annual Consumer Price Index (CPI) each year you continue to be disabled. This option is available only on long-term plans and is sometimes referred to as an *inflation rider*. Watch for significant differences among policies offering this rider. Check whether the increases are calculated on a simple interest basis or compounded—it makes a big difference. The compounded inflation adjustment will more likely track actual inflation, and will cost more but will provide you with better protection. Also check for limits on how high the increases can go.

Automatic Increase in Benefits

With this option, after you purchase your policy, the benefits are automatically increased each year for a limited period of time, such as a 3 percent increase each year for five years. This is a lower cost, lower benefit option than the CPI option.

Guaranteed Insurability

This option allows you to purchase additional monthly benefits periodically subject to the insurance company's issue and financial underwriting requirements but without evidence of medical insurability. This option is strongly recommended. It helps to ensure that your disability benefits keep up with your increasing income and obligations.

Return of Premium Rider

This option is appealing if you are among those who cannot conceive of being disabled—the "I'm as healthy as a horse" group. Because you never expect to make a claim on your policy, you will like the feature that promises to return a portion of your premium, less claims paid, at future dates, such as every five years. These riders do not come cheap. For example, you could have a return of premium rider that guarantees you a 60 percent return of premiums paid if you have no claims for five years. It could cost you $100 per month more than the cost of your base policy, or $6,000 over the five-year period. If the refund feature was to pay you back $8,000 at the end of five years you might be tempted. The problem is that the $8,000 due you from the policy may only be payable *if* the policy is still in force (it won't be if you can't afford it) and only *if* you have not made a claim. These "ifs" create the risk that the payment will not be made. The downside risk of 100 percent loss of the extra money you invested in order to have this rider usually makes it unacceptable.

The rider may influence you not to make a legitimate claim when you deserve to be paid. This could mean that the cost of the return of premium rider came out of your own pocket and so did the benefit because in order to get your refund, you passed up claiming benefits that should have been paid to you because of disability. In most cases you would be better off putting the extra $100 per month in a good stock mutual fund.

Caution: The higher the rate of return the insurance company is offering on the extra money invested in the return of premium rider, the less likely the policy is to pay off. There is no "free lunch." Examine carefully every contingency under which the policy will not pay before you make any purchase.

THE DISABILITY INCOME INSURANCE INVENTORY

Complete the inventory shown in Figure 2–1 for all disability income policies you or other household members currently have in force. Record who is insured, the insuring company, policy number, the monthly income, when benefits start, how long benefits last, and the premium's cost. Circle the numbers that indicate the important features of the policy.

FIGURE 2–1

The Disability Income Insurance Inventory

Company/ Insured	Policy Number	Monthly Income	Benefits Start	Benefits End	Annual Premium	Features of Disability (circle as many as apply)
						1 2 3 4 5 6 7 8 9 10
						1 2 3 4 5 6 7 8 9 10
						1 2 3 4 5 6 7 8 9 10
						1 2 3 4 5 6 7 8 9 10
						1 2 3 4 5 6 7 8 9 10

Total: ☐

60% of my gross monthly income is $_____. My disability benefits represent ____% of my total income and are adequate/inadequate.

Features of Disability

1. Personal Policy
2. Noncancelable and Guaranteed Renewable
3. Your Own Occupation
4. Guaranteed Insurability
5. Inflation Rider

6. Residual Disability
7. Partial Disability
8. Group Policy
9. Association Policy
10. Any Occupation

When you have completed the inventory of existing disability income insurance policies, it is time to review them in light of the previous discussion. If you have circled 1, 2, and 3, it would appear that you, the insured, have purchased quality disability income insurance. Number 1 indicates a personal policy; number 2, a noncancelable guaranteed renewable contract; and number 3, a policy that insures you against the inability to work within your own occupation. If you also circled 4 or 5, 6, and 7, indicating that your policy has a guaranteed insurability rider, an inflation rider, and either a partial or residual disability rider, you have selected some of the most important riders currently available within disability income policies. If the circles are all 8s, 9s, and 10s, you should be concerned about the quality of the coverage.

The Insurance Company Is Important

Keep in mind that the quality of your policy is dependent upon the quality of the insurance company that writes it. You expect your insurance company to deal with you fairly in the event of disability. In some circumstances it will be difficult to determine whether you truly are disabled. Individually, of course, you prefer to have the insurance company always err in your favor. However, it is also the obligation of your insurance company to stay in business so that it will be around to pay your benefits. The insurance company must not pay unwarranted claims if it is going to stay in business to pay just claims. It also has an obligation to offer insurance at reasonable prices, which it will not be able to do if it pays unwarranted claims. Information regarding the ratings of the financial strength of insurance companies is provided in the final chapter of this book and is an important consideration in selecting disability insurance. Keep track of what the various rating agencies are saying about your company, not only at the time of purchase but thereafter.

The Changing Marketplace

The disability income marketplace is changing and it has *not* been improving for the consumer. The cost of this type of coverage has been increasing. Recently it has been reported that companies have increased men's rates 6 percent to 10 percent and women's rates as much as 35 percent. The majority of companies that charge the same rates for men and women have experienced more moderate increases. If you lock in today's rates with a quality contract, you will be extremely happy that you had the foresight to do so. The ability to "lock in" rates to age 65 from your current age is rapidly disappearing. Act now!

Ways to Reduce Cost . . . and Benefits

Being created to fill the gap caused when companies cease to offer guaranteed renewable and noncancelable contracts are disability income policies that are guaranteed renewable but *not* noncancelable, meaning that the company can increase the premium later on, if necessary. That privilege allows the company to charge you less now because it retains the right to charge you more later.

Another tool used by the companies to offer you more economical premiums is to mandate that disability benefits from other sources, such as social security, will reduce the benefit the company has to pay you. This is referred to as *integration*. You will find integration used more and more in insurance.

If integration was not used and you were disabled while working and driving your car, think of all the places that might owe you disability benefits. There could be benefits from social security, worker's compensation, state compensation, group disability, and individually owned disability insurance. If each had to pay 100 percent of what was owed to you under each plan, you could find yourself being paid more to be disabled than you were being paid to work. As a result, there would be no economic incentive for a disabled worker to go back to work. This would be an undesireable situation for workers and taxpayers at large: they would be the ones who would end up paying for your excessive benefits.

Integration allows the systems of reimbursement to work together to make sure that adequate—but not excessive—benefits are paid. This helps keep down the cost of insurance for us all. You may remember the days prior to integration when people could collect medical reimbursement from more than one source: being sick could actually be profitable. Integration came to medical insurance in order to eliminate that costly practice.

There is a trend away from the payment of benefits solely on the basis of your ability to perform your occupation and toward a requirement that your income must have dropped by at least 20 percent, and to insist that you work in a reasonable occupation if you can do so.

Insurers are limiting benefits payable for mental disorders and substance abuse (such as maximizing coverage of 24 months) and other so-called "inside limits" that eliminate or reduce benefits under various circumstances.

The following are some other ways for *you* to reduce the cost of your disability insurance:

+ Instead of lifetime benefits, choose benefits for a more limited period of time, such as age 65, or even as short as 5 years.
+ Accept a smaller monthly benefit.
+ Limit the options added to the policy.
+ Extend the waiting period beyond 90 days.
+ Accept more restrictive definitions of disability.
+ Make sure you take advantage of all discounts available to you. For example, if you get two other people in your office to sign up and your employer agrees to deduct premiums from your paychecks, you could save up to 20 percent.

An example of someone redesigning a policy to reduce cost follows. A 40-year-old was offered a $3,000 per month lifetime benefit policy with a 60-day waiting period, cost-of-living increase rider, residual benefits, and option to buy more insurance for a total cost of $2,273 per year, which was almost 4 percent of his annual income. To reduce costs, the agent requoted the policy with benefits of $3,000 per month to age 65, a 180-day waiting period, and elimination of all the riders. The cost came to $788 per year, a little over 1 percent of his annual income. The lower cost policy was doable, so he now has a core benefit policy that he can build on with employer or association group contracts.

To reduce premiums, you could also accept a graded premium policy that starts at a lower cost and goes to a higher cost five years later, or you could opt for a term insurance disability plan. There are many options and a professional agent, well versed in the disability income marketplace, will *earn* his or her commission helping you get the right policy for you.

IF YOU OWN IT NOW... KEEP IT

If you already own a noncancelable and guaranteed renewable disability policy... hold onto it! It is likely that you have better benefits and lower costs than you could obtain today. If you have any questions, seek the advice of a disability income insurance professional.

If you are shopping for new policies and are tempted to accept the guaranteed renewable only type of contract (premiums can be changed by the company in the future), understand that you are purchasing what could be compared to an adjustable rate mortgage with no caps. There is no guarantee that your premiums will remain low cost. The insurance company, subject to state approval, has the right to raise your premium in the future. Just consider how happy you would be if you could buy auto or medical insurance that could never increase in cost. You can't, and one day you may not be able to buy disability insurance that will be guaranteed not to increase in cost.

TAKE ACTION

In order to put a disability income policy in force, you may need to contact an agent licensed to sell disability income policies in your state. A professional salesperson should be able to help you find quality coverage from a quality company, assist you in completing the paperwork and requirements of application, help you through the underwriting process, and assist you in understanding your policy and buying what is appropriate for you. The salesperson should provide ongoing service, such as taking advantage of your guaranteed insurability options and assisting you at claim time, if necessary. In short, the professional should help you put the correct coverage in place and keep your policy in force. A good disability income insurance professional can be an invaluable assistant to a lawyer trying to help a client cope with this type of insurance. The sample action letter in Figure 2–2 may be of value to you in dealing with these professional salespeople.

F I G U R E   2–2

Disability Income Action Letter

Dear _____ :

I am a full-time _____, born _____, male/female, earning approximately $_____ per year. I am in the process of evaluating my disability income insurance, and I would appreciate your assistance.

In the event of my disability, it is my objective to have disability income benefits of approximately 60 to 70 percent of my income, with the strongest definition of disability available. Preferably, the policy should insure me within my occupational specialty for the duration of the benefit period.

I would appreciate a quote for quality individual, noncancelable, guaranteed renewable coverage in the amount of $_____ per month for the longest payment period possible, preferably for life. Please quote a 30-, 60-, 90-, 180-, and 365-day waiting period. Your quote should include any supplemental benefits that you would recommend for me along with descriptive material and premiums.

Please mail the information to me from _____ quality companies. I would appreciate your recommendations regarding which suit my needs best.

Sincerely,

WHAT IS HAPPENING NOW

Disability insurance is getting tougher to get! Availabilty varies in different areas of the country depending on where and why insurance companies are losing the most money. If you're a California or Florida physician, hold on to whatever disability insurance you have . . . It is probably irreplacable, generally speaking:

- Physicians and dentists are less desirable risks today because costs are up, benefits are down, underwriting is tougher because of AIDs and also because of excessive medical and disability claims. Such professionals should never terminate their existing disability contracts.

- Replacement ratios (the percent of your income that will be replaced) are down, paying 50 to 60 percent now whereas it used to be 60 to 70 percent.

- Lifetime benefits are not as readily available as they used to be.
- Own occ coverage is much more difficult to get.
- Residual riders are more limited.
- Claims are up. Southern California and Florida claims exceed the expected rates by 20 percent.
- Mental, nervous, drug, and alcohol benefits are becoming severely limited.

CHAPTER THREE

Long-Term Care Insurance/Functional Disability Insurance

The Need Is Real

Currently, there are 29 million people over the age of 65. In the year 2000, there will be 34 million people over the age of 65.

U.S. Census Bureau, 1991

Patients are discharged from hospitals as soon as possible, driving up the demand for recovery time in a long-term care facility.

Journal of Ambulatory Care Marketing, 1991

40 percent of all people over age 65 will enter a nursing home. In seven of ten couples, one spouse will need nursing home care for an average of 2½ years (half for less than three months).

U.S. Department of Health and Human Services, 1991

One in seven men and one in three women who turned age 65 in 1990 are expected to spend at least one year in a nursing home.

The New England Journal of Medicine, February 28, 1991

By the year 2000, 40 percent of functionally disabled Americans will be under age 65.

United States Health Cooperative, Washington, DC, September 1988

Depending on the area of the country, a one-year stay in a nursing home costs between $26,750 and $80,200. The daily cost can be as much as $214. A 2½-year stay costs between $66,875 and $200,500.

Costs surveys conducted by CNA 1992

The average nursing home stay has reached 4 years.

The New England Journal of Medicine, February 1993

Depending on where you live, the average annual cost of a nurse to provide home health care is $5,000 to $14,000.

Broker World, May 1991

Medicaid pays 41.5 percent of nursing home expenses.

Health Care Funding Review

Wisconsin recovered $3.3 million from 433 estates in fiscal 1993 for medical payments.

Jane Bryant Quin, *Washington Post*

Sixty-seven percent of the people needing long-term care are age 65 or older. Don't fall for the myth that long-term care is only for the elderly; this statistic means that 33 percent of those needing care are under age 65.

The average cost for long-term care throughout the country was about $32,000 per year in 1995, with average costs reaching $60,000 in high cost-of-living areas such as New England and California.

For a 65-year-old the chances are two in five that you will spend some time in a nursing home during your lifetime. And you will pay the high costs for long-term care. You pay almost 95 percent of these bills either individually, with your family's help, or as a taxpayer. Statistics indicate that upon entering a nursing facility, the typical patient pays the bill from personal or family savings. When the personal and family savings have been exhausted and the patient has "spent down" all personal assets and must finance care using Medicaid, now you, the taxpayer, pay the bill. Sanford J. Schlesinger and Barbara J. Scheiwar, in their book *Planning for the Elderly or Incapacitated Client,* report that "approximately 75 percent of elderly cannot afford to finance even one year in a nursing home." Families and individuals typically are not prepared to meet the resulting need. State welfare Medicaid funds are insufficient to meet the demands being put upon them. Medicare is not the answer: It is paying less than 2 percent of total long-term care costs. Long-term care insurance is a way of offsetting your risk of financial devastation because of needing long-term care.

The "over age 65" group is the fastest growing segment of our population. Statistically speaking, two thirds of the people who have ever reached age 65 from the beginning of time are alive today. This group can look forward to 30 years of life after retirement. A lady in France celebrated her 120th birthday in a nursing home. Comedians joke about people at age 120 taking care of their 140-year-old parents with their 100-year-old children still living at home. Someday you can expect to reach a point of diminishing capabilities. Just as we all needed care when we came into this world, it is likely that we will need care prior to leaving this world.

The actual bills from an average-cost nursing home in Florida come to over $48,000 per year. That cost is what many people would consider a comfortable retirement income for two. Now, it has become a frightening annual bill for a caregiving spouse.

THE STORY BEHIND THE BILL

The care-giving spouse in this situation had promised that she would never put her husband into a nursing home, but the short circuits began to occur—ministrokes that cut off parts of her spouse's brain, vision loss to less than 10 percent, hearing loss also. Her spouse could not tell night from day. He could forget how to walk in midstep. He would stay awake for 72 hours at a crack and keep her up too. One night when the two of them fell, she thought she had broken her shoulder. She called her only daughter to help, as well as all the home agencies in her area. Neither could provide the required care. The only answer for her spouse was 24-hour-a-day professional help in a nursing home staffed and equipped to provide it.

Thankfully, her spouse now considers "the home" to be home. She cares for him every day. She would not be so anxious if they had just had some long-term care insurance to cover part of the $48,000 annual expense.

The moral of this story is that you have a choice to make. You can use the "head in the sand" approach and do nothing about long-term care, which means that you will pay costs out-of-pocket and hope that your pockets are deep enough, or you will depend on your fellow taxpayers to help you via Medicare or Medicaid. In time, you are likely to learn that your fellow tax-payers can't afford to pay your long-term care bills so, for other than the *really* destitute, government assistance will not be available.

In 1940 there were 40 taxpaying workers to support 1 retiree. In 1970, it was 7 workers per retiree. Now it is about 3 workers per retiree and by 2030, according to the U.S. Department of Commerce, it will be 1.5 workers per retiree. It is interesting to note that at that point, statistically, you will in essence be depending on your own children to support you. If you do not provide for long-term care, your children will have to pay your way, sacrificing *their* security and increasing the likelihood they will be dependent on their children. The cycle will go on.

It is important to you to send an action letter like that in Figure 3–1. Find out the costs and benefits of joining with others who have the same problem in an insured long-term care plan.

LIFE INSURANCE LIVING BENEFITS

Do not depend upon a payout of part of the death benefits of your life insurance policy to cover long-term care costs unless your physician gives you a life expectancy of only 6 to 12 months. It would be easier for the care-giving spouse *economically* if she knew her functionally disabled husband only had six months to live, but she does not; he may live 10–20 more years. Life insurance living benefits will not help her. Accelerated benefit riders are generally available from most insurance companies. They pay a portion of the death benefit, such as 75 percent, during the last months of a person's life. The benefits could be taxable unless the

FIGURE 3–1

Long-Term Care Insurance Action Letter

Dear _____:

We are in search of a quality long-term care insurance policy. We would appreciate it if you could provide us with quotes and information.

I was born in _____, and am a male/female smoker/nonsmoker in good health. My spouse was born in _____, and is a male/female smoker/nonsmoker also in good health.

I would like quotes on guaranteed renewable long-term care policies providing benefits of _____ per day after a waiting period of _____ days, for a benefit period of at least _____ years. I would like to have the benefits payable regardless of whether the nursing home I use is classified skilled, intermediate care, respite, or a custodial care home. I would like to have benefits payable if the required personal care is provided in our own home or in an adult day-care center. I wish to avoid any policies that have exclusions for Alzheimer's disease or organic brain disease of any sort, and policies that include preentry requirements such as the three-day hospitalization requirement.

I would like to know of any preexisting condition limitations and the requirements for application. I would appreciate your recommendations in regard to any supplemental benefits the policy should offer, such as an inflation rider.

Please call me if you have any questions. I look forward to receiving your proposals in the mail so that I may review them with my advisor. We will then ask you to visit with us to respond to our questions. Thank you for your assistance.

Sincerely,

U.S. Senate passes HR 1215. At death, the advances plus interest will be recovered by the insurance company from the total death benefit due to the beneficiary.

LONG-TERM CARE INSURANCE POLICIES

Prior to 1989, long-term care policies were inadequate. They were full of requirements that prevented the payment of benefits, such as a requirement that benefits were available only after a three-day hospital stay. Then, with pressure from consumers and the National

Association of Insurance Commissioners, long-term care policies began to improve. Today they are much more reasonably priced and provide better benefits. The message here is that if you have an early policy, review it in light of today's long-term care policy environment and see whether your insurance company will adjust your policy to a more beneficial design. The following are some of the features of the policies you will want to examine.

Length of Benefits

As with disability income insurance, benefits payable for life would be your first choice, but economics and age could make a lifetime policy unavailable. You will want benefits payable for as long a period as you can possibly afford. The normal choices run from two years to your lifetime.

Amount of Benefit

The basic measure of the amount of benefit is how much the policy would pay per day if you were admitted to a nursing home. These benefits currently range from $50 to $400 per day. Your choice is likely to be dependent upon both what you can afford and what nursing home costs are in your area. Keep in mind that the quality professional care you hope to receive if institutionalized will go up in cost in the future.

Your choice of benefits may be influenced by long-term care income tax rules being considered in 1995 in the "Contract with America" legislation. The income tax status of long-term care insurance is still uncertain at the time of this writing. The Contract with America legislation (HR-1215) could classify long-term care insurance as health and accident insurance, which would allow employers to purchase it for employees, tax-deductible to the corporation and tax-free to the employee. It would make individually purchased long-term care insurance premiums tax-deductible on Schedule A of your federal income tax return to the extent that your total medical deductions exceed 7.5 percent of your adjusted gross income. It would make the benefits of long-term policies income tax-free. There is some pressure to limit these favorable tax rules to long-term care policies providing only up to $200 per day benefits. Benefits above this amount would be taxable.

Inflation Riders

These are critical for insureds up to at least age 70. These riders increase the benefit by either a simple or a compound inflation factor each year the policy is in force.

Suppose you were considering a $100-per-day benefit policy that provided no inflation rider. That means that 15 years from now you would still receive only a $100-per-day benefit. Alternatively, you could purchase an $85-per-day policy with a compound inflation rider at a comparable price. The following shows the significant difference this will make to you as you get older and the risk of your need for long-term care becomes greater.

No Compounding		5% Simple	5% Compound
Year 1	$100	$ 85	$ 85
10 years	$100	$127	$138
20 years	$100	$170	$225
30 years	$100	$212	$385

It is easy to see the importance of the compound inflation rider when you consider the substantial possibility that many people today will live well into their 90s, and that is when they probably will need long-term care.

Home Healthcare

One of the problems with many of today's policies is that they require riders and an extra premium to provide care alternatives other than admission to a nursing home. People who do not have the riders may find themselves forced to seek admission to a nursing home so that they can receive benefits. In effect, the terms of the policy are forcing policy owners into institutionalization. Avoid this type of policy; there are better ones on the market. We would suggest you seek the "pot of money" type of policy design.

"Pot of Money" Policies

These policies take the amount of benefit you have purchased and multiply it times the number of days you have contracted for in order to calculate the maximum amount the insurance company would be called upon to pay out. That amount becomes your pot of money or reserves to be drawn upon for your long-term care needs. If all that you require is home health care, adult day care, or some other lesser level of care, the insurance company will work with you within your community to find the care you need. Then, only the required funds will be drawn from your pot of money to pay for the required care. This system of payment is better for all concerned.

The following is an example of when benefits are payable. These "benefit triggers" are indicated when any one of the following conditions exist:

- Inability to perform two of seven (bathing, dressing, feeding, toileting, continence, transferring and taking medication) activities of daily living (ADL).
- Cognitive impairment.
- Medical necessity.

Benefit Triggers

It takes a benefit trigger to cause benefits to begin being paid. It is a way of measuring your functional disability. The question becomes whether you are capable of performing or remembering to perform, the activities of daily living, such as eating, dressing, transporting, and toileting. Avoid policies that require "medically necessary" as a benefit trigger, because often care is not medical but custodial.

Managed Care Comes to Long-Term Care Policies

Managed care should work well in the administration of long-term care policies because most of us would prefer to be as independent as possible and avoid becoming a nursing home resident. For those of us who have been through the need to find help for a functionally disabled friend or relative, we know the need comes on quickly. Most of us are ill-prepared to cope with the situation. What if we could find a professional paid to know community resources and how and when to use them? Better yet, what if our long-term care insurance company provided the assistance as a part of our policy? Professional care coordinators do exist, and professional care coordinator benefits exist in some long-term care policies. In fact, you receive some benefit improvements when you use the coordinator, e.g., waiver of elimination periods, 100 percent benefit rather than 80 percent benefits, etc. The "managed care" provided by the care coordinator should work particularly well with long-term care because you and the care coordinator have the same objective. You want to get the care you need but still maintain as much independence as possible. You want that needed care to intrude on your life as little as possible.

Deductibles and Waiting Periods

Just as in disability income insurance, the cost of the policy will be lower the longer you are willing to wait before the insurance company begins to pay benefits. Waiting periods of 20 or 100 days are typical. One hundred days goes by quickly, and you may find that a waiting period of this length is cost-effective if you have adequate financial reserves.

Nonforfeiture Features

Nonforfeiture benefits provide some value to insureds who cease paying their insurance premium or surrender their policies after some extended period of time. Although that may be beneficial to some policy owners, it will drive up the cost of long-term care insurance to all policy owners.

The National Association of Insurance Commissioners (NAIC) is somewhat hung up on making sure you have nonforfeiture benefits. Efforts are continuing to find a way to keep benefits in force if you forget to pay premiums or if you are unable to pay premiums after keeping the policy in force for many years. A current solution is to have you designate a friend or relative who should be notified if you forget to pay your premium so that they can assist you in keeping your policy in force.

Couple Policies

Some companies will offer a discount if both a husband and a wife buy policies. Such arrangements may offer additional benefits such as the survivorship benefit, which provides that, after premiums have been paid for 10 to 15 years and one spouse dies, the survivor's policy automatically becomes paid up.

Contact Your State for Information

You can use your state insurance commissioner's office as a source of information regarding long-term care policies. This type of coverage has created a great deal of interest, and rapid changes in policies have resulted in much confusion and political involvement. State insurance commissioners throughout the country have been sympathetic to the plight of people shopping for this type of policy; many have put together studies designed to help you purchase good policies. Call your state insurance commissioner's office and ask for help.

ANNUITY ALTERNATIVE TO LONG-TERM CARE INSURANCE

Mary is age 75 and has an income of $20,400 per year coming from $340,000 in bank certificates of deposit (CDs) generating 6 percent interest. She has $10,000 in annual social security income. Although she is managing financially at $30,400 per year, there is no room for inflation or for paying the $2,000 or more per year for even minimal long-term care insurance. Paying such premiums would reduce her current standard of living, to say nothing of the fact that she does not think she can pass the required physical exam to obtain a policy. She and her son are concerned that she will run out of money if she ends up needing nursing home care. Her son was ready to pay up to $5,000 per year for a top-quality long-term care policy for her, but she would prefer to avoid that.

The solution to Mary's problem could be one of the new life annuities the insurance industry has developed. It would work as follows.

Mary could invest $240,000 into an annuity contract and change her income from $30,400 per year to:

Social security:	$10,000
$120,000 in CDs:	$ 7,200
Annuity contract:	$20,400 ($14,000 not subject to income taxes)
Total:	$37,600

The $37,600 represents an immediate increase in income of $7,200 per year, an increase of almost 24 percent. This means that Mary does not have to reduce her standard of living through the purchase of a long-term care policy. She can, using her own resources, increase her standard of living and be assured that her total income, in or out of a nursing home, will be approximately $100 per day.

If Mary does not live to age 85, the contract provides a death benefit of about 65 percent of what she paid into the contract less the payments she has already received. Should she need a lump sum after the annuity payments have started, up to age 85, she has the right to stop the payments and make a withdrawal based upon the market-adjusted value of her account at the time of her withdrawal.

Alternatively, she could put all of her $340,000 into an annuity and have a life income, including her social security, of $45,000 per year, a 48 percent increase in income. Mary's mother lived to age 95; Mary could live longer. Mary's son says that $45,000 could change his mother from an aging, concerned women to a dynamic, wealthy-feeling grandmother. He would like that because he is more concerned about his mom running out of money than he is about receiving an unneeded inheritance. Thus, Mary and her son can choose between doing nothing, buying the long-term care policy, or using the annuity to ensure a lifetime income equivalent to or greater than long-term care policy benefits.

LIFE INSURANCE ALTERNATIVE
TO LONG-TERM POLICIES

Today you can pay a single premium into a life insurance policy and have convalescent care benefits paid for by having the cost of a long-term convalescent care insurance rider deducted from the policy value. The cost of the rider is considered a distribution subject to income taxes and the company will report it to you and the IRS. The result is that both the cost of the rider and the benefits when/if paid are currently taxable. For example, if you were a woman age 75, you could make a $50,000 (if you had it) one-time payment into a policy with a $73,000 death benefit. You would have convalescent care benefits of $100 per day for four years, total convalescent care benefits of $146,000. This will occur only if the policy performs (earns a reasonable rate of interest) as the insurance company has illustrated. For a woman age 56, the cost for the same benefits would be about $22,000; for a male age 60, about $31,000.

The policy provisions require that benefits are payable after you become functionally impaired and have required care for 90 days or more in a nursing home, in your own home (50 percent of daily benefit), or in an adult day care center. This operates like a 90-day elimination or waiting period.

Functional impairment means that you need "continual assistance in performing two or more activities of daily living (ADLs)" such as feeding, dressing, bathing, toileting, and transferring, or that you suffer from cognitive impairment such as Alzheimer's or irreversible dementia. Your doctor must attest to your condition. Be aware that cognitive impairment is the largest cause of the need for long-term care and care is likely to be required for 12 years.

In order to allay your fears regarding lower interest rates and your policy not earning enough to provide the benefits, the insurance company has instituted a number of guarantors:

- At *quoted rates*, the policy will continue in force for your lifetime.
- If rates decrease, the insurance company will inform you and recommend a lower benefit level that the policy can maintain, while guaranteeing that the benefit level will

never be less than the policy face amount, such as $73,000. If you maintain your coverage at the insurance company's recommended level and do not withdraw or borrow from the policy, the insurance company will guarantee its continuation for your lifetime.

◆ If you choose to terminate the policy, you have the guarantee that the amount you receive will never be less than your original premium less any convalescent care benefits paid if you maintained your coverage at the insurance company's recommended levels and did not withdraw or borrow money from the policy.

Tax-Free Exchange of Existing Life Insurance

Some people have a certain amount of money inside of existing life insurance and may be able to make an income tax–free exchange of a policy with similar benefits but without provisions for convalescent care, to a policy with the convalescent care benefits. Before you make such an exchange, learn from your existing insurance company whether that insurer can provide similar benefits. If a great number of people choose to exchange existing coverage for this type of life policy, you can bet the companies will find a way to incorporate this benefit into an existing policy.

Another policy design for a 60-year-old couple allows them to put a $50,000 single premium into a $128,000 face amount policy and allows each spouse to withdraw up to 2 percent per month ($2,560 monthly, or about $85 per day) for nursing home care or 1 percent per month for home healthcare to a maximum of the policy's face amount. Unused long-term care benefits pass to beneficiaries as life insurance proceeds, income tax-free. These benefits are built on a second-to-die life insurance policy. Single premium and annual premium policies are available. The benefits paid from the policy would be subject to income taxes.

In order for these policies to provide the promised benefits, the company issuing them must be able to earn a reasonable interest rate and be profitable. If it cannot, you risk losing coverage or receiving reduced benefits. Be cautious and critical when you consider one of these policies.

GROUP/EMPLOYER-PROVIDED LONG-TERM CARE INSURANCE

Policies provided by employers or groups to cover long-term care is an area that still is in its infancy and the offerings have been limited, old-fashioned policies that have not been kept up-to-date by employer and insurer, and that have been insufficiently discounted for the employees. Insurers and employers can do a better job in this area. It is hoped that there will be better news for you in this area in future editions, and that those of you who are finding credible employer offerings will communicate your findings for inclusion in future editions.

IS MEDICAID AN ANSWER TO THE LONG-TERM CARE PROBLEM?

Medicaid is a program for people who have no means of paying for their own care. As our population ages (two-thirds of all those who ever attained age 65 are alive today, and this group will double in the next 40 years), the Medicaid system will be called on to pay much more than the taxpayers can afford. People have resorted to Medicaid more and more frequently because most people resort to Medicaid assistance within 22 months of entering a nursing home. More of your tax dollars today are being used to pay for these expenses. Medicaid officials are doing more to see that aid goes only to those with real need. The practice of protecting assets for survivors instead of financing their owner's long-term care needs is rapidly being legislated out of existence. The answer to the question is that Medicaid is not the answer to your long-term care problems unless your assets truly are exhausted.

However, if you are right up against this problem, call your state Medicaid official and ask for help in understanding your rights under your state's Medicaid laws. Find out which assets may be protected and which cannot, spousal allowances, disqualified periods, and what actions can and cannot be taken. The law in this area is changing too quickly for you to depend on any general rules that could be described here. The situation is grim and if you can use long-term care insurance or annuity arrangements to make sure adequate resources are available to pay your own way, the dismal circumstance of functional disability will not be compounded by the problem of financial disaster.

When Medicaid Is the Only Answer

Suppose that the nursing home expenses were likely not only to impoverish the patient but in the process impoverish the spouse so that the result would be two people dependent on the tax-payers. What steps could be taken in most jurisdictions to try to protect the patient's spouse?

The law does try to protect the spouse by making sure that your state does not take away all the essentials of daily living such as home, transportation, and basic income prior to approving Medicaid payments. Therefore, it's sensible to make sure that your mortgage is paid off and your home is in tip-top shape. Pay off any car loans and/or replace the car. To the extent that these actions keep the care-giving spouse from being dependent on the government, it is in the best interest of everyone.

State Initiatives

Call your state Medicaid office to find out if your state is one of the few that adopted a special state-certified, long-term care policy that provides, in effect, that if you buy the policy it will offer asset protection (not income protection) from Medicaid. This is done either by agreeing not to require the use of assets equal to what the insurance company pays (the Connecticut Plan) or if you buy the policy for at least $100 per day for at least 3 years ($50 per day for 6 years for home healthcare) all of your assets will be protected (New York Plan). All of a person's *income* above what the spouse is allowed to keep must continue to go to paying the nursing home. This program of Medicaid waivers was terminated by 1993 federal legislation so new programs will not be started.

TAXATION OF LONG-TERM CARE BENEFITS

To date taxpayers have no income tax guidance from the IRS with regard to the taxation of any long-term care benefits. They may be subject to income taxes when received. There is substantial pressure being put on your regulators to see to it that benefits paid from long-term care insurances of any type are not subject to income taxes; however, legislation has not passed as yet. Inform your elected officials where you stand on this issue.

The House Ways and Means Committee has approved HR 1215, which would clarify the tax treatment of long-term care. It would enable employers to provide long-term care insurance tax-free to employees, and provide that those paying for it themselves could consider the cost a medical expense on Schedule A of their federal tax return, deducting it if it exceeds the 7.5 percent of adjusted gross income threshold. It also will ensure that individuals who buy and pay for their own long-term care policies with post-tax dollars will receive long-term care benefits income tax-free. This was passed by the U.S. House of Representatives and the U.S. Senate. It is probable that tax legislation favorable to long-term care insurance will be signed by the President.

The Special Concerns in a Second Marriage

You have cared for a spouse going through long-term care and you have made it. You're not impoverished and after your spouse has passed away it is time to get on with the rest of your life. Then the impossible happens: Someone special comes along and you contemplate remarriage. Well, you're older and wiser, so a prenuptial agreement would make sense, but under such an agreement if the new spouse gets sick will you be liable for financing the new spouse's long-term care?

The answer is yes. Medicaid is not the least bit interested in your prenuptial agreements. Title XIX of the Social Security Act, 42 U.S.C 1396R-5(c) stipulates that each spouse is considered to own one-half of the total resources, regardless of who holds legal title to the resource. Medicaid says *all assets* held by persons that are married are considered joint assets and are accountable under Medicaid laws. So, in addition to those prenuptial agreements, make sure your prospective spouse has a good long-term care policy. You know what the personal burden is of being a caregiver and you can't do much about it, but you can avoid the financial burden.

CONCLUSION

Having money left over at the end of your life is not a problem. Having life left over at the end of your money is.

The good news with long-term care is that as the need is growing bigger, more palatable solutions are being found to finance that need. We are likely to see vast improvements in this field in the future. As you read the following chapters on auto and fire insurance, which most of you would not be without, keep in mind that the odds are about 1 in 240 that you will need your auto insurance and 1 in 1,200 that you will need your fire insurance, but they are 2 in 5 that you will use your long-term care insurance. You need to understand that:

- The annual cost of nursing home care ranges from $30,000 to over $50,000 and is continuing to increase.
- Medicaid will pay for long-term care only after you are impoverished.
- Medicare only covers long-term care costs for Skilled Care only for a limited time and only after hospital confinement. It does not cover custodial or intermediate care.
- Long-term care insurance is medically underwritten and any significant changes in your medical condition may make such coverage unavailable after a later date.
- Premiums for long-term care insurance are age-rated, meaning that it will be more expensive to purchase coverage tomorrow than it is today.

CHAPTER FOUR

Medical Insurance

The basic objective of medical insurance is to make sure that you and your family are never exposed to medical bankruptcy.

With this objective in mind, the first specification for a policy is that it have an "unlimited" maximum. Such coverage is not always possible and, in fact, it used to be more readily available than it is now. Many insurance companies have reduced their lifetime maximums to $1 million. Although the $1 million maximum sounds like a significant amount, it is not necessarily enough. Your insurance strategy is to go for the best, request the unlimited, and compromise only if you find that the best is unavailable or impractical.

Optimally, the policy should cover all physician-prescribed treatments to diagnose and correct a medical condition. In an *indemnity plan* (in which the insurance company reimburses you for your expenses after you are treated by your chosen provider), the insurance company should pay your bills after you have paid an acceptable deductible. In addition, you will participate in the payment of the bills up to some percentage, called *coinsurance*. The coinsurance percentage you pay could range between 10 percent and 50 percent. The insurance company pays the balance of those bills. It is entirely possible that you could go medically bankrupt paying the coinsurance percentage of unlimited bills. As a result, you hopefully will find a "stop-loss provision" that obligates the insurance company to pay 100 percent of the bills for the balance of the calendar year, after some stipulated limit on your coinsurance payments. It is important that you know how much would have to be paid out of your own pocket in the way of deductibles and coinsurance if you and others in your family suffered a number of severe illnesses in one year. Once you have determined the maximum "out-of-pocket" amount, you can make sure that you have an emergency fund sufficient to provide for this worst case scenario.

SPECIFICATIONS AND LIMITS FOR MEDICAL COVERAGE

Our specifications for medical coverage are for an unlimited maximum, comprehensive coverage, reasonable deductibles, and an acceptable stop-loss. Complete your Medical Insurance Inventory in Figure 4–1 to see how you are doing on meeting the specifications.

Preexisting Conditions

Preexisting conditions may be an obstacle you will have to face. Often when you apply for insurance coverage you have to answer questions regarding your medical history. This will reveal anything that has happened in your past that would affect the insurance company's ability to provide health insurance for you profitably. You may not have to complete medical questions on employer-provided group medical insurance, but the policy is likely to state that it will not pay benefits for conditions that manifested themselves before the policy was put in force.

Preexisting conditions may be excluded entirely or they may be excluded only for a certain period of time. In some cases, insurance companies will pay some benefits for preexisting conditions but limit the amount of the total payments. Any condition that has been diagnosed by a physician should be revealed on the application. It does not pay to turn in fraudulent applications to insurance companies. When you file a claim for an unrevealed preexisting condition, the insurance company will, and

FIGURE 4–1

Medical and Dental Insurance Inventory

Insured	Company	Policy Number	Policy Maximum	Deductible	Coinsurance	Stop-Loss	Annual Premium
1							
2							
3							
4							
5							

Total Annual Family Premium: _____

must, refuse to pay. You are much better off being candid and thorough with the insurance company, so that if and when it does issue a policy, you have reasonable assurance that the promised benefits will be paid and the policy will not be rescinded because of any erroneous or misleading statements on the application.

The fact that insurance companies exclude preexisting conditions has caused many people to become disenchanted with the insurance industry, resulting in pressure for reforms and health insurance legislation. Legislators have tried to reduce the impact of preexisting conditions on your medical insurability by not allowing insurers to make such exclusions or by reducing the time period during which they can be considered. This is just one of the many healthcare issues with which your government representatives have been concerned. In 1995 80 bills pertaining to healthcare were presented in California alone.

Inside Limits

Many policies today contain "inside limits" that restrict the benefits payable for a number of conditions. Limits on benefits paid for mental or nervous disorders and also drug and alcohol problems, are common. Insurance companies have found that bills for these types of problems can be unending. Conditions that are difficult to diagnose and difficult to treat with measurable results are often excluded within a policy and/or subject to limits on what the insurer will pay. Know the limits in your policy.

Guaranteed Renewable

Individual health insurance policies may be guaranteed renewable, meaning that the insurance company cannot cancel or change the policy benefits once it is issued. However, the insurance company does reserve the right to change the *cost* of the policy on what insurers refer to as a *class basis*. This means that all people with similar policies would be exposed to the same cost increase at the same time. In effect, the insurance company would not select you *individually* for a rate increase. The company must file the cost change with your state insurance commissioner and get approval before the insurer can impose a change.

EMPLOYER-PROVIDED MEDICAL INSURANCE

The best source for medical insurance today is your employer-provided policy. If you have access to an employer-provided medical insurance policy, it is highly likely that the employer is subsidizing it. The advantage to this arrangement is that you need not report what the employer pays for that policy as taxable income as long as the employer is treating all employees equally. The employer also is allowed to deduct the cost as an employee benefit. Costs that are deductible by your employer and not taxable to you as income are about as good as it gets. Your employer is the efficient purchaser of medical insurance from an income tax standpoint.

Medical insurance plans usually are one of four types: indemnity plans, service provider plans, preferred provider plans, or health maintenance organizations. Let's look at each one individually and then at how they are put together and offered by employers.

Indemnity Plans

After you have experienced a loss, indemnity plans reimburse you for that particular loss in accordance with the policy provisions. Indemnity plans offer you the advantage of selecting your own physician and/or hospital. You may choose the best provider, even though "the best" may also be the most expensive—this is both the advantage and the problem with indemnity plans. The giver and receiver of care have no personal incentive to keep costs reasonable. More recent medical insurance plan designs involve both you and the caregiver in providing cost-efficient medical care to bring down the costs. These generally are referred to as "managed care" plans and the more "managed" they are, the less they usually cost.

Service Provider Plans

Blue Cross/Blue Shield service organizations offered some of the first "fee for service" types of plans in which the *insurance organization* is also the *provider* of care. Blue Cross/Blue Shield provides participants with the facilities of the member hospitals and physicians for a monthly subscriber's fee. If the insurance company and the provider are one and the same, the insurance company has a better opportunity to control costs. Theoretically, this makes them better able to estimate the charge to subscribers. Many Blue Cross organizations contract with the hospital to provide the benefits required by its plan. Because the insuring organization is supplying that provider with a substantial amount of business, it will negotiate discounted rates with that provider, thus reducing costs below that of an indemnity plan.

Preferred Provider Plans

Preferred provider organizations (PPOs) are arrangements established by commercial insurance companies following the Blue Cross/Blue Shield example. Coalitions of insurance companies negotiate with providers to obtain discounted rates for their insureds based on the fact that they will be able to send a substantial number of patients to those providers. You will be encouraged to use these preferred providers because of the lower deductibles than the indemnity plan, lower coinsurance, and, often, less paperwork. The preferred providers agree to charge less so they can get the "business." You agree to use the preferred provider because it costs you less and it is less hassle than the indemnity plan.

Health Maintenance Organizations

A health maintenance organization (HMO) is an assemblage of insurers, physicians, and hospitals joined in one business arrangement to provide medical care to its members on a prepaid basis. In effect, HMOs state to their members that they will "maintain their health" for a stipulated amount of money per month.

HMO arrangements can work well if the organizations are economically sound and have good facilities and personnel. However, if any of these factors deteriorate, the whole system may deteriorate. In 1989, a major HMO failed financially, leaving hundreds of thousands of people in doubt about their coverage. Imagine how members of a failing HMO would feel if their health were failing at the same time!

Gatekeepers...The Keeper of the Keys in Managed Care

In PPOs and HMOs, management of your care is primarily through a primary care or "gatekeeper" physician. All your medical services are funneled through this physician. If you need a specialist, this gatekeeper will assign that specialist; and if that specialist wants to take an X-ray, he will ask permission of your gatekeeper to do so. If the organization providing your care works properly and all participants are confident in each other's fairness, permission will be granted for your X-ray. However, don't be surprised if the gatekeeper doctor demands that the request for the X-ray be in writing and insists on responding to that request in writing, a process that could delay your X-ray 10 days or more.

Managed care is in a constant process of balancing costs with medical benefits. If the cost side of the equation is emphasized too much, you find hassle and delay that can result in unsatisfactory medical care and thus higher costs than would otherwise be the case. Figure 4–2 reports an example of this problem.

Currently the gatekeeper system deserves very poor grades. The more people need the continuing care of specialists, the more they are sent back to gatekeepers who end up interfering with rather than facilitating your care. CIGNA, a major provider of health insurance, had only one individual that could approve a

FIGURE 4–2

The "Downside" of Managed Care

Associated Press   August 25, 1995

PORTLAND, Ore.—Jane Harrison was surprised that she had to fight with her doctor to see a specialist about her multiple sclerosis.

Although diagnosed 15 years ago, Harrison never had seen a neurologist who specializes in the debilitating nerve and muscle disease.

She finally found one on a list provided by her insurer, a health maintenance organization, but they ran into a problem: Her primary care doctor wanted her to see his clinic's neurologist—one who did not specialize in MS.

She had to change primary care doctors before she got to see the specialist.

critical chemotherapy drug in 1995. A patient needed that drug while the approver was on vacation. The battle the family had to put up to get that drug was detrimental to all concerned and drove up the cost of care.

HMO Limitations

When you enroll in an HMO, you have accepted that organization as your exclusive provider of care for some period of time, usually one year. If the organization has a talented staff and is healthy financially, you are likely to be a satisfied member. However, if the HMO is not healthy financially, it will begin to lose talented physicians and you may find that your gatekeeper seems to be more concerned with costs than with your health. When you think about the boom going on in new HMO offerings, keep in mind that when the HMO starts up and enrolls new members, there is a lot of money coming into the organization and little going out. The new enrollees are healthy so demands on services are relatively low. It is easy to be profitable under these conditions and profit entices startup companies into this business. However, over time, the population of the HMO grows older and sicker and, although incoming revenue may not be increasing, services—and costs—will be. If you're in an HMO facing these problems and you become seriously ill, you may become unhappy with your HMO. The fear of this situation has caused many potential members to avoid the HMO type of plan.

All HMOs are going to have to work together and police themselves if they are going to keep concerns such as this from appearing in the paper and scaring their health membership away. These problems have encouraged the development of hybrids of HMOs. The PPO and indemnity plan combination (often referred to as a *point of service plan*) gives you more choice and control so that you can use the HMO and/or PPO options with less fear of losing control.

Point of Service Plan

The combination indemnity plan/PPO option, or point of service plan, is an alternative offered by many commercial insurance companies and adopted by many employers. Under this arrangement, you do not commit to the indemnity or the PPO plan in advance. You decide which to use at the time care is needed. The employer will attempt to "steer" you toward the PPO by means of lower deductibles and lower coinsurance than are available under the indemnity plan, but ultimately the choice is yours. If the care is needed for something you feel can and will be handled well by the PPO, the PPO will be the choice. You can expect the services to be cheaper and easier because the benefits are often delivered without annoying paperwork (no claim forms) and with low, or no deductibles and coinsurance.

This freedom of choice *encourages* you to use preferred providers and to go through gatekeepers rather than *mandating* it as is the case with an HMO. What has happened is that more people are willing to use PPOs under these circumstances and, as doctors have seen more of their patients willing to use PPOs, they have affiliated with the organizations, thus increasing the available talent. Indeed, many doctors have found that they generally are better off negotiating their rates up front with a PPO and collecting what is due them rather than staying on their own in an individual practice and maintaining their own collection department to try to collect their billings. You may be staying with the indemnity plan so that you can choose your own doctor, but one day you'll probably find that your own doctor is in your optional PPO. Then you can use his or her services at a discounted rate.

The indemnity plan with the PPO option is referred to as the dual option plan or point of service plan. You may, however, be given the option to choose between the indemnity, PPO, or HMO—a triple option. Cost-wise and benefit-wise, you will be encouraged to move from indemnity to PPO to HMO. If you elect the HMO you'll probably have to live with that election for at least a year, but then you can move back.

COBRA

On April 7, 1986, the U.S. Congress enacted the Consolidated Omnibus Budget Reconciliation Act (COBRA). It is a federal law applicable to employers providing health benefits to groups of 20 or more employees. It allows an employee to continue group insurance even after his or her employment has terminated. The insured pays the full cost of what the employer was paying for the plan and possibly up to 2 percent more for administrative expenses. The continuation of coverage may extend up to 18 months. The insured's spouse and children may have up to 36 months of continued health insurance. As a rule of thumb, if you qualify for COBRA, sign up. *Don't go even one day without health insurance!*

The second rule of thumb is to get other health insurance in effect as soon as possible. Your COBRA coverage has a "brick wall" at the end of your allowable coverage. If you are using COBRA and are healthy enough to get your own coverage, switch off COBRA (with the brick wall) and obtain your own coverage (without a brick wall), because your own or your family's health may deteriorate while you are on COBRA. In such a case, you may find yourself unable to obtain coverage because of ill health as the end of COBRA coverage approaches. If this happens to you, see the discussions of conversion and state programs.

The COBRA provisions are a boon to employees whose employment is ending and their dependents because they make health insurance available *regardless* of a family's physical condition. Premium payments to continue the coverage must be made promptly. It has been estimated that an employee or dependent covered under COBRA receives $2 in benefits for each dollar of premium paid. As a result, employers have been advised to terminate employees' COBRA coverage if they don't pay their premiums on time, so don't be late! Table 4–1 summarizes COBRA provisions.

Employer and Employee COBRA Responsibilities
Of the lawsuits related to COBRA, approximately one-third involve inadequate completion of the "initial notice" requirements that serve to outline the rights of COBRA-qualified beneficiaries and their responsibilities. It is up to the employee to notify the employer in case of divorce or when a dependent is no longer eligible for regular group coverage.

It is up to the employer to provide "initial notice." COBRA guidelines dictate that the notice be mailed via first class mail to employee and spouse. It is the "and spouse" part that has created problems. Envelopes not properly addressed to include the spouse, new spouses the employer did not know

TABLE 4–1

COBRA–Qualification and Eligibility Period

COBRA Qualifying Event	Qualifying Individual	Maximum Time Period
Death of a covered employee	Covered dependent spouse and covered children	36 months
Termination of the covered employee's employment (other than for gross misconduct) or reduction in a covered employee's hours of employment	Covered employee and covered dependents	18 months / 29 months*
Divorce or legal separation of covered employee from spouse	Covered dependent spouse/children losing coverage	36 months
The covered employee's group health coverage terminates due to coverage by Medicare	Covered dependent spouse and/or covered children	36 months
The dependent child ceases to be an eligible dependent under the terms of the employer's group health plan	Covered dependent child ceasing to be eligible	36 months

* Or 36 months if disabled at the time of termination or reduction of hours

about, and other administrative foul-ups have created havoc for employers. It is important for employers to administer COBRA carefully. A $100-million class action suit was filed against a company by 2,000 former spouses and dependents alleging lack of compliance with the notice requirements of COBRA. The COBRA statutory penalty against employers for COBRA violations is $100 per day per beneficiary.

Conversion
In many states, your final chance to continue your health insurance without having to requalify medically comes at the end of your COBRA benefits or the state-mandated continuation for employers with fewer than 20 employees. This is the

right to convert to an individual policy. Typically, these conversion policies are relatively expensive and the benefits are very
restrictive. The conversion privileges are of value only to those
who cannot obtain health insurance in any other way.

State Programs

Many states have passed legislation for employer groups of fewer
than 20 employees that is patterned after COBRA so that employees have a right to continuing healthcare benefits after termination.
For example, Illinois provides for a nine-month extension of health
coverage. Your employer's insurer will provide you with the information and paperwork you need.

Should none of these alternatives for health insurance be available to you, the next step is to contact your state insurance commissioner's office and ask for the enrollment materials, price list,
and benefits description of the state-sponsored health insurance
pool. Most states have created state pools for those who cannot get
health insurance elsewhere. You can get the papers and sign up for
the state pool, but while you are awaiting acceptance, keep trying
for alternative coverage for each member of your family.

INDIVIDUAL MEDICAL INSURANCE

If employer-provided health insurance is not a viable alternative,
you will apply directly to an insurance company for an individually issued policy. The advantage of this procedure is that
you can more or less dictate the type of benefits you want. The
disadvantage is that you have no employer to help pay for the
insurance. Unfortunately, individual insurance policies are
most readily available if you are healthy. When you apply for
an individual health insurance policy, the insurance company
will ask you a dizzying array of medical questions. The insurer
will want to know your personal health history and that of everyone in your family. It is in your best interest to divulge everything because even if you have a particular health condition that
the insurance company might not wish to cover, the insurer
may be able to issue the policy with an exclusion rider. The policy

FIGURE 4–3

Individual Medical Insurance Action Letter

Dear _____:

I am in need of private medical insurance. I am male/female born
_____. I am a smoker/nonsmoker in excellent/good/fair health.

My spouse is a male/female born _____ and is a
smoker/nonsmoker in excellent/good/fair health.

We have/do not have children. Their names, dates of birth, gender, and basic
health condition are listed on the back of this letter.

I would like a comprehensive major medical policy that is lifetime guaranteed
renewable and has an unlimited life-time maximum.

Other plan features are:

1. Individual deductible $100/$200/$500/$1,000/$2,000/$_____.

2. Coinsurance provision 80/20 (Insurance company pays 80%, I pay 20%)

3. Stop-loss provision—What is my maximum out-of-pocket requirement?
   For the family _____
   For how long _____

4. A PPO and/or HMO option.

Please send me quotes from a number of companies including any descriptive
material you have on the plans along with enrollment forms and instructions.

I would appreciate your evaluation of the coverages regarding which ones you
feel are fairly priced and sufficiently comprehensive to provide for my family.

Sincerely,

---

would cover everything except that particular condition, which
is certainly a better alternative than no health insurance at all.
Another advantage of an individual policy is the availability of
a guaranteed renewable contract that allows the insurance company to adjust the costs for the insurance as long as it does so
on a class basis and has the approval of your state insurance
commissioner to make the change. The action letter in Figure 4–3
is designed to help you define your medical insurance needs to
a provider or insurance agent.

The action letter to request quotes regarding private health insurance first lists the specifics regarding those who need health insurance (dates of birth, smoker or nonsmoker, health conditions) for all members of the family. It then requests a comprehensive major medical policy that is guaranteed renewable throughout your lifetime and has an unlimited lifetime maximum. You then select an appropriate deductible. You can ask the insurance professional to provide you with quotes at various deductibles so that you may choose the one that is most cost-effective for you. It states your requested coinsurance provision—that is, how much of the medical bills you would pay and how much the insurance company would pay, stipulating the most typical split, 80 percent insurance company/20 percent you. Keep in mind a 50/50 split normally will cost you less but may not increase your out-of-pocket maximum. You would pay a greater percentage of the smaller bills but then shift responsibility to the insurance company. The letter next asks for your maximum out-of-pocket exposure so that you would know what your medical costs could be under a worst-case scenario.

ASSOCIATION MEDICAL INSURANCE

Another alternative for obtaining medical insurance may be through an association of which you are a member. Some organizations sell insurance to provide an extra benefit for their membership and/or in order to make a profit for their organization. You obviously would prefer the former reason. Some of the less savory fare offered by associations are policies that pay you a stipulated amount of money each day you are in the hospital. Keep in mind that the average stay in the hospital is less than 10 days, and a $50 per day indemnity policy paying you $500 is not going to be much help. Generally these policies are not worth what they cost. Also, beware of policies that will pay benefits only if your medical condition is caused by an accident or some specific illness. These policies cost less but are not as inexpensive as they ought to be. They are a high-profit item to the insurance companies issuing them. They play on your fear of a specific illness, such as cancer. Avoid these types of policies—rather, obtain high-quality comprehensive (covers whatever illness affects you) coverage instead.

MEDICARE: FEDERAL GOVERNMENT-PROVIDED MEDICAL INSURANCE

Both federal and state governments provide medical insurance benefits. The Medicare program of the federal government provides mandatory basic hospitalization benefits for most U.S. citizens over the age of 65 and some other special classes of individuals. The hospital coverage, referred to as Part A, is supplemented by Part B of Medicare at a cost to you of $46.10 per month (at the time this was written in 1995). Part B is a voluntary program that provides for the payment of doctor bills. All eligible individuals should sign up for *both* of these plans three months prior to their 65th birthday. Medicare normally is insufficient by itself. It's advisable to purchase a supplemental plan.

Caution to Medicare Participants

Medicare has been an indemnity insurance plan primarily. Your chosen doctor and hospital are reimbursed for the services they provide to you within the benefits approved by Medicare. But, managed care is coming to Medicare: Now Medicare patients can experience the problems of dealing with gatekeepers. HMOs all over the country are soliciting your business and telling you in wonderful ads what good care they will offer you, but be careful. Ask HMOs whether signing up with them mandates that they must be your exclusive provider and, if so, when and how you could terminate the relationship. What freedoms would you be giving up? What happens when you get sick away from home? You will also want to know how solvent financially HMOs are and whether they are a new startup company or one with a mature patient base and a good reputation for quality care. No, it is not easy for Medicare patients to select a provider today. Too many new providers are trying to leverage seniors' fear of costly illness into business for themselves. Shop with a healthy degree of skepticism.

Which Medigap Plan?

There are 10 standard Medicare Supplemental Benefit Plans. Table 4–2 highlights the benefits each provides. The most cost-effective choice is Plan F. It covers all the basics plus 100 percent of

TABLE 4-2

The 10 Standard Medicare Supplement Benefit Plans

CORE BENEFITS	Plan A	Plan B	Plan C	Plan D	Plan E	Plan F	Plan G	Plan H	Plan I	Plan J
Part A Hospital (Days 61–90)	X	X	X	X	X	X	X	X	X	X
Lifetime Reserve Days (Days 91–150)	X	X	X	X	X	X	X	X	X	X
365 Life Hospital Days at 100%	X	X	X	X	X	X	X	X	X	X
Parts A and B Blood	X	X	X	X	X	X	X	X	X	X
Part B Coinsurance—20%	X	X	X	X	X	X	X	X	X	X
ADDITIONAL BENEFITS										
Skilled Nursing Facility Coinsurance (Days 21–100)			X	X	X	X	X	X	X	X
Part A Deductible		X	X	X	X	X	X	X	X	X
Part B Deductible			X			X				
Part B Excess Charges						100%	80%		100%	100%
Foreign Travel Emergency			X	X	X	X	X	X	X	X
At-Home Recovery				X			X		X	X
Prescription Drugs								$250 Deduc. 50% to $1,250	$250 Deduc. 50% to $1,250	$250 Deduc. 50% to $3,000
Preventive Medical Care					X					X

the Part B expenses—the doctor's bills. Doctor bills can far exceed what Medicare mandates as "reasonable and customary," and it's a significant area of exposure for you. Another reason for selecting Plan F is that it does not include the at-home recovery, prescription drugs, and preventive medical care benefits which usually are too limited to be worth what they typically cost. You may have a good reason for choosing the more costly and comprehensive Plan J. If you know that you will use up the full prescription drug limitation of $3,000 per year each year or really want the extra benefits of the more comprehensive plans then by all means select one of them.

One reason for a Medigap policy is the need for coverage for that portion of the doctor bill that Medicare deems "excessive." A doctor who accepts just what Medicare allows is a "participating" physician; others are "nonparticipating." About one out of every three physicians is participating. It is probable that this number will fall as Medicare continues its cutbacks. When Medicare refuses to pay too often, it becomes impossible for these physicians to maintain their practices.

You can obtain a good Medigap policy for approximately $80 to $100 per month. You should be able to locate a good one by consulting your doctor or better yet his billing department to find out which ones they and their patients like best. But select only one plan; multiple Medigap policies are a waste of money. Figure 4–4 provides a sample inquirer letter for Medigap policies.

The good news about Medigap policies is that if you apply in time (start three months prior to your 65th birthday) or without a break in your existing coverage, you can get a policy without any medical questions asked. Make sure you apply promptly. Even after you have a plan, you can move to another without medical questions or preexisting condition limitations as long as there is no break in coverage.

Here's one more caution. Doctors in some areas are signing their patients up for "wellness" benefit plans, annual physicals, and so on, for a monthly or annual retainer and a promise to waive the Medicare deductible. First, the deductibles for Medicare may be picked up by your Medicare supplement insurance. Second, if the doctor is selling "insurance," it is probably not legal. Third, it is probably not worth the money. If any of you have

FIGURE 4–4

Medigap Action Letter

Dear Sir or Madam:

I am in need of private Medigap insurance. I am a male/female born
_____. I am a smoker/nonsmoker in excellent/good health.

My spouse is a male/female born _____ and is a
smoker/nonsmoker in excellent/good/fair health. I would like a comprehensive
Medigap policy that is lifetime guaranteed renewable and has an unlimited
lifetime maximum.

Other plan features desired are:

1. Cost-effective benefits that fill in the gaps by paying what Medicare Parts
    A and B commonly exclude.

2. Usual and customary expense coverage so that the Medigap policy will
    pay the excess charges between the usual and customary costs and the
    more limited Medicare-eligible expenses.

Please send me quotes from _____ companies including any
descriptive material you have on the plans along with enrollment forms and
instructions.

I would appreciate your evaluation of the coverages regarding which one(s)
you feel is/are fairly priced and sufficiently comprehensive to provide for my
family.

If you have any questions, please call me at _____. I look
forward to hearing from you. Thank you for your assistance.

Sincerely,

---

knowledge of such a plan that you consider a fair, legal arrangement, it is hoped that you will communicate your knowledge for inclusion in future editions. If you are aware of those that are not, take the issue up with your state insurance commissioner.

A WORD ABOUT THE NATIONAL HEALTHCARE CRISIS

"Crisis?" Yes, it's a crisis. The only people that you will encounter that do not think healthcare is in crisis are those who have not personally been affected or had someone they care about fall through the cracks of the current U.S. healthcare system. However, crisis does not mean it can't get worse. It *is* getting worse as we continue to ignore it.

You see, health insurance as it is structured today is not insurance. *Insurance* by definition is a pooling of your payments with those of others to have your losses, if any, paid by the insurer because you have paid a premium. But most consumers obtain their health insurance through their employers. Health insurance can, and will, terminate when employees become too sick to work (after COBRA, potential conversions, and so on). It will cease to reimburse employees for losses even though they paid the premiums while they were healthy and employed. During an illness, the insurance company legally can refuse to accept employees' insurance payments, terminate our coverage, and cease paying for the illness (loss) incurred while the patients were healthy and insured. You have health insurance while you are a healthy, employed, fortunate worker. In fact, because the cost is deductible it costs you no more than 70 cents per dollar after the tax benefit, assuming you're in the 30 percent tax bracket.

But, when you get sick, the current healthcare system ignores the fact that you paid for "insurance" while healthy, and the insurer systematically starts to eliminate your coverage. The insurer finds a way to no longer accept your premium and to cease to pay benefits. First, the insurer increases your cost. It gives you an opportunity to pay for COBRA, conversion insurance, or state pool health insurance with your *after-tax* earnings. You not only have to pay 100 percent to 102 percent of the cost of your coverage but also full income tax on the money with which you pay the premium. In the 30 percent tax bracket, you have to earn $1.42 in order to spend $1 to buy health insurance.

How is that for public policy? Health insurance costs you $.70 per $1 of premium if you are a healthy, employed worker but twice that much if you're too young, too old, or too ill to get your health insurance through an employer.

The obstacle course that the healthcare insurance system puts you through as your health deteriorates and employment terminates serves to push you into the ranks of the uninsured and uninsurable. Those of you that this has happened to are too quiet. Somehow, some victims even feel that it is their own fault and embarassment keeps them quiet. It's not! It is time more people, particularly your legislators, heard from you.

This does *not* mean that you want government being the *provider* of health insurance or healthcare. There are two reasons. One, dollars that go through government are eaten up by inefficient bureaucratic expenses. Two, you can't complain to city hall about city hall. Government's function should be to do what it does best: serve and protect you if the private healthcare system lets you down.

What kind of private system would work? One that could not get rid of you no matter what happened. As a result of the healthcare system receiving your monthly capitation fee from whatever source, the insurer would be *required* to provide your care forever. Economically, in such a system, it would be best for the system to keep you healthy, and if you became sick to get you well as soon as possible . . . which is just the opposite of the motivation of the current system.

What's wrong with this new system? There is no room for "little" systems. They have to be big so they can serve you throughout the country. They must spread the risk and be efficient. You won't get to choose your own doctor. Professionals who want to make you well will choose for you. And, worse yet, you will have to agree to pay for your coverage forever, even if it is out of welfare, healthcare stamps, or charity. There's the rub . . . there can be no "free lunch" in the new healthcare scenario. Spreading the risk and spreading the cost are essential.

There must be constant pay, constant coverage, and professionals directing your treatment. Uncle Sam should be there to measure, evaluate, and report quality of coverage and results, as well as to assist you when the system fails to provide quality care. The competition among the systems will be to keep their populations healthier at lower cost than the other systems. Efficiency and quality will pay. You will have no choice regarding participation, provider, or paying. But this scenario is impossible! Americans won't accept it! What do you mean? It sounds like social (medical) security.

Of course, you can keep your present system. You can hope you and yours won't fall through the cracks of the system dragging all of you down emotionally and economically. The current system does allow you to choose your own doctor, choose not to pay directly, and choose not to be covered—and these features obviously are important to you.

CONCLUSION

Although you may not be seeing healthcare reform on the evening news anymore, you can be sure that it is still proceeding. Insurers, legislators, healthcare providers, employers, and combinations of all these players are working daily to devise systems of delivering healthcare more effectively. Managed care is the jargon of the day. This is your new medical care world and you are going to have to cope with the following:

- Networks rather than individual physicians.
- Financial incentives to accept more controlled (by providers and payors, not you) care.
- Change, as the providers work at trying to balance quality of care with cost of care.
- Gatekeepers, the general or primary physician, who will approve your use of specialists.
- Utilization review to determine the "necessity" of the medical care you are receiving.
- Preadmission certification.
- Dental PPOs.

The bottom line on medical insurance is that you shouldn't go a day without it. A lack of medical insurance can be hazardous to your economic health.

CHAPTER FIVE

Residence/Real Estate Insurance

The objective of real property insurance is to make sure that you have adequate insurance coverages related to where you live and what you own. Real estate insurance is all about fire, theft and being sued, all related to where you live. You may be a home-owner, condo owner, or a renter, but in any case you need this coverage. In fact, if you are a homeowner and have a mortgage, the bank will not lend you the money or continue your mort-gage unless you show proof of adequate (protecting the lender adequately) real estate insurance. If you're a renter, chances are that only one in four of you reading these words has a renter's policy. That is despite the fact that half of you admit that it is likely that some of your possessions could be lost or stolen this year. Why don't you insure? Is it because you never got around to it? Do you think it is too expensive? Or don't you think you have much? Well then, get around to it! It is not too expensive. You can probably expect to pay about $40 per year for a typical one-bedroom apartment with about $25,000 worth of property in it. You may think that what you own is not worth that much, but you would find that it is worth much more than you think if you had to replace all of it.

Are you parents of uninsured adult children, with children and pets? You say you still need motivation to encourage your children to get that renter's policy? What happens when they get burned out of their apartment because they were grilling on the patio and destroyed their own apartment building because of their negligence? That's right, they come to live with you (the cost of your homeowner's insurance goes up) and they stay with you because they have no money and are being sued for damages to the apartment building—and they stay a long time. On the other hand, what happens if your children have a good renter's policy with adequate liability coverage? They come, they replace their possessions that were lost in the fire, the insurance company deals with their landlord, and they find another place to live and leave much more quickly, for their sake and your own. One great benefit of adequate insurance is peace of mind.

CASUALTY INSURANCE INVENTORY

If you already have a homeowner's or renter's policy, you need to examine the essential information within that policy. Complete the inventory in Figure 5–1 to evaluate your coverage and determine whether there are any ways to improve it.

To complete the inventory, go to the most recent declarations page of your policy. It will be provided on the anniversary date of your policy. There you will find the information required for the inventory.

As you look at your inventory now, does it mention every piece of real estate you own? I can hear your answer. "Yes, all but that lot we bought in the mountains of Colorado a year ago . . . but it is not worth much. It's just vacant land with a 2,000 foot mine shaft that the kids like to play around." If that is your answer, you have a liability risk that is uninsured. Call your insurance company and correct it now!

DETERMINING YOUR INSURANCE NEEDS

The real estate action letter in Figure 5–2 specifies what you want in coverage for your residence and other real estate holdings. Generally, you should send these specifications to your property/casualty insurance provider regardless of what you find on the inventory that you completed. It is possible that the maximum amount the insurance company will issue today is higher than what you

FIGURE 5–1

Casualty Insurance Inventory for Residence/
Real Estate Insurance

Insurance Company/ Real Estate	Policy Number	Policy Type	Liability Maximum	Property Maximum	Medical Maximum	Special Riders	Annual Premium
1							
2							
3							
4							
5							

FIGURE 5–2

Real Estate Insurance Action Letter

Dear _____ :

I am evaluating my property casualty insurance, and I would appreciate your assistance.

My specific desires concerning my real estate coverage are as follows:

1. Maintain my *liability* at the maximum amount available or the amount that would best coordinate with a personal umbrella or comprehensive liability policy.

2. Make sure my property is insured for 100% of replacement cost and includes an inflation endorsement making the insurance company responsible for keeping my policy at that level.

3. Make sure that the coverage is of the most *comprehensive all-risk* variety. I would like the most comprehensive HO form including coverage for personal property losses and indirect losses resulting from the loss of use of personal property.

4. Loss payments are to be made on a *"replacement cost"* basis rather than on an "actual cash value" depreciated value basis for all coverages including personal property.

5. Please let me know if there are any discounts available for the following:

	I Have	**Do Not Have**
CO_2 Fire Extinguishers	_____	_____
Detectors	_____	_____
Deadbolt Locks	_____	_____
Other Protective Devices	_____	_____

6. Do I require any special coverage for our household domestic help and/or other occasional workers we hire for household work?

7. Please recommend cost-effective deductibles.

8. Please maximize guest medical.

9. Please let me know the cost of *earthquake* and/or *flood* coverage and your recommendations.

10. Your recommendation regarding special items of value that should be included on a personal property rider (as follows):

Real Estate Insurance Action Letter (Concluded)

Item	Value	Appraisal Method	Date
——	——	————————	——
——	——	————————	——
——	——	————————	——

11. Do you recommend any business pursuits endorsements?

12. Please include coverage providing benefits if we are forced to bring our property up to code after a loss.

Sincerely,

were able to purchase when you originally obtained the policy. It is prudent to send this written request to make sure your policy is up-to-date. In most cases, the cost differential to increase your policy from its present levels to the more adequate levels for today are so minor that it doesn't make economic sense not to bring your policy up to date. It gives your property/casualty provider an opportunity to ensure that your coverage conforms to the specifications in the action letter and is current.

For you folks in California, it is not going to be that easy. In your state, as in some others, you must contact your governor's office and the state insurance department and put pressure on them when needed insurance is unavailable. Some of the laws passed in these states have caused insurance companies to avoid doing business in the state, thus making some needed coverages unavailable or difficult to find. It is essential for you to work with a good insurance professional in those states.

Real Estate Liability

You of course want to maximize your liability coverage. You have liability insurance because you, or a member of your family, might make a mistake that injures someone else. The law requires that people behave as reasonable and prudent individuals and if you do not, your error can constitute negligence. If that negligence leads to the injury of another person or the property of another individual, you may be held liable for damages. Not only will you be held liable for your own actions but also for the actions of your relatives who are residents in your household under age 21 and in your care, or for the actions of someone else who is a resident of your home. You may be held liable for the animals for which you are legally responsible and also for the negligent operation of your insured, unlicensed vehicles that are used with your consent. If you own an unlicensed three-wheel, all-terrain vehicle that the neighborhood kids use, you are exposing yourself to a big lawsuit! It is best handled by the "don't" control technique. That is, "Don't own it!"

Take a mental inventory of your household. How many people are you responsible for? Are any of them teenagers? Do any of them do things that you would describe as not reasonable and prudent or, more importantly, that your neighbor would describe as not reasonable and prudent? Do you have any animals that could injure someone? What about toys, bikes, boats, all-terrain vehicles, snowmobiles, and so on? What about equipment such as the lawnmower and the snowblower? Do you allow others to use any of your possessions, on your own insured property or, more hazardous still, off your own insured property?

You need to know how your policy will protect you from economic loss in any circumstance for which you may be held responsible. Also know the difference in protection that you have if unlicensed vehicles are insured and operated on your property with your consent, as opposed to the degree of protection that you have if they are operated on property other than your own. Ask your property liability insurance professional about liability where homeowner's policies were not effective in providing protection. The bottom line is, don't risk a lot for a little. The "little" is the little additional premium you will pay when you ask for the maximum amount of the most comprehensive type of coverage.

You will note that the action letter asked for the liability maximum to be increased to "the maximum amount available or the amount that would best coordinate with a personal umbrella or comprehensive liability policy." We recommend that you obtain an umbrella liability policy or a comprehensive personal liability policy coordinated with your other property casualty insurances. The cost of such a policy is frequently related to the quantity and quality of your underlying property/casualty insurances. Your agent can evaluate the increases in costs resulting from increasing your underlying policy and compare those increased costs with the resulting decreased cost of the umbrella policy. The coordination of the two should provide the most cost-effective package for you.

Real Estate Medical Payments Coverage

The medical payment provision protects you by requiring that the insurer pay reasonable medical expenses, including funeral expenses, incurred by persons who are injured on your premises with your permission (or permission from someone else who is also covered by your policy). It also will pay if someone is injured away from your premises but the injury results from your activity or from the activities of someone insured under your policy. The medical payments provision will not pay benefits to you or your other insureds. It is designed to reimburse others for injuries related to people and pets in your household. The action letter asked your agent to maximize your medical payments provision. You will find that the additional cost to go from minimal to maximum coverage is not significant. Don't take a chance by rationalizing that everyone has medical coverage. More than 39 million people in the United States do *not* have medical insurance, and the number is increasing rather than decreasing. Another 65 million people were temporarily without medical insurance during 1994 according to the October 1995 Report in the National Underwriter Magazine. If the person making a claim against you is uninsured, he or she has no one other than you to look to for reimbursement. Again, don't risk a lot for a little.

The "HO" Puzzle

The homeowners coverage diagram in Table 5–1 illustrates the varieties of homeowner's coverage. The diagram refers to policy types HO-1 through HO-8; they provide differing levels of coverage for various types of residences. If you have an HO-1 policy, all you have is "basic coverage."

TABLE 5–1

Homeowner's Coverage

	100% Dwelling Coverage A	10% of A Other Structures Coverage B	50% of A Personal Property Coverage C	20% of A Loss of Use Coverage D
HO-1	Basic	Basic	Basic	Basic (10% of A)
HO-2	Broad	Broad	Broad	Broad
HO-3	All risk	All risk	Broad*	All risk
HO-4 (For Renters)	Not applicable	Not applicable	Broad (Basic Coverage)	Broad (20% of C)
HO-5	All risk	All risk	All risk	All risk
HO-6 (For Condo Dwellers)	Not applicable	Not applicable	Broad	Broad (40% of C)
HO-8 (For Properties Not Qualifying for HO-1, 2, 3 or 5)	Basic (ACV only)	Basic	Basic	Basic

*HO-15 converts broad to modified all risk.

The HO-1 Policy

The HO-1 type of policy was the first of the homeowner's series and provides basic coverage—protection against only the specific perils listed, such as fire and lightning, vandalism, malicious mischief, glass breakage, theft, and volcanic eruption.

The HO-2 Policy

The HO-2 policy, which improved upon the HO-1, is called "broad-form" coverage. The HO-2 policy includes all the perils named in the HO-1 and adds six more. It also covers losses caused by falling objects; weight of ice, snow, and sleet; heating or air conditioning system damage; water damage; frozen plumbing; and injury by artificially generated electricity. It also eliminates the exclusion under the HO-1 policy for smoke damage from fireplaces. The HO-2 policy was an early improvement, and you will find many HO-2 policies still in existence today—too many. Today you need to upgrade your policy from HO-2 to HO-3.

The HO-3 Policy

Probably the most cost-effective homeowner's policy today is the HO-3 policy, which pays benefits for all losses except those specifically excluded by the policy. It does not define the specific perils for which the policy will pay benefits, as do HO-1 and HO-2. HO-3 is referred to as "open perils" or "all-risk" coverage applicable to your *dwelling*, your *other structures*, and *loss of use*. The other structures provision provides an amount of insurance equal to 10 percent of the amount on the dwelling itself for other detached structures on the property, such as a garage. The loss-of-use coverage provides funds up to 20 percent of the amount of coverage on the dwelling to pay any outside living expenses you require as a result of the loss and *in excess* of your normal living expenses.

The *personal property* coverage under an HO-3 policy provides for payment up to an amount equal to 50 percent of the coverage on the dwelling to reimburse you for losses caused to your personal property. Personal property coverage is on a broad form, rather than an all-risk basis. This coverage for personal property may be extended by various riders but, in order to get true all-risk coverage for personal property, you may find that you have to pay a great deal more than you are willing to pay. The high cost results from the fact that all-risk coverage to personal property may include the risk of your own personal carelessness, which can mean frequent claims. Thus, this coverage can become very expensive and is probably impractical. The solution is to add (to your HO-3 policy) an HO-15 endorsement that converts your "broad form" personal property coverage to a "modified all-risk" design.

The HO-4 Policy

Renter's insurance is referred to as an HO-4 policy. It provides broad form coverage for your personal property, and reimbursement of any *loss of use* of your rental property to the extent of 20 percent of your personal property coverage. Renters frequently need riders that provide adequate protection by extending and increasing the benefits of the standard HO-4 policy. The standard HO-4 rental policy and HO-6 condominium dweller's policies provide no liability coverage automatically, so renters and condominium dwellers should make special arrangements for a general liability policy.

The HO-5 Policy

The highest quality homeowner's policy is the HO-5 policy. It provides all-risk coverage for the dwelling, the other structures, personal property, and loss of use. This policy is available only in limited circumstances. Your insurance agent may be unable to offer it because the insurance company has determined that it results in too many claims. When the HO-5 policy is available, it is relatively expensive, but it is the most comprehensive policy.

The HO-6 Policy

Condominium owners are responsible for the physical repair of everything within the walls of the condominium unit; therefore, owners should have coverage (HO-6) that provides indemnification in case of the interior destruction of their unit. Condominium owners also have a responsibility for the common elements of their condominium complex, insurance for which is normally provided by their condominium association. Your condo is *your* property and you would be wise to make sure that adequate coverage has been obtained by your association. You may purchase "loss assessment" insurance that will pay up to a stipulated amount for assessments made against you by your association for both common element losses and liability suits filed against your association.

The HO-8 Policy

Many privately owned freestanding homes will not qualify for an HO-1, HO-2, HO-3, or HO-5 policy, either as a result of their location or their construction. Replacement, either partially or wholly, of these properties would be impractical or impossible. For example, you might have a historic landmark home with irreplaceable, elaborate woodwork and stained glass windows or an older home in a remote area that has no market value. It could be an elaborate home, expensive to replace, built in a neigh-borhood where it would not now be replaced, even if it could be, if it were totally destroyed. Insurance companies have found, under these circumstances, that their risk of such struc-tures being destroyed by fire increases dramatically.

As a result, insurers seek to limit their exposure by provid-ing a special contract for such structures, referred to as an HO-8 policy. The HO-8 policy limits the amount under Coverage A that provides for the replacement of the dwelling. Reimbursement under Coverage A will be provided only for the basic risks listed in the policy, and reimbursement will be on actual cash value only, that is, the replacement cost less depreciation.

If you own such a structure, discuss its coverage with your property/casualty insurance professional. Be aware of the limits of your coverage and the extent to which you are self-insuring the dwelling. With this type of structure, control techniques become your primary risk-management tool because financing techniques (insurance) are limited.

Real Property Loss

Dwelling coverage, or Coverage A under your policy, indicates the maximum amount the insurance company will pay in the event of the total destruction of your property. Do not relate the adequacy of the amount recorded to the "market value" of your home. This is a common error. The insurance company relates property coverage to the "replacement cost" of your prop-erty. The amount recorded should adequately cover 100 per-cent of the "replacement cost" of your home. If it does not, and your home is totally destroyed, the insurance company will not pay more than the amount stipulated under Coverage A unless your policy includes a valuable rider usually referred to as an *inflation guard endorsement*. In that case you would, by pay-ing a premium for that endorsement, make the insurance com-pany responsible for keeping your coverage at 100 percent of replacement cost.

In determining replacement costs, the insurance company will ask you for information about the construction of your home and its location. Typically, an assessor will inspect the home and/or request pictures of it. The insurer will use this information, along with information in its data banks regarding construction costs in your particular area, to estimate a replacement cost figure for you. You should insure your home for that amount and add an inflation guard endorsement to your policy. With the inflation guard endorsement on your policy, you can be confident that if the insurer's estimate of the replacement cost of your home proves inaccurate at the time of your loss, it will be the insurance company's responsibility to make up the difference, not yours. If you have the proper coverage in the event of the total destruction of your home, you are more likely to have the proper coverage if partial losses occur. For example, a fire that causes a $20,000 loss to a home that has a replacement value of $100,000 and is fully insured for that amount would pay the full amount of the $20,000 loss, less the policy deductible.

The 80 Percent Rule

An 80 percent rule that applies to partial losses. This rule states that a $20,000 claim would still be fully paid even if this $100,000 home was insured for only $80,000, or 80 percent of its true replacement cost. However, what would happen if the owner of this home was risking a lot to save a little and had the home insured for only $40,000? Under these circumstances, the insurance company would not pay the entire loss but would share the loss with the insured. The insurance company would pay an amount related to the amount of insurance required to receive full reimbursement, $80,000 (on the $100,000 replacement value house), to the amount of insurance this homeowner chose to carry, $40,000. Because the insured was carrying one-half the amount of insurance required, the insurance company would reimburse for one-half the loss ($10,000 of the $20,000 loss) less the applicable policy deductible. Your action letter will help by asking your property insurance provider to make sure that your home is insured at 100 percent of replacement cost, and includes the inflation guard endorsement.

Personal Property

Your action letter asks that your coverage be of the most comprehensive, all-risk variety available for property, personal property, and indirect losses resulting from loss of personal property. You want to be insured against all the risks the insurance company will possibly insure you against; however, you also want to discuss the cost-effectiveness of the riders that provide this coverage. The premium effectiveness question comes up twice—once when you are paying the premium and once again when you are making a claim, with 20/20 hindsight.

Endorsements and Floaters

The standard provisions under the homeowner's coverage relating to what will be paid for other structures (10 percent) of dwelling coverage, personal property (50 percent), and loss of use (20 percent) may be inadequate for you. You may increase the coverage by purchasing floaters or endorsements to your policy.

A *floater* is actually a separate policy that you purchase to extend and broaden the coverage you have under your basic policy for high value items that you own. Your jewelry, silverware, valuable collections, and so on should be itemized on a floater policy with an appraisal or bill of sale and a photograph. You can expect to pay from $1 to $5 per $100 of value depending upon property type and where you live.

Endorsements are additions to your existing policy and extend coverage that otherwise might be excluded or limited under your base policy. These days you are likely to need endorsements for your computer, home business, or waterbed, for the "mysterious disappearance" of your valuables, and for earthquake damage.

Replacement Cost versus Actual Cash Value

You are advised to purchase the *replacement cost* endorsement mentioned in the action letter so that reimbursements will be made on a replacement cost basis rather than on an actual cash value/depreciated value basis for all coverage, including personal property. Unless you have requested this replacement cost coverage, the policy will contain provisions relating to reimbursing you on an *actual cash value* basis of your lost property. Actual cash value means that your reimbursement for losses will be made on the basis of current replacement cost less depreciation. For example, if your 10-year old TV set were destroyed and it would cost you $1,000 to replace it today, the insurance company might say that the set had depreciated at the rate of 10 percent per year and now was valued at $100. Because this was equal to your deductible, you might receive a check for nothing. Replacement cost coverage, on the other hand, would mean being reimbursed $1,000 for the loss, minus your deductible. In order to avoid this problem, the replacement cost rider assures indemnification for the full replacement cost of the item without any deduction for depreciation at the time of the loss.

The personal property reimbursement section of your homeowner's policy will have interior limits on the amount that it may reimburse you for certain items as Table 5–2 itemizes.

You may own certain items that cannot be adequately provided for within these limitations. Inventory those items, such as jewelry, silverware, and firearms, with appraisals and request that a rider or endorsement to your policy be added to provide adequate coverage for these particular items.

TABLE 5–2

Personal Property Limitations under Homeowner's Policy

Item	Dollar Limit of Indemnification
1. Money, bank notes, bouillon, coins, and metals	$ 200
2. Securities, manuscripts, stamp collections, and valuable papers	1,000
3. Water craft including their trailers, equipment, and motors	1,000
4. Trailers	1,000
5. Grave markers	1,000
6. Property on the residence premises used for business purposes	2,500
7. Property away from the resident premises used for business purposes	250
8. Loss of jewelry, watches, fur, and precious and semiprecious stones by theft	1,000
9. Loss of firearms by theft	2,000
10. Loss of silverware, silverplateware, goldware, goldplateware, and pewter by theft	2,500

Earthquake and Flood Insurance

As you review the exclusion section of your policy you may find some disconcerting exclusions, such as earth movement and water damage. You may obtain some relief from the earth movement exclusion by buying an earthquake rider, which is widely available. However, you may experience more difficulty as you seek to reduce exposure to water damage and flooding. Commercial insurance companies have not been able to provide flood insurance profitably because people who live on mountains don't buy it, and those who live in river valleys and lowlands are more inclined to buy it. As a result, the federal government has a federally subsidized program for flood insurance.

The federal program provides basic protection and safety; it does not replace elaborate basement recreation rooms. Those of you who are living in lowlands where the coverage is particularly desirable will find, as expected, that your costs will be significant. The action letter asks your insurance provider to let you know the cost of both earthquake and flood insurance. It gives the provider the opportunity to address your needs for that type of coverage. Table 5–3 will give you an idea about the coverage available and the approximate costs under the federal program.

Residential Worker's Compensation

Another confusing aspect of homeowner's insurance is the requirement in some states to have worker's compensation insurance if you hire domestic help or other occasional workers to do household work for you. You may be liable in these situations whether or not you are aware of the requirement. It is wise to be prepared for the problem. For this reason, the action letter asks that your insurance professional inform you of any requirements that might be unique to your particular area.

Safety Devices Reduce Homeowner Policy Premiums

You have the opportunity to reduce the annual cost of your homeowner's insurance policy using the "control" treatment of risk rather than the "financing" treatment that insurance represents.

TABLE 5-3

Coverage Limits and Premium Costs for Earthquake and Flood Insurance*

Building/Contents Without Basement	Premium
$20,000/$5,000	$ 80
$30,000/$8,000	$105
$50,000/$12,000	$135
$75,000/$18,000	$155
$100,000/$25,000	$170
$125,000/$30,000	$185
$150,000/$38,000	$200
$200,000/$50,000	$220
$250,000/$60,000	$235
Building/Contents With Basement	**Premium**
$20,000/$5,000	$105
$30,000/$8,000	$130
$50,000/$12,000	$160
$75,000/$18,000	$180
$100,000/$25,000	$195
$125,000/$30,000	$210
$150,000/$50,000	$245
$250,000/$60,000	$260

*Terms:

Building deductible: $500. Contents deductible: $500. The deductibles apply separately to building and contents.

Only one of the coverage combinations may be purchased. A probation surcharge applies to preferred risk policies whenever applicable.

Replacement cost coverage applies *only if* the building is the principal residence of the insured and the building coverage chosen is at least 80 percent of the replacement cost of the building.

Why not reduce your exposure to loss by instituting safety procedures and purchasing safety devices? You will be able to reduce the annual cost of your homeowner's policy by purchasing and installing smoke detectors, CO_2 detectors, fire extinguishers, deadbolt locks, and possibly other protective devices. This approach, too, is included in the action letter, both to inform you and to encourage you to adopt such procedures and make such purchases. It also lets your insurance provider know that you have done so.

Home Businesses

It is important for you to inform your insurance provider if you are conducting any business pursuits within your home, so that appropriate business insurance protection may be purchased. Home businesses are growing in popularity and opportunity, and they require appropriate insurance coverage.

CONCLUSION

In reviewing your residence and real estate insurance, make sure that the declarations pages of your policies specifically refer to each piece of real estate that you own personally. If a particular piece of real estate is not listed on any of your policies, you are exposed to losses for which you are personally liable without the assistance of insurance.

There are certain actions that you must take if you do experience a loss. These are listed within the conditions and exclusions area of your policy. It is important to comply with these conditions in order to collect any claim you make against your insurer. The steps that you can expect to see within your policy are as follows:

1. Give immediate written notice of the loss.
2. Protect the property from further damage.
3. Separate the damaged property from the undamaged.
4. Furnish an inventory of the damaged property with its costs, values, description of damage, and losses sustained.
5. Provide written proof of loss within 60 days with detailed information about the loss, such as the time of occurrence, origin, your insurable interest, occupancy, other insurance contracts in force, and so on.
6. Exhibit to the insurer the property and books of account.

Follow the steps specifically outlined in your policy. Cooperate fully with the insurer; do procedures in writing and do them promptly.

If you need help beyond what you can get from your insurance agent or insurance company, contact the National Insurance Consumer Hotline between 8:00 A.M. and 8:00 P.M. Eastern time at 1-800-942-4242 and if your problem is not resolved, contact your state insurance commissioner's office, lodge a complaint in writing, and discuss your situation with an attorney.

Actual Cash Value   The cost of your property, minus deprecation.

Appraisal   An evaluation to determine the insurable value of property or to determine the amount of a loss.

Claim   A demand to recover for a loss covered by an insurance policy.

Conditions   The provisions of an insurance policy stating your rights and duties and those of the insurance company.

Coverage   A synonym for *insurance* indicating how much protection the insurance provides. This may mean either the dollar amount purchased or the type of loss covered.

Deductible   The amount of money the policyholder agrees to pay toward the total amount of an insured loss.

Depreciation   The decrease in the value of property due to wear and tear, and age.

Endorsement   An amendment attached to an insurance policy to add to the terms of the policy contract.

Exclusion   An event or loss that your insurance policy does not cover.

Floater   An insurance policy, separate from the basic homeowner's or renter's policy, which covers specific items of personal property. The coverage "floats" with the property—that is, it applies to the property wherever it is located, within the limits stated in the contract.

Homeowner's Policy   A package of insurance coverages providing homeowners with a broad range of personal property, dwelling, and liability protection.

Household Goods Policy   Insurance coverage for personal property; excludes liability coverage.

Insured   A person or organization covered by an insurance policy, including the "named insured" and any other parties for whom protection is provided under the policy terms.

Insurer   The insurance company providing the coverage.

Liability   Any legally enforceable obligation.

Liability Insurance   Insurance that pays when you are legally responsible for an accident in which you have injured someone or damaged his or her property.

Limits   The maximum amount of insurance that will be paid for a covered loss.

Medical Payments Insurance   A coverage to compensate people who sustain an injury while on your property or whom you injure accidentally. This coverage excludes those who live in your house.

Named Perils   Perils specified in a policy as those against which the policy insures you.

Peril   The cause of a loss insured against in a policy.

Policy   A legal contract that sets forth the rights and obligations of both the policy holder and the insurance company.

Premium   The amount of money you pay to the insurance company in return for insurance protection.

Renter's Policy   A homeowner's policy adapted to the needs of people who rent. It usually provides protection for both your personal property and/or personal liability. Also called a *tenant's policy.*

Replacement Cost   The amount it would cost to replace damaged property at today's prices, without a deduction for depreciation.

Risk   The chance of injury, damage, or loss. Also used to refer to the insured or to property covered by a policy.

Umbrella Liability   A policy that insures losses in excess of amounts covered by other liability insurance policies; also protects the insured in some situations not covered by the basic liability policies.

CHAPTER SIX

Vehicle Insurance

Most states have laws that require the registered owners of vehicles to have insurance. Many states also have financial responsibility laws that allow for the revocation of your license and registration unless you can demonstrate your ability to pay any judgments that may result from an accident. Vehicle insurance is a must for vehicle owners. There are 34 million accidents each year, 5.5 million injuries, and 1.5 million cars stolen. Your personal losses as a result of being uninsured could bankrupt you for life.

Make sure that every vehicle you own—including motorcycles, airplanes, boats, jet skis, and so on—is in the inventory shown in Figure 6–1.

WHO IS COVERED?

Covered persons are you, referring to all the name(s) listed on the declarations page of your policy; your spouse who is a resident in your same household; and other family members related by blood, marriage, or adoption, including a ward or foster child who is a resident in your household. The term *resident* has a special legal connotation and may extend beyond the confines of the insured's dwelling. A son or daughter away at school or in the military may still be considered a resident of the household as long as the household is considered "home"

FIGURE 6–1

Vehicle Insurance Inventory

Insurance Company/ Vehicle	Policy Number	Liability Maximum	Medical Maximum	Collision Deductible Premium	Comprehensive Deductible Premium	Under-/ Uninsured Motorist	Annual Premium
1							
2							
3							
4							
5							

and there is an intent to return to the household. Although the covered person definition does not make reference to a requirement of permission, the policy normally will exclude coverage of anyone operating a vehicle without a reasonable belief that he or she is entitled to do so. The coverage applies to the operation of both the covered vehicle and nonowned (borrowed or rented) vehicles.

In certain situations, suit for liability may be placed against the driver of the vehicle and, if that driver is on company business, the driver's employer. If that employee was driving a vehicle owned by someone else, that employee would be covered as an insured under his or her own policy while driving the nonowned vehicle and coverage may be extended to that driver's employer. However, if you routinely drive for your employer, the property/casualty agent for both you and your employer should be made aware of the situation to ensure that proper coverage is in force.

Legal Separation Affects Auto Insurance

In order to be eligible for the packaged personal automobile policy, a vehicle must be owned by an individual or by a husband and wife "who are residents of the same household." When a husband and wife are not legal residents of the same household, their qualifications for a personal auto policy for a jointly owned vehicle may terminate. In this case, alternative coverage should be sought immediately. Contact your agent.

The Potential for Loss Is Large

If any of these covered people should happen to injure a bright, young medical student to such an extent that the medical student is prevented from practicing medicine for the rest of his or her life, you could find yourself the object of a judgment that could force you into personal bankruptcy. However, even personal bankruptcy would not relieve you of the obligation of paying the judgment as a result of the injuries to that young student. Such a judgment could follow you the rest of your life. Substantial coverage is essential to your economic health.

TYPES OF COVERAGE

Liability Coverage

Liability coverage is of primary importance because this is the area in which you have the most to lose. The action letter shown in Figure 6–2 recommends that you increase your liability coverage to the maximum practical limit coordinated with your umbrella or comprehensive personal liability policy. You will find hundreds of examples of automobile accidents and injuries that have resulted in judgments against car owners for $1 million and more. However, not many insurance companies will issue an automobile policy with that much liability coverage. Thus, you should obtain a personal umbrella liability policy or the personal comprehensive liability policy, discussed in more depth in the next chapter.

Your vehicle insurance policy contains different kinds of liability coverage. *Bodily injury liability* pays medical costs, loss of income, and compensation for pain and suffering of those to whom you have caused injury with your auto. It also will pay for your legal defense under these circumstances. *Property damage liability* pays for the claim and legal defense when you are at fault of and have caused damage to property with your auto.

Liability insurance often is sold with split limits. When you see your coverage reported to you as $250,000/500,000/100,000 it means that your policy provides up to $250,000 of protection for any one person you are at fault of injuring, $500,000 for all the people you have injured, and $100,000 for all the property damage you have caused. Most states require that drivers carry $20,000/$40,000/$15,000. You can see right here that you are going to need to carry maximum uninsured/underinsured motorist coverage because most drivers will have insufficient liability coverage to protect you from their negligence. This is covered in more depth later in this section.

Visualize this situation. An accident occurs. You are *not* at fault but the other party sues you anyway. You have purchased the minimum required liability coverage so the insurance company's maximum loss exposure is $40,000. Thus, it is

FIGURE 6–2

Vehicle Insurance Action Letter

Dear_____:

I am evaluating my property casualty insurance, and I would appreciate your assistance.

My specific desires concerning my *vehicle* coverages are as follows:

- Provide the maximum available uninsured and underinsured motorist coverage.
- Provide the maximum available medical payments coverage.
- Make collision and comprehensive insurance cost-effective.
- I would also like to use cost-effective deductibles.
- Increase my liability coverage to the maximum practical limit, keeping in mind that I would like to have it coordinate with my personal umbrella policy.
- Please let me know exactly how my auto policy covers me when I rent cars for business or pleasure, or a combination of the two.

Sincerely,

your personal assets that are exposed to loss above that amount. At the same time, the insurance company has other lawsuits going where the insureds bought maximum coverage so the insurance company's exposure is $500,000. To which case will the insurance company assign their most talented attorney— the case that exposes the insurer to a potential loss of $40,000 or the one that exposes it to a possible loss of $500,000? Will you like being represented by an attorney and insurance company relatively uninterested in your case because although you have much to lose, the company has little to lose?

Medical Payments

This is a special form of accident insurance that provides coverage for medical expenses and funeral expenses for *you* and *your passengers* injured in an accident regardless of who is at fault. The standard limit for most policies is $1,000 per person; however, this limit can be raised by the payment of a small additional premium. Basically, the medical payments provision is designed to pay reasonable expenses incurred for necessary medical and funeral expenses because of bodily injury caused by accident and sustained by a covered person. It usually limits the payment of these expenses to within three years of the date of the accident.

Vehicle insurance medical payments coverage, unlike a homeowner's policy medical payments coverage, *applies to the named insureds*—you and your family members—who suffer bodily injury caused by an accident while occupying an automobile covered by the policy. The coverage also will apply to you and your family members if, while you are pedestrians, you are struck by a motor vehicle designed for use on the public roads or by a trailer of any type. Additionally, *people* other than the named insured and family members are covered for medical payments while *occupying your auto.*

There are a number of circumstances under which you will not be covered by this provision. You will not be covered for vehicles that have fewer than four wheels. Get rid of that three-wheel, all-terrain vehicle. You will not be covered in autos that are used for carrying people or property for a fee or if you are injured in your employer-provided vehicle. Business vehicles require business policies. Additionally, you will not be covered in an auto that you are operating without a reasonable belief that you are entitled to do so.

Your vehicle insurance action letter asks for the maximum medical payments coverage available. You will be surprised at the small additional cost it takes to increase this coverage significantly above the $1,000 minimum to an amount that would provide reasonable protection ($100,000) against the substantial risks to which you are exposed.

It could be argued that because most people are covered under some form of individual health insurance, medical payments coverage is redundant. However, there are too many circumstances in which you, your family members, or the passengers in your vehicle may be temporarily without medical coverage. For example, your dependent child may be a recent graduate who no longer fits the definition of "dependent and in school" and therefore may not be covered under your employer-provided group medical insurance. If Murphy's Law prevails, that is when an accident will occur. This is another area where the general rule, "don't risk a lot for a little," is applicable.

Collision Coverage

Collision coverage is to indemnify you for losses caused by the upset of your covered auto or its collision with another object. This coverage is provided regardless of who is at fault in the accident and will apply when you cannot recover damages from another party whose negligence was the cause of your loss. This provision ensures that you can get your vehicle back in operation as quickly as possible. Your insurance company may make a claim against the negligent party's insurance company and seek reimbursement from that company.

Some people elect out of this coverage when the replacement value of their vehicle is so low that they prefer to self-insure that amount rather than pay the premium to insure it. That's fine, but don't forget that you have done it. If you replace the car with a new one, adjusting your coverage, you don't want to have an accident in the new car and find that you still have no collision coverage!

Comprehensive Coverage

If you sustain a loss other than as a result of the upset of your vehicle or its collision with another object, you will be reimbursed under the comprehensive section of your policy.

You would make a claim under the comprehensive section of your policy for such occurrences as broken glass, losses caused by missiles or flying objects, fire, theft, larceny, explosion, earthquake, windstorm, hail, water, flood, malicious mischief or vandalism, a riot or civil commotion, or contact with a bird or an animal.

Because the deductible on your comprehensive coverage can be lower than the deductible on your collision coverage you may prefer to make a claim under your comprehensive coverage.

However, be aware of a number of exclusions under comprehensive coverage, such as the theft or destruction of special radio, sound, and video equipment within your vehicle. If you drive with this type of valuable equipment, you will want to request additional riders to make sure that it is covered.

The amount that you can expect your insurer to pay for physical damage to your vehicle will be either the actual cash value of the damaged or stolen property—meaning its replacement value less an allowance for depreciation—or the amount required to repair the property. You will prefer the latter.

Deductibles

The cost of both collision and comprehensive insurance is affected by the amount you self-insure: the deductible. For example, you probably will have a choice of $100, $250, and $500 deductibles. By accepting the $500 deductible instead of the $100 deductible, you self-insure an additional $400. It would not be surprising to find that your annual premium would be reduced by enough so that if you went accident free for two years, you would save the $400 in premium. Paying the extra $400 in premium is a certain loss. Self-insuring that amount and practicing defensive driving exposes you to an uncertain loss . . . drive carefully.

Uninsured/Underinsured Motorist Coverage

People still drive motor vehicles without insurance despite the mandatory insurance laws and financial responsibility regulations in practically all states that require people to have either adequate insurance or resources to satisfy judgments against them. Nationally, at least 1 driver in 10 has no liability coverage. In Cook County, Illinois, which includes Chicago, it has been reported that half of the drivers on the road do not have insurance. In California, it is estimated that 2 million of the 11 million vehicles registered are uninsured. Typically, it is the people without resources that drive motor vehicles without insurance.

If you were to have an accident in either the Chicago area or California under those circumstances, the odds are pretty high that the person who hit you would be one of those people without insurance and without resources. How, then, and from whom are you going to be reimbursed for your losses? Look at your inventory of vehicle insurance. Have you filled in the section under uninsured/underinsured motorist coverage? If you have recorded $15,000/$30,000, which is the amount that we see much too often, you are severely underinsured.

How can you be sufficiently covered with a limit of $15,000 per person, and $30,000 per accident as the maximum that your insurance company will reimburse you? Underinsured motorist coverage is *to protect you,* not others. The action letter requests the maximum uninsured/underinsured motorist coverage available. The declarations page in your policy will state how much you are paying for that coverage at the present time. You probably can increase the reimbursement to $100,000/$300,000 for a relatively insignificant increase in premium. If some uninsured driver hits you or any of your other insureds, you will realize the insignificance of that extra premium.

The underinsured provision in your coverage exists because some people have insurance with limits that are too low to protect you adequately. If you or your family sustain losses exceeding the other driver's coverage, you may find yourself making a claim under your own coverage.

This coverage provides protection to you, your passengers, and your family members. For you and your family members, it even protects you as a pedestrian and against the hit-and-run motorist. Maximize the coverage.

NO-FAULT INSURANCE

No-fault insurance has received a great deal of attention in the press. Indeed, you might be a resident of a state that requires no-fault coverage to some degree. The personal auto policies issued in such states will be in compliance with the state regulations. Your policy should be flexible in its provisions because you may not be involved in an accident in your own state.

The concept of no-fault insurance is to save money by not having to go through the process of determining who is at fault. The conventional means of indemnification, which necessitates determining who is at fault and who pays, takes time and also may involve substantial legal fees. No-fault insurance in its pure form means that it does not matter who caused the accident that resulted in bodily injury. The insured party suffering the loss would seek recovery for medical expenses, loss of income, and other expenses from his or her own insurer, and there would be no claim for general damages or suffering. This pure form of no-fault coverage has not been popular. People just don't wish to give up the right to sue a driver who causes them general damage and suffering.

Modified no-fault, however, provides limited immunity from the requirement to establish blame in the event of an automobile accident. Under modified no-fault, a certain amount of expense will be reimbursed by your own policy regardless of fault. Beyond that "limit" amount, liability would be determined and you would seek recovery from the party at fault. Treatment of claims for pain and suffering vary from state to state under the modified plans. The catch-22 in no-fault coverage is that although we all would like to eliminate the expense of lawyers and the legal process necessary to obtain just compensation, the idea that a negligent driver does not have personal responsibility is repugnant to most of us.

Another pseudo form of no-fault insurance is expanded first-party coverage. This type of coverage expedites the claim for injuries after an accident, allowing the individual to make claims against his or her own insurance company. However, the insurance company may then sue the negligent driver's insurance company to recover the amount paid to its insured who was not at fault. This is not really no-fault coverage because the negligent driver is not freed of responsibility.

Those of you in states that have no-fault laws will often find a requirement that you buy *personal injury protection,* which covers you with broader coverage including lost wages, medical care, and the cost to replace the services normally performed by the person injured in the accident.

WHICH VEHICLES ARE COVERED?

Any vehicle that is shown on the policy's declarations page is covered. Check your inventory. Are all vehicles that you own listed on the inventory, and are they included in the declarations pages as covered vehicles under appropriate policies?

In addition to the vehicles indicated on the declarations page, you will be insured for any vehicle for which you acquire ownership during the policy period, providing you ask the insurance company to insure it within 30 days of becoming the owner. This will apply to private passenger cars and, as long as they are not used in business, it also will apply to pick-ups, panel trucks, and vans. Also covered is any trailer that you might own and any nonowned auto or trailer being used as a temporary substitute for any vehicle described above that is out of normal use because of breakdown, repair, service, loss, or destruction. Remember that your coverage will be the same as your personal auto, so if you elected out of collision coverage you had better drive cheap cars or you'll have a problem.

Rental Cars

Anytime you rent an automobile, you are encouraged by the rental agency to purchase a collision damage waiver to eliminate your liability for the deductible or any uninsured losses to which the rental car agency is exposed. The typical charge of $9 per day totals up to $3,285 per year, which is a rather significant premium to have to pay for a potential loss of $500 to $3,000. In most cases, your personal auto policy or family auto policy will provide coverage to indemnify you for the payment of any of these deductibles. However, problems can occur when you return to the rental agency on a Sunday night with a damaged vehicle and have difficulty proving that you do have coverage to pay the bill. The rental agency could demand immediate damage payment.

To avoid these problems and, indeed, in response to these problems, credit card agencies have included (and in some cases later have withdrawn) automatic coverage in their package of benefits, stipulating that if you rent a car using their credit card, they assume this liability. In most cases, the rental car agencies have accepted this type of coverage and have not hassled the renter for immediate payment. This appears to be a satisfactory solution to the problem. Check with your credit card company for the availability of this benefit and check with your insurance company regarding how your policy protects you when you rent cars.

Reasons to Buy Rental Company Insurance

Your insurance may not cover you for amounts the rental company charges you for the money it loses while the car you wrecked is out of service. Also, your insurance company may not pay quickly enough to satisfy the rental company, so it may insist on immediate payment from you if you did not buy the agency's insurance.

Other Vehicles

You will want to make sure that all motorcycles, mopeds, all-terrain vehicles, snowmobiles, and other miscellaneous vehicles that you own, are covered by your policy or an endorsement on your policy referred to as a "miscellaneous vehicle endorsement." There is *no coverage* under the endorsement *for rented or borrowed vehicles* of this type. Caution is advised whenever you rent a recreational vehicle. Read the waivers you are asked to sign and consider the risks that you may be taking. For instance, don't sign for your neighbor's children—their own parents should be there to do it for them.

STEPS TO TAKE AFTER AN ACCIDENT

An automobile accident normally is a traumatic experience and most of us do not think clearly when involved in one. Therefore, it is wise to know what you have to do in the event of an accident.

1. Promptly notify the police and obtain care for the injured.
2. Cooperate with the authorities on the scene.
3. Take reasonable steps to protect the vehicle and equipment from another loss.
4. Record everything at the scene, including details of the accident and identification of autos and people involved including names and badge numbers of all emergency personnel. Take pictures if possible.
5. Insist on breath tests if drugs or alcohol are suspected to be involved.

6. Do not accept money. Do not accept fault and do not agree to forget about the accident.

7. Acquire a copy of all police reports.

8. Have the insurance company inspect and appraise the damage before any steps are taken to repair it.

9. Cooperate with the insurer in the investigation, defense, or settlement.

10. Promptly send the insurer copies of any notice or legal papers received in connection with a loss.

11. Submit to physical examinations by physicians selected by the insurer as often as the insurer reasonably requires. The insurer pays the cost of examinations.

12. Authorize the insurer to obtain medical reports and other pertinent records.

13. Submit proof of loss as required by the insurer.

CONCLUSION

Don't drive without vehicle insurance! All vehicle insurance is costly, but to upgrade from minimal coverage to the best coverage really is not that much more expensive and represents a wise purchase—one that you will appreciate at claim time.

Know what insurance is going to cost you before you buy a vehicle. One of the best ways to save money on insurance is to select carefully the vehicles you drive. The make and model of your vehicle greatly influences the cost of your policy. If insurance costs influence your choice, chances are you'll be saving more than just the premiums. You'll be saving all the other costs associated with high insurance–cost vehicles such as high purchase price, high repair bills, low gas mileage, and so on.

The factors that will influence your auto insurance premiums are:

• **Sex and age**—Young males are charged more than are young females. A 17-year-old male can expect to pay three times what a 30-year-old male would pay. Apply for good student discounts. Discounts are also often available between ages 50 and 65 for those with good driving records.

United Services Automobile Association reports that the following are imprecise examples of the costs you may find for drivers with clean driving records in medium-size metropolitan areas with liability limits at state-required maximums. (The state-required maximums are too low to be practical.)

Age	Under 20	21–24	25–29	30 or older
Sex	*Male/Female*	*Male/Female*	*Male/Female*	*Male/Female*
Annual Cost	$2,000/$1,500	$1,500/$1,000	$900/$800	$800/$800

- **Marital Status**—Insurance is cheaper when you are married.
- **Driving Record**—Accidents and moving violations increase costs, usually for three years.
- **Type and Amount of Driving**—Work-related driving versus personal driving affects costs, as does the number of miles driven per year.
- **Discounts**

  Good Student—B average students under age 25.

  Driver training and defensive driving courses.

  Good Record—no accidents or convictions, usually for three years or more.

  Mature Driver—Ages 50 to 65.

  Multicar Coverage—insure all vehicles with one insurer if possible.

  Restricted Mileage—less than 7,500 miles driven per year.

  Carpooling.

  Anti-Lock Brakes.

  Seat Belts and Air Bags.

  Antitheft Systems.

  Car Out-of-Service.

  Not a "Muscle Car."

  Not a "Theft Likely" Car.

GLOSSARY OF AUTOMOBILE INSURANCE*

Actual Cash Value   In many insurance policies, the amount awarded for property damage losses. This amount usually equals the cost to replace the damaged item with a new one, minus depreciation.

Assigned Risk   Often known as a nonvoluntary insured. An applicant for auto insurance who cannot find a company willing to insure him or her voluntarily—perhaps because of a poor driving record or lack of driving experience. The state in which the applicant lives will assign this risk to an insurance company doing business in that state.

Automobile Insurance   A contractual relationship that exists when an insurance company, for a premium, agrees to reimburse an insured or policy holder for automobile-related losses. The six major automobile insurance coverages are bodily injury liability, property damage liability, medical payments and no-fault coverage, noninsured/underinsured motorist protection, collision, and comprehensive physical damage.

Automobile Shared Market   A program in which all automobile insurers in each state participate to make coverage available to car owners who are unable to obtain auto insurance in the regular marketplace. Usually called *assigned risk plans, joint underwriting associations*, or *reinsurance facilities*. (See Assigned Risk.)

Bodily Injury Liability   Coverage that protects you against financial loss and pays legal defense costs when you are legally liable for injuring other persons in an auto accident. In auto insurance, both bodily injury (BI) and property damage (PD) liability insurance are usually required by law. The two are often referred to simply as *liability insurance.*

Claim   A policy holder's formal demand to recover, from an insurer, losses covered by the insurance policy.

Collison Insurance   Automobile insurance coverage that reimburses you for damage to your own auto when the damage results from overturn or collision with another object—not necessarily an auto.

Comprehensive Insurance   Insurance coverage that reimburses you for damage to your own auto from causes other than collision, overturning, or general wear and tear. Comprehensive insurance covers perils such as hail,

---

*Some of the definitions in this glossary are from the *1991 Property/Casualty Fact Book,* published by the Insurance Information Institute (III), and from *Auto Insurance in Texas, a Guide for New Drivers,* published in 1994 by the Texas Automobile Insurance Service Office and III.

flood, theft, fire, glass breakage, falling objects, missiles, explosions, earthquakes, windstorms, vandalism or malicious mischief, riot or civil commotion, and collision with a bird or animal.

Coverage   A synonym for *insurance* indicating how much protection a policy provides. This may mean either the dollar amount purchased or the type of loss covered.

Deductible   The amount you pay before the insurance company begins paying on a loss. For example, a $200 deductible means that in a loss totaling $1,000, you would pay the first $200 and the insurance company would pay the remaining $800. However, if the loss were only $200, you would pay the entire loss and the insurance company would pay nothing.

Depreciation   The decrease in value of a car of its parts due to wear and tear, and age.

Exclusion   An event or loss that your insurance policy does not cover.

First-Party Coverage   Insurance coverage under which you are compensated for your losses by your own insurance company rather than by the insurer of another person who caused an accident. Collision and comprehensive insurance are two examples.

Hazards   An act or condition that will increase the likelihood or severity of a loss. For instance, ice on a bridge is a hazard because it increases the chance of a car skidding.

Insured   A person or organization covered by an insurance policy.

Liability   Any legally enforceable obligation.

Liability Insurance   Insurance that pays claims against you and your legal defense costs when you are responsible for an accident in which you have injured someone or damaged his or her property.

Limits   The maximum amount of insurance that can be paid for a covered loss. For example, if you have a $5,000 dollar loss and the limit on your policy is $3,000 dollars, then $3,000 is the maximum amount the insurance company will pay.

Loss   The basis for an insurance claim. For example, a loss occurs when the quality or value of an automobile is reduced by an accident. Insurers also refer to losses as *payments made on behalf of insured*.

Medical Payments Insurance   A coverage available in various liability insurance policies. It reimburses you and your passengers—regardless of legal liability—for medical or funeral expenses stemming from bodily injury (BI) or death by accident.

No-Fault Insurance An insurance concept designed to speed payment to accident victims and lower the cost of auto insurance by reducing the number of lawsuits for minor claims. Under a no-fault system, each insured's own insurance company pays for certain financial losses—such as medical expenses and lost wages—regardless of who caused the accident. In exchange for these benefits, the right to sue may be restricted.

Peril The cause of a loss. Perils include theft, glass breakage, floods, hail, fire, and negligence.

Personal Injury Protection (PIP) A broader form of medical payments insurance coverage that implements the no-fault concept. PIP offers protection for expenses actually incurred, up to a specific, per-person dollar amount. States that have no-fault laws require drivers to purchase PIP. It is also offered as an optional coverage in some states without no-fault laws. This coverage varies from state to state.

Policy A legal contract that sets forth the rights and obligations of both the policy holder and the insurance company.

Policy Holder A person who pays a premium to an insurance company in exchange for insurance protection detailed in an insurance policy.

Premium The amount of money paid for an insurance policy.

Property Damage Liability Insurance that protects you against financial loss because of your legal liability to others for auto-related damage to another person's property.

Renewal In insurance, a policy renewal can take place when a new policy is written or when a standard certificate is issued, stating that the same conditions of the old policy will stay in effect for a specified time.

Risk The chance of injury, damage, or loss. Also used by insurance companies to refer to the insured or to property covered by a policy.

Tort A wrongful act, resulting in injury or damage, on which a civil action may be based. Does not apply to a breach of contract.

Umbrella Liability Insurance Insurance that covers losses in excess of amounts covered by primary liability insurance policies. Also protects the insured in many situations not covered by the primary automobile liability policies.

Uninsured/Underinsured Motorist Coverage Uninsured motorist coverage pays for damages sustained by you and your passengers that were caused by an uninsured motorist or a hit-and-run driver. Underinsured motorist coverage pays when you or your passengers are injured as a result of the negligence of someone who didn't have sufficient liability insurance. The definition of an underinsured motorist varies from state to state.

CHAPTER SEVEN

Liability Insurance

We all face the risk that our behavior could result in injury to another person or damage to someone's property. We are responsible for the results of our behavior. What is unique about liability risk is that it has no predictable maximum. If you have read or heard about large liability suits, you probably have thought about what would happen if you were the subject of such a suit. If a judgment was won against you, the claimant could take everything you own in addition to being awarded damages under whatever insurance you might have. You, your spouse, and your family members cannot be expected to behave as reasonable and prudent individuals at all times. Each of us will, at times, be negligent. If someone else is subject to a loss as a result of your negligent act, you can expect to be sued and you can expect that the courts will hold in favor of the claimant. To be negligent doesn't mean that you are a bad person; it merely means that you failed to exercise the proper degree of care required under a certain set of circumstances. You made a mistake and mistakes are costly.

Therefore, make sure you have an "umbrella" or comprehensive personal liability policy to enter in the inventory shown in Figure 7–1. They are available in amounts of $1 million to $10 million of coverage.

FIGURE 7–1

Comprehensive Personal Liability Insurance Inventory—"Umbrella" Liability Policy

	Insurance Company/Insured	Policy Number	Liability Maximum	Deductible	Special Features	Remarks	Annual Premium
1							
2							

WHO IS INSURED?

In your comprehensive personal liability/umbrella liability inventory, first determine who is insured under your umbrella policy and what company is providing the coverage. If you do not have a liability policy, sign and send the liability insurance action letter shown in Figure 7–2 so that your property casualty insurance agent or company can give you a quote on a personal liability policy and let you know what is required to put it in force as soon as possible. The letter inquires about the cost of $1 million of coverage and also asks the cost of the maximum amount of coverage that you could purchase.

The minimum recommendation is a $1 million policy. Increase that recommendation based upon what is available to you, your lifestyle and public profile, and what your property/casualty

FIGURE 7–2

Liability Insurance Action Letter

COMPREHENSIVE PERSONAL LIABILITY (UMBRELLA) POLICY:

Dear_____:

I would appreciate it if you would put in effect a comprehensive personal liability policy for my family and me. Besides the cost and amount you would recommend, I would like to know if this coverage will increase my existing vehicle/real estate liability coverages.

Will it supplement these coverages by providing protection against certain liability exposures not covered under those policies such as personal injury, invasion of privacy, and liability for most non-owned property in my care, custody, or control?

What is the amount you recommend? $_____ Cost? $_____
What would be the maximum I could purchase? _____
Cost?_____

I would appreciate any further recommendations that you can make to help me accomplish my objective of being adequately insured for all situations involving potentially severe losses.

Sincerely,

insurance professional recommends. The higher your standard of living, the more you have to lose. The higher your profile, the more the public expects of you, and the more people will react negatively as a result of you *or your family's* personal negligence that results in damage to another. The more people expect of you, the greater the suit. Don't risk a lot for a little—maximize this coverage!

WAS THERE A LOSS?

Once negligence has been determined, there must be actual damage or loss as a result of the negligence. In most cases this is measured by the actual monetary loss suffered by the injured party. When someone suffers a bodily injury as a result of the negligence of another, the injured party may sue for compensatory payments and for *specific damages,* such as medical expenses and loss of income. These are relatively easy to measure. In addition to these specific damages, the injured party may also ask for *general damages* to compensate for the intangible losses resulting from pain and suffering, disfigurement, mental anguish, and loss of consortium. The monetary value of these losses is more subjective. *Punitive damages,* the third form of damages that may be assessed against the negligent parties, are a form of punishment. An injury to a party that results from gross negligence or willful intent is likely to result in sustainable claims for all three types: specific damages, general damages, and punitive damages.

In most cases, the burden of proof of negligence is on the injured party. However, if you break the law and cause an injury, your action may be referred to as *negligence per se.* The injured party in this case might not have to prove negligence. The fact that you broke the law may be sufficient to establish negligence. In other cases, there is absolute liability. Such liability may be imposed simply because an accident happens. Liability is imposed regardless of whether you actually can be determined to be at fault.

The bottom line is that we all need substantial liability insurance and we all need to know when such insurance will *not* protect us.

WHEN INSURANCE WON'T HELP!

Liability insurance coverage is not likely to assist you if your behavior, which is deemed to be negligent, occurred while you were breaking the law—committing a criminal or public wrong. You cannot expect insurance companies to come to your aid if you commit intentional acts to harm others. Nor will it cover any bodily injury or property damage arising out of a business pursuit of any insured. Business pursuit liability insurance needs immediate, proper handling by a qualified property/casualty insurance agent.

COMPREHENSIVE PERSONAL LIABILITY INSURANCE POLICY

Comprehensive personal liability coverage can be acquired by purchasing a separate comprehensive liability policy or, at times, by purchasing a rider on your individual homeowner's policy. You should consult with your property/casualty insurance professional to find out which is more appropriate under your personal circumstances.

Under this type of policy, the insurance company will promise to pay, up to the limits of liability set in the policy, all payments that become the insured's legal obligation because of bodily injury or property damage falling within the scope of the coverage provided by the policy. In addition, it will pay the legal expenses and attorney's fees for the insurance company's chosen counsel. The insurance company has the right to settle a claim or suit against you that it decides is appropriate. In addition to the expense, the contract will pay the interest on judgments plus certain other legal costs.

The insureds under your comprehensive liability policy are you, your relatives who are residents of your household, and any other person under age 21 who is in the care of a resident of the household.

The policy will pay all medical expenses, including funeral expenses, incurred by persons who are injured while on the premises with the permission of any insured, or injured away from the premises if injury results from activity of an insured or member of the insured's family. In addition to the claim costs, the policy also will pay for the first-aid expenses incurred by the insured, related to any bodily injury covered under the policy. The policy may even pay some minor amount, usually up to $500, for damage to the property of others for which there is no legal obligation on the part of the insured, but which the insured might feel a moral obligation to pay.

CONDOMINIUM/COMMON PROPERTY OWNER'S POLICY

If you own a condominium, your condominium association could be sued as a result of an injury occurring to someone on the condominium common property; in turn, the condominium association may have to assess you in order to obtain funds to pay that judgment. Your comprehensive personal liability policy would provide coverage up to $1,000 to pay those assessments; $1,000 is inadequate. You will want to request an endorsement purchasing additional coverage.

A comprehensive personal liability policy is particularly appropriate for people who do not own their own home or automobile and thus do not have liability protection under a homeowner's or auto policy. Comprehensive personal liability policies do not assume any underlying coverage. The coverage also is appropriate for renters and condominium owners.

UMBRELLA LIABILITY POLICY

The personal umbrella liability policy expands the liability coverage home and auto owners normally have within their homeowner's and auto policies. It exists because anyone may be subject to a liability claim of catastrophic proportions. The umbrella liability policy originally was developed for business purposes and, at one time, was exclusively underwritten by Lloyds of London. It is a broad form of liability coverage covering both general liability and automobile liability, purchased in addition to the separate liability protection provided by the typical auto and homeowner's policies.

In order to qualify for the umbrella liability policy, you will be required to purchase certain kinds of underlying liability protection within your homeowner's and/or automobile policies. Each insurance company has its own customary practices regarding the underlying coverage required before it will write an umbrella policy. The objective is to have the umbrella policy written as excess coverage, over the limits of the required basic contracts, with a high limit of liability ranging from $1 to $10 million.

Umbrellas Provide Additional Coverage

The umbrella policy serves two separate functions. It adds to your basic coverage and thus fulfills its first function of "excess coverage" because it will pay in addition to the basic coverage if the basic coverage proves insufficient to pay the claim. For example, if you have $500,000 of coverage under your basic policy and a $1 million umbrella policy, your total coverage for any one liability claim would be $1.5 million.

Umbrellas Provide Expanded Coverage

The second function of your umbrella liability is to establish broader coverage than that provided under the basic contracts. The liability insurance action letter specifically asks your insurance professional to explain how the proposed umbrella policy will work. Will it extend or increase the existing coverage? Will it supplement your existing coverage by providing protection against certain liability exposures that are not covered under your underlying policies? Answers to these specific questions are necessary because umbrella policies are not as standardized as auto and homeowner's polices. It is essential that you ask for an explanation of the specific coverage under your policy.

You want your umbrella liability policy to expand your protection in the areas of slander, defamation of character, invasion of privacy, and damages caused by use of nonowned property in your care, custody, and control. An example of the latter is a situation in which you borrow equipment from a neighbor—such as a lawnmower or snowblower—and, while it is in your care, custody, and control, a neighbor's child is hurt with the machine. You would be liable for that injury, subject to suit, and if a judgment was awarded against you, your homeowner's policy would probably not provide coverage, whereas your umbrella liability policy should provide protection.

If you are in the public eye, quoted in the public press, or simply outspoken, you may be interested in the coverage provided for libel, slander, and invasion of privacy. Libel is written defamation of character; slander is spoken defamation of character. Invasion of privacy may be claimed by anyone who feels that his or her piece of mind has been invaded. People have a right to privacy in personal matters and feel that they should not be commented on or scrutinized in public without their consent. Additionally, if you are exposed to claims of plagiarism or violation of copyright laws, your comprehensive personal liability or umbrella liability policy could provide protection. It is unlikely that protection would be offered under your homeowner's or auto policy.

ONE AGENT/ONE COMPANY

Ideally, you will find one capable and competent insurance professional to fill your residence, automobile, and liability insurance needs. It also is preferable to have all three policies with one insurance company. The advantage of one agent and one insurance company is that the agent should take a greater interest in your affairs as a result of having all your business.

Furthermore, having all of your coverage with one insurance company eliminates the question of which insurance company should pay which claim. Because only one insurance company holds all three policies, that insurance company alone is liable, no matter which of your policies happens to pay the claim.

In most cases, a discount is offered to package all three of these types of policies together with one insurance company. If you have only one agent and one company for real estate, vehicle, and liability insurances you can use the combined vehicle, real estate, and liability action letter shown in Figure 7–3 and record your findings in the inventory of Figure 7–4.

FIGURE 7–3

Combined Vehicle, Real Estate, and Liability Action Letter

Dear _____:

I am evaluating my property/casualty insurance, and I would appreciate your assistance.

My specific desires concerning my *vehicle* coverages are as follows:

◆ Provide the *maximum* available *uninsured* and *underinsured motorist* coverage.

◆ Provide the *maximum* available *medical payments* coverage.

◆ Make collision and comprehensive insurance cost-effective. I would also like to use cost-effective deductibles. What changes would you recommend to bring my insurance into compliance with these two objectives?

◆ Increase my *liability* coverage to the *maximum* practical limit, keeping in mind that I would like to have it coordinate with my "personal umbrella" policy.

REAL ESTATE INSURANCE

Please provide me with residence/real estate insurance coverage based on the following parameters:

◆ Maintain my *liability* at the maximum amount available or the amount that would best coordinate with a personal umbrella liability policy.

◆ Make sure that the coverage is of the most *comprehensive all-risk* variety. I would like the most comprehensive HO form including coverage for personal property losses and indirect losses resulting from the loss of use of personal property.

◆ Loss payments are to be made on a *replacement cost* basis rather than an actual cash value depreciated value basis for all coverages including personal property.

◆ Please let me know whether there are any discounts available for the following:

	I Have	Do Not Have
Smoke Detectors	_____	_____
Fire Extinguishers	_____	_____
Deadbolt Locks	_____	_____

Combined Vehicle, Real Estate, and Liability Action Letter (Concluded)

CO_2 Detectors ＿＿＿＿　＿＿＿＿

Other ＿＿＿＿　＿＿＿＿

- ◆ Do I require any special coverages for our household domestic help and/or other occasional workers we hire for household work?

- ◆ Recommend *cost-effective* deductibles.

- ◆ Maximize *guest medical* coverage.

- ◆ Let me know the cost of earthquake and/or flood coverage and your recommendation regarding them.

- ◆ Special items of value that should be included on a personal property rider are as follows:

Item	Value	Appraisal Method	Date
＿＿	＿＿	＿＿＿＿＿＿＿	＿＿
＿＿	＿＿	＿＿＿＿＿＿＿	＿＿
＿＿	＿＿	＿＿＿＿＿＿＿	＿＿
＿＿	＿＿	＿＿＿＿＿＿＿	＿＿

- ◆ Do you recommend any *business pursuits endorsements?*

COMPREHENSIVE PERSONAL LIABILITY (UMBRELLA) POLICY:

I would appreciate your providing a quote on a comprehensive personal liability policy. Will this coverage increase my existing vehicle/real estate liability coverages? Will it also supplement them by providing protection against certain liability exposures not covered under those policies, such as personal injury, invasion of privacy, and liability for most nonowned property in my care, custody or control?

What would be the cost for $1 million in coverage? $＿＿＿＿＿

What would be the maximum I could purchase? ＿＿＿＿ Cost? ＿＿＿＿

I would appreciate any further recommendations that you can make to help me accomplish my objective of being adequately insured for all situations involving potentially severe losses.

Sincerely,

Enclosure(s): Copies of current declarations pages from existing real estate, vehicle, and liability policies.

F I G U R E   7–4

Casualty Insurances Inventory

Residential/Real Estate Insurance:

	Insurance Company/ Real Estate	Policy Number	Policy's HO Type	Liability Maximum	Property Maximum	Medical Maximum	Special Riders	Annual Premium
1								
2								
3								
4								
5								

Vehicle Insurance:

	Insurance Company Vehicle	Policy Number	Liability Maximum	Medical Maximum	Collision Deductible /Premium	Comp. Deductible /Premium	Un-/Under- insured Motorist	Annual Premium
1								
2								
3								
4								
5								

Comprehensive Personal Liability Insurance— "Umbrella" Liability Policy:

	Insurance Company/Insured	Policy Number	Liability Maximum	Deductible	Special Features	Remarks	Annual Premium
1							
2							

CHAPTER EIGHT

Life Insurance

life insurance:

Insurance providing for payment of a stipulated sum to a designated beneficiary upon the death of the insured.

Webster's Third International Dictionary

A more pragmatic definition of life insurance may be that it is "insurance company money to be received by a beneficiary upon the death of the insured."

The Life Insurance Investment Advisor, Baldwin and Droms, Probus, 1988

WHY HAVE LIFE INSURANCE?

The answer to the question, "Do I need life insurance?" depends on your answers to two more questions. The first is, "In the event of my death, will anyone experience an economic loss?" If the answer to that question is "yes," that is, someone will experience an economic loss, then you are ready for the second question, "Do I care?" If you do not, then you have determined that you do not need life insurance.

Life insurance provides cash to the person who would have otherwise suffered an economic loss in the event of your death. Replacing human life value is the primary purpose of life insurance. Replacing human life economic value is unique to life insurance.

Determining the amount of life insurance you want for your beneficiary is a very personal decision. Completing Figure 8–1 can assist you in determining the amount that will satisfy your objectives, but the final decision will be a value judgment of your own.

COMPLETING A LIFE INSURANCE INVENTORY

Inventory all your life insurance policies using the figure. If you have difficulty determining the type of your policy, look at the bottom of the front page of the contract. Usually you will find a short statement of exactly what type of policy it is, such as whole life, term insurance, universal life, fixed-premium variable life, or variable universal life.

The asset value of the policy is the amount that the insurance company would pay you for that policy if you cashed it in for its cash surrender value. If you have borrowed against the policy, record the amount of the policy loan in the next column. If your policy is other than term insurance and increases in cash value each year, record the latest annual increase in cash value in the next column. Next, record the annual premium and the annual dividend if the policy provides for one. Record the *gross* annual premium, not the annual premium reduced by the dividend. In the section at the lower part of your inventory page beside the number 1, record the primary beneficiary for policy number 1, the secondary beneficiary, and the policy features such as waiver of premium, accidental death benefit, option to purchase additional insurance, the existence of any surrender charges or contingent withdrawal charges, and so on. Do this for each policy. Carefully check those beneficiary provisions; you would be surprised how often they turn out to be other than what you want. Finally, record the interest rate that the insurance company would charge if you should take a policy loan.

The best way to make sure you have accurate information is to send the following Request for Policy Information form in Figure 8–2 directly to the insurance company. The insurer will respond, in time, and possibly with some prodding, with a report on your policy with the information you need for your inventory and forms that you need to bring your policy up-to-date.

FIGURE 8-1

Life Insurance Inventory

Company	Type of Policy	Policy Number	Register Date	Death Benefit	Asset Value	Policy Loan	Annual Cash Value Increase	Annual Dividend	Annual Premium
1									
2									
3									
4									
Total									

	Primary Beneficiary	Secondary Beneficiary	Policy Features	Loan Interest Rate
1				
2				
3				
4				

FIGURE 8-2

Request for Policy Information

TO: _____   Date: _____
    (Company Name)

_____   Re: _____
    (Address)(Insured)

_____ Policy No.: _____

Please forward the following information on the above Policy for the items below:

[1] Kind of policy _____
    Is accidental death included? _____ Disability premium waiver? _____

[2] Register date _____ Age at issue _____

[3] Face amount _____

[4] Commuted value of any family income type provision or decreasing term as of
    current date _____ Expiration date _____

[5] Owner of policy _____

[6] Successive or contingent owner _____

[7] Beneficiary: Primary _____ Secondary _____

[8] How settled? (If other than single sum please indicate withdrawal rights, power of
    appointment, and terms of simultaneous death provision)

    _____

[9] Assignments _____

[10] Summarize any physical or occupational ratings _____

[11] Amount of premium _____ Payable _____

[12] Premium paid to _____

[13] Current dividend election _____

[14] Amount of current year's dividend _____

[15] Supplemental one-year term insurance now in force through use of dividends

    _____

[16] Cumulative amount of dividends now credited to policy:
            Paid-up additional insurance _____
            Cash value of additional insurance _____
            Accumulations at interest _____

[17] Please send form for new dividend election, policy loans, and change of
    beneficiary/owner.

[18] Outstanding loans _____

[19] Guaranteed cash value, as of previous year, current year, next year and age 65.

    _____

[20] Provide policy cost basis _____

[21] Provide gain/loss position as of this time _____

Please send the requested information and/or necessary forms to:

_____

_____

_____   X_____
                                           Policy Owner's Signature

Once you have completed the inventory, total your present life insurance. If you are in doubt about the beneficiary provision on your existing life insurance, ask for a change of beneficiary form and complete it as it should be stated.

Completing this inventory will help you answer the questions posed in the coming pages. Has the life insurance you purchased in the past been right for you? Is there any way that you can improve your current life insurance? Do you have enough for your present/future circumstances? Do you have the right kind of life insurance in light of your present and future needs?

DETERMINING YOUR LIFE INSURANCE REQUIREMENTS

Now that you have inventoried your policies and made the logical corrections to have them serve your family, it is time to determine their sufficiency. How much life insurance do you need based upon *your* requirements? Start with the objective form in Figure 8–3 that will assist you in considering specific needs.

Probate and Administration Expenses

When you die, you undoubtedly will own real estate and/or personal property that will have to pass to the ownership of others. No, you cannot take it with you. Probate property is property that is not jointly held property, beneficiary property, or living trust property. On those latter types of property you already have designated who should be the succeeding owner at your death via a beneficiary provision, a joint ownership arrangement, or a living trust provision.

The probate process is concerned with assets that you own in your individual name only and on which there are no directions about where the property is to go at your death. Your will provides the only instructions available to determine the proper disposition of probate property at your death. Some readers may conclude that they have no probate property; everything they own is either in joint tenancy with the right of survivorship or controlled by a beneficiary provision or a living trust and thus they do not require a will. This assumption is erroneous! All of us own some

FIGURE 8-3

Life Insurance Needs Analyzer
Funds Required for Cash Expenses and Sinking Funds

1. Probate and Administration Expenses:	
a. 5% of Probate Property	_____
b. 2% of Nonprobate	_____
c. ?% for Complexity	_____
2. Funeral Expenses	_____
3. Special Obligations	_____
a. Pledges	_____
b. Contracts	_____
c. Divorce	_____
d. Business	_____
4. Debts/Insurance Loans/Current Bills	_____
5. Income Tax Liabilities:	
a. Year of Death Return	_____
b. Retirement Plan Payout	_____
c. IRA/KEOGH/TSA Payouts	_____
d. Deferred Annuity Payouts	_____
e. Tax Shelter—Liability Exceeds:	
1. Basis	_____
2. Fair Market Value	_____
6. Federal Estate Taxes	_____
7. State Inheritance Taxes	_____
8. Education Fund (Calculated or today's cost estimate)	_____
9. Mortgage(s)	_____
10. Extra Fund for Error/Family Emergency Fund	_____
Total Funds Required for Cash Expenses *and Sinking Funds*	_____

personal effects. These personal effects can have substantial value. It would be irresponsible, expensive, and a disservice to your beneficiaries to leave the disposition of these assets up to the probate court and the state laws. You really cannot know the size of your probate estate, that is, what you will own in your own name at death. If your death is caused by an accident and your estate places a suit against a negligent party, a judgment could be won in favor of your estate that would increase its value beyond what you ever contemplated during life. Another "good news, bad news" scenario that would substantially inflate the value of your estate would be that you won the lottery, the excitement caused a heart attack, and you died. Who should receive your lottery winnings? Either you have stated your wishes in your will or the probate law of your state will assume control.

In short, you need a will. You also need a properly qualified and licensed attorney to assist you in drafting that will. Forget the do-it-yourself forms—that comes under the category of risking a lot for a little. The "no-will" will shown in Figure 8–4 paraphrases what could happen to your family and your assets if your probate estate has to be distributed under the provisions of the probate code of your state of residence. It is adapted from the "no-will" will that appeared in an add for the Chicago Title and Trust Company many years ago. It is intended to emphasize the importance of having a will drafted. By all means, do not do your loved ones the disservice of dying without a will.

The probate process is the legal system's way of making sure that your assets go to the right people. The courts do this by confirming that your will is a properly prepared and executed legal document that clearly expresses your wishes and that your beneficiaries and creditors are treated fairly. The probate process can entail legal fees, court costs, bonds, and so on, and it can be more expensive than other ways of passing assets to your heirs. It is also public; all potential beneficiaries and creditors need to be informed so that they can present their claims to the court. Probate can cause a great deal of delay because it can take a long time to settle conflicting claims. For these reasons, assume that probate costs could run up to 5 percent of the value of the property that will have to pass through your probate estate on its way to your beneficiaries. It could be a great deal less because many states have instituted simplified probate processes for smaller and/or uncontested estates. Adjust this number to whatever you and your attorney feel is reasonable.

Nonprobate Administration

The expenses connected with your nonprobate property, such as joint tenancy and beneficiary property, can be estimated at from zero to 2 percent because they will pass more efficiently and without delay or publicity.

FIGURE 8–4

Your "No-Will" Will
Written for You by Your State of Residence

I hereby do make, publish, and declare this to be my Last Will and Testament by failing to have a Will of my own choice prepared.

First Article

I give my wife only one-half of my possessions, and I give my child or children the remaining one-half. If my wife is not living, all goes to the children, (or their children if they are not living), equally. If I have no spouse and no children, then all I have is to go to my parents, double share if only one is living, and to my brothers and sisters equally, or to the children of any deceased brothers and sisters.

    I appoint my wife as guardian of my children, but as a safeguard, I require that she report to the Probate Court each year and render an accounting of how, why, and where she spent the money necessary for the proper care of my children.

    As a further safeguard, I direct my wife to produce to the Probate Court a Performance Bond to guarantee that she exercises proper judgment in the handling, investment, and spending of the children's money.

    As a final safeguard, my children shall have the right to demand and receive a complete accounting from their mother of all of her financial actions with their money as soon as they reach legal age.

    When my children reach age eighteen, they shall have full rights to withdraw and spend their share of my estate. No one shall have any right to question my children's actions on how they decide to spend their respective shares.

Second Article

Should my wife remarry, her second husband shall be entitled to his marital share of everything my wife possesses.

    Should my children need some of this share for their support, the second husband shall not be bound to spend any part of his share on my children's behalf.

    The second husband shall have sole rights to decide who is to get his share, even to the exclusion of my children.

Third Article

Should my wife predecease me or die while any of my children are minors, I do not wish to exercise my right to nominate the guardian of my children.

    Rather than nominating a guardian of my preference, I direct my relatives and friends to get together and select a guardian by mutual agreement.

    In the event that they fail to agree on a guardian, I direct the Probate Court to make the selection. If the court wishes, it may appoint a stranger acceptable to it.

Fourth Article

Under existing tax law, there are certain legitimate avenues open to me to lower death taxes. Because I prefer to have my money used for governmental purposes rather than for the benefit of my family, I direct that no effort be made to lower taxes.

                                     NO SIGNATURE REQUIRED

The Complexity Cost

With regard to "complexity," if your estate is difficult to value and/or could create disputes among creditors and/or beneficiaries at your death, the expenses and delays can be expected to increase exponentially. If you do not have a will, you probably should allow for such expenses here. The less you prepare your estate prior to death, the more it will cost your survivors.

Funeral Expenses

Record about $10,000 for funeral expenses. Some of you will think this sum is ridiculously low; others, inordinately high. The proper amount will, in the end, be determined by you and whatever arrangements you personally find suitable.

Special Obligations

In this section, record any pledges you have made to charity that you wish to see completed, any contractual obligations that you might have, any requirements binding you under divorce decrees, and also any business obligations that you wish to see completed. Do you have any children or other relatives who have special needs that you wish to provide for? If so, value those needs and enter the amounts here.

Debts, Insurance Loans, and Current Bills

Record the actual debts and loans that need to be paid off in the event of your death. Add to that amount a sum equal to two or three months of average household bills. This will provide your family with sufficient funds for a few months after your death to get reorganized.

Income Tax Liabilities

Uncle Sam is not sympathetic. In the year of your death, there still will be income tax liabilities. If your beneficiaries are required to take payouts from your retirement plans, pension

plans, profit-sharing plans, IRAs, Keogh plans, and tax-sheltered annuity plans, they must pay income taxes on those distributions. Such income taxes will diminish the value of these
assets by as much as one-third or more.

The changing tax laws, the economy, and tax-sheltered
investments (such as limited partnerships) may have caused
you problems. Those problems do not cease at death. If you
own a tax shelter on which you have borrowed money in excess
of your cost basis, your death will trigger an income tax liability—another of those less-than-pleasant surprises that may
occur to your beneficiaries in the event of your death. You may
lessen such shocks by making sure sufficient assets are made
available to pay the income tax liability and that all records
are easy to locate.

Federal Estate Tax

If *every single thing* you own—including the full face amount
of your life insurance policies—is worth less than $600,000 on
the date you die, you will not have to worry about federal estate
taxes as long as you have not previously used up your $600,000
exemption by giving gifts. An exemption allows you to give
up to $600,000 to anyone, during your life or at death, and
not pay any estate or gift taxes on that transfer. If you are married at the time of your death, you still may give that
$600,000 to someone other than your spouse without incurring
estate taxes. Also, you may transfer to your spouse an unlimited amount of assets without incurring any estate taxes. Thus,
an unlimited amount may pass to a spouse without incurring
estate or gift taxes, and $600,000 may pass to someone other
than a spouse without incurring gift or estate taxes either
during life or upon your death.

If your assets total less than $600,000 (including the full death
benefit of all your life insurance), federal estate taxes are not of
concern. You may skip the balance of this section unless you expect
your assets to grow to more than $600,000.

Those whose property exceeds $600,000 in value, however,
must face the fact that Uncle Sam will claim a substantial portion of those assets at your death via the federal estate tax. The

percentage of the tax bite goes as high as 55 percent of the asset value. The problem with federal estate taxes is that, in addition to being substantial, they are due within nine months of the date of your death. Uncle Sam wishes to be paid in cash. If your estate comprises marketable securities, bank accounts, cash, and so on, the estate may have no difficulty raising that cash in time to pay the bill. However, if your estate comprises of real estate, a nonpublic business interest, or some other material assets that are not readily convertible to cash, then your beneficiaries may have to sell these assets at greatly reduced prices to raise cash within nine months to pay the tax bill. For you life insurance and proper planning is essential if you intend to preserve your estate. Even if your estate has plenty of cash so that more than half of it can be conveyed to Uncle Sam within the nine-month deadline, does it make sense to let it happen? Robert E. Hales, Esq., a noted estate planning attorney from San Francisco and Saratoga, California, explains it this way:

> As the attorney for your estate, Whose money do I use? It makes no difference to me, it is not my money. But, frankly, it makes no sense to me to use your money if insurance company money is available. I can keep your multimillion dollar estate free of probate, minimize death taxes, and make sure your assets go to who you want them to go to, but what good is all of this, if at your death I have to tell your beneficiaries to liquidate and convey to the IRS half of everything you own?
>
> I don't understand. You insure your cars and homes so that you do not have to use your money to replace them at time of loss but you don't have yourself adequately insured at death, which is certain to happen, whereas the loss of your automobile or house is an improbable loss.
>
> I had a client once who owned 60 single-dwelling homes. I asked him, "Whose money do we use to pay death taxes?" He answered that all he had were his homes. Not having given it much thought before, he was curious as to how many of his homes would have to be sold to pay his death taxes.
>
> I noted approximately 30 to 35, recognizing that selling 30 homes in nine months would probably deflate that market, not counting the costs of selling those homes. I asked him to list the homes that would need to be sold. When he got to number 10, he found it very difficult to continue.

I told him to stop and go back to the top of his list and just sell the first three homes he checked. "Can I pay all of my death taxes just by selling three homes?" he queried. "You told me you would have to sell 35."

I said, "Yes, that's the difference."

"If you will sell the three homes now to get enough equity out of your estate to purchase all the life insurance you need to pay your death taxes, your family won't have to sell 35 homes when you die."

So many times, estate planning attorneys have reduced taxes, eliminated probate, and have seen to it that the estate is distributed as the clients wanted. But in so many cases, we have seen that those beneficiaries have had to sell the 35 homes instead of the father selling the three. Isn't it easier for someone to sell $20,000 of stock to buy a million dollar policy than it is for the attorney to sell a million dollars worth of stock to pay the death taxes? Isn't it easier for the dairy person to sell five cows a year to pay his insurance premiums than it is for an attorney to sell his whole herd when he dies?

Robert E. Hales, Esq.

Hales, Hales & George, San Francisco & Saratoga, California

State Death Taxes

State death taxes are unique to each state. The federal government allows a credit up to a certain amount if you are required to pay that amount to your state in death taxes. Most state governments then require that you pay them whatever amount the federal government will give you credit for. It makes little difference to you whether the taxes must be sent to the federal or state government. Although state death taxes in most states are generally less of a concern than federal estate taxes, they cannot be ignored. Work with your attorney and estate advisors to plan your estate and minimize all taxes.

Education Funds

You may be familiar with the "Rule of 72." This rule states that 72 divided by a particular interest rate will yield the number of years required for money to double at that interest rate. For example, if the interest rate you were considering was 10 percent, you would divide 72 by 10 percent and determine that money compounding at 10 percent would double in 7.2 years or money compounding at 7.2 percent will double in 10 years. Similarly, if your child's college education costs $10,000 per year today, and you expect education costs to escalate at 10 percent, expect educational costs to increase to $20,000 in approximately 7.2 years.

In calculating what you will need for college education funds, consider what it would cost to send that child to college at the present time. The instructions for your survivors would be to segregate this sum from your total estate and invest it in a fund that ideally would earn at least enough to keep pace with yearly increases in education costs, generating sufficient funds to provide for the child's college education. The more conservative you are, the larger your fund should be at the outset.

Mortgage Funds

As you consider your estimate for money required to pay off mortgages, you may decide that you prefer, and that it would be more sensible economically, not to pay off the mortgages. Your survivors must then be able to service the mortgage; that is, they must be able to pay the principle, interest, taxes, insurance, and other property maintenance costs. Make sure that your beneficiaries have the flexibility to achieve this. It is wise to have a mortgage fund so that your beneficiaries and their counsel may debate the merits of either position—paying off the mortgage or continuing the mortgage—from a position of economic strength rather than from a position of economic weakness.

Family Emergency Fund

Even though you have done your best to accurately estimate the various cash funds required at your death, invariably you will be wrong. The function of the family emergency fund is to make sure that your errors are not economically devastating to your survivors. Normally, a family emergency fund of six months' gross income is recommended. Many people gasp at this amount. However, if it is instead called an emergency/opportunity fund and these same people are reminded of the times in their lives that they were forced to pass up a good opportunity because they didn't have sufficient liquid cash to take advantage of it, they understand our recommendation. If you have six months' gross income and an outstanding opportunity comes along, you will not mind risking up to one-half of the amount on the opportunity because you know that a basic emergency fund of three months' gross income remains.

The total of all the amounts just described are what you feel your family's cash needs are in the event of your death. These represent what you perceive as economic security for your family. Your next concern is the monthly income needed by your survivors to provide for their day-to-day living.

Survivor Income Funds

The need for survivor income funds obviously depends on the economic circumstances of the survivors. If you leave a spouse who is every bit as capable of earning income as you are, with no surviving children dependent upon that survivor, then survivor income funds may be unnecessary. However, in many families today economic survival depends on the continued earnings of both parties.

When you consider the income funds needed for your family, consider the following three basic time periods. Period one is up until your youngest child attains age 18. The second is the period between the youngest child's age 18 and the spouse's age 60. The final period goes from the spouse's age 60 for the rest of his or her life, which is estimated to be higher than you used to estimate. These three periods are designed the way social security payments are made: Social security is payable to the families of workers while children up to 18 years of age are being cared for. Benefits then cease and are no longer payable until the surviving spouse reaches at least age 60.

Period One

Period one covers the period of time until the youngest child attains age 18. The spouse of a deceased worker will receive a social security benefit personally up until the youngest child attains age 16. Children's social security benefits continue until age 18. You can estimate the payments at $300 per eligible beneficiary with a maximum of three per family. This is an inaccurate, but conservative, number. To use more accurate numbers, obtain a report of your benefits from the Social Security Administration. A form is available from your local social security office which you should complete and send in at least once every three years to verify that your Social Security account is accurate.

Social security income can be supplemented by the spouse's own continuing income. Remember: A spouse's earnings in excess of a certain threshold may reduce or eliminate social security benefits. However, if your spouse is capable and desirous of earning substantially more than the threshold amount, this, of course, is advisable. Compare the sources of income to your income objective. Is there any unfunded income objective remaining? If there is, funds need to be made available to provide for it.

Knowing the amount of income required and the time period during which it is required, use a 5 percent assumed interest rate and discount that required stream of income to its present value.

If you wish to factor in inflation, use an inflation discount. For example, a nominal return of 5 percent or 6 percent minus the average inflation rate of 3 percent, will net approximately 2 percent or 3 percent inflation-adjusted interest rate.

The lump sum calculated will provide sufficient capital so that a monthly income may be paid from that capital sum to the surviving spouse during the required period. At the end of that period, both the capital sum and the interest it earned will have been used up. A zero balance will remain at the end of the payment period which is why this is referred to as the "annuity method."

Period Two

Period two is unique. During this period—in which children are over age 18 and the surviving spouse is under age 60—no social security benefits are payable. The only support for the spouse during this period is earned income and other miscellaneous income that may be available. Of course, at this time, the spouse will have fewer parental responsibilities and will be freer to seek a career and a higher income job. During this second period the objective may be to provide just enough supplemental income to allow the surviving spouse to terminate an unsatisfying position and/or to take the time to obtain the education required to get a better-paying position. The amount of funds required for this period is calculated in the same way shown for period one; however, a second step is required in this calculation. The lump sum calculated is not *currently* required—it will be required at the time in the future when there are no longer any children under age 18. Therefore, discount the lump sum future value back to the present value using your chosen interest rate and the number of years between the present time and the time when it will be required. This will tell you that you will have to put aside x dollars as of the date of death to earn 6 percent so that your spouse will have the required income.

Period Three

Income period three starts when social security becomes available again to the surviving spouse. This can be as early as age 60. Also at age 59½, IRAs and other retirement plan benefits become payable without penalty. Of course, you will have the spouse's earned income and any other assured income that may be available to that individual. Total up these four sources and check their adequacy against your objectives. If they are insufficient to provide for your surviving spouse's standard of living, you may wish to add to them. The calculation for the amount of the retirement fund is similar to that for period two—the discounted present value method. The numbers needed for this calculation are the amount of income required per month, the time period, and the interest rate.

The discounted present value method gives you the lump sum required at the beginning of period three. This capital will not be needed until the surviving spouse is age 60, and you then discount the lump sum needed at age 60 back to the present. Schedule the income to stop and the principal to be exhausted at an assumed age at death. If you choose age 85 and your beneficiary lives beyond that age, those last years could be tough. Factor in today's higher life expectancies.

Capital Retention Method

An alternate method for determining how much capital you would like to have for your surviving spouse is referred to as the *capital retention method.* The capital retention method assumes that you will not invade principal. You will use *only the interest* on the funds to provide income. In order to calculate the amount required for your survivors under this method, review the incomes required for periods one, two, and three. Pick the highest income required for any of the three periods. For example, if the highest income required from supplemental funds in any of the three periods were $1,000 per month ($12,000 per year), how much capital at 5 percent would be required to generate $12,000 income per year without invading principal? By dividing $12,000 by the interest rate assumption of 5 percent, you will find that you need $240,000 in capital to generate $12,000 a year in income at 5 percent. That $240,000 worth of capital could generate that income right from the start, through all three periods, and never diminish its principal.

If some income periods require less than that, the surviving spouse is more than adequately provided for, can reinvest the excess income, and can work on protecting his or her income stream from reductions in purchasing power because of inflation. The effects of inflation can be provided for further by adding to capital all earnings in excess of the 5 percent rate, so that the capital base, from which the 5 percent is being used, grows. If you are more concerned about inflation, assume a lower interest rate and provide sufficient capital to do the job at the lower assumed rate. For example, a 5 percent nominal interest rate less a 3 percent assumed inflation rate gives an approximate inflation-adjusted rate of 2 percent. Instead of $240,000 of capital in the previous example, you would need $400,000. For quick calculation purposes, you can assume that it is going to take at least $100,000 in capital to provide for every $500 per month you want for your survivors using a 6 percent interest assumption, $120,000 per $500 per month using a 5 percent interest assumption.

Comparing What You Need to What You Have

Now that you have determined the total amount of capital your family needs in the event of your death—the lump sum and the income requirements—you may start subtracting what you already have accumulated for their benefit, such as your present invested capital, the net benefits of your existing life insurance, and the cash generated by your retirement funds. The difference between what you decide is required and what you have accumulated is your shortage or surplus. The most immediate way to provide for that shortage is to pay a premium for a life insurance policy with a face amount equal to what you are lacking in capital. Once the insurance company has accepted you as an insured and issued your policy, that total amount of capital is immediately available at your death for your family's benefit. There is no other economic tool that can do this for you. The next question is: "What kind of life insurance will do this best?" To begin your search for the "right kind," you would edit and send the action letter in Figure 8–5 to the insurance providers from whom you are considering purchasing your life insurance.

FIGURE 8–5

Life Insurance Action Letter

Dear_____:

I am evaluating my life insurance and would appreciate your assistance.

I would be interested in your recommendations regarding the type of life insurance I now own, keeping in mind that my principal objective is to own enough to provide adequate security for my survivors at minimum after-tax cost for the protection.

I have not decided whether I need or want any additional life insurance. Please send me an illustration showing the cost of $_____ of yearly renewable and convertible term insurance for a male, nonsmoker/smoker, age _____ and $_____ for a female, nonsmoker/smoker, age _____.

If you have an alternative policy that you would recommend, please send me the information, including a ledger statement for any contract you are recommending. If you will be offering a universal life or universal variable policy, I will need a statement of monthly charges, mortality cost, credits, account values, and surrender values and a statement disclosing the assumptions being used in the statement.

Sincerely,

Enclosure(s): Inventory life insurance policies to be reviewed.

CHAPTER NINE

What Kind of Life Insurance?

All life insurance has at least two costs: costs for mortality and those for expenses. The money paid into a policy is applied to these two costs with any excess held in reserve. If you pay in more than is required for the current year's mortality and expense charges, the surplus is invested in an account within the policy.

Expense charges are incurred in issuing and maintaining the policy. Mortality charges, or life insurance costs, are calculated by the insurance company to cover the amount the life insurance company promises to pay under your policy at your death. The insurance company, in effect, has pooled you with others of your same age, sex, smoking habits, and physical make-up. Individually you and I don't know if we are going to die next year, but if enough of us are grouped together, the number of people who will die in any one year from among this large group can be predicted with great statistical accuracy. The insurance company has taken an uncertainty on our part, and turned it into a certainty on their part. Therefore, if you all contribute "x" to the fund held by the insurance company, there will be sufficient dollars in the fund to pay the death benefits to those who will die in the coming year. That's the mortality cost, the cost of the "life insurance."

These two aspects, mortality costs and expenses, are a part of *every* life insurance policy. They cannot be avoided or the insurance company would go out of business. You do not want your insurance company going out of business before you do.

TERM LIFE INSURANCE

Term insurance is the type of insurance for which you pay just the mortality and expense charges, and no more. Typically, the most efficient form of term insurance is yearly renewable and convertible term. With this type of policy you pay the mortality and expense charges for the current year only, and you accept the fact that as you get older, your mortality costs will go up. In each succeeding year, you can expect the premium on this type of policy to go up also.

If you want inexpensive term insurance, don't ask the insurance company to do anything more than to pay the death benefit. As a result of not having to make any extra promises, the insurance company will be able to minimize your cost.

Renewable Term Insurance

If, however, you want more from the insurance company, such as the promise to accept your premium in the coming years and to allow your insurance to continue (*renewable* term insurance), you will have to pay a little bit extra for the promise of renewability. You should willingly pay extra for this renewable feature; you never know when you may go from "insurable" to "uninsurable." Uninsurability may be a result of the deterioration of your health, your latest avocation, or your current occupation. The insurance companies may not wish to provide life insurance for you at any cost. At that time, that renewable privilege on your existing policies will become particularly important.

Convertible Term Insurance

You also may want to pay for the convertibility feature in a life insurance policy. This enables you to change your term insurance policy into any of the other types of contracts that are issued by the same company that issued your term insurance policy. This means that if you are dealing with an insurance company that has an incomplete portfolio of products or does not have the type of product you would want to replace your term insurance, the convertibility feature is of no value to you. Deal with an insurance company that has a complete portfolio of products or at least the type of product that you may wish to use in the future.

Level-Premium Term Insurance

Some term insurance policies charge a level premium for 5 years, 10 years, or even as long as 20 years. The insurance company has taken a look at the yearly renewable and convertible term rate required each year and has averaged it out over the time period of the policy. The insurer then charges you for an average level premium for the 5, 10, or 20-year period. The insurer will take more than is required in the early years of the policy so it can afford to take less in the later years. If you keep the term insurance policy for the total period of time, it might be a fair arrangement. However, because many people adjust their term insurance policies from year to year, paying this additional premium in the beginning of the period when you may not own the policy at the end of the period can be a waste of money. Also, when you come to the end of the level-premium period you might run into a "brick wall" in the form of substantial increases in premium cost. Whenever you see the word "reentry" in your term insurance policy, you will find that the insurance company has erected a significant "hurdle." In order to continue your term insurance at the time of reentry at a reasonable premium level, you may have to pass another physical or requalify financially—or the insurance company can, even if you qualify physically and financially, just charge you a much higher cost. The "reentry" provision gives the insurance company the opportunity not to renew your policy. You should call reentry term "out-of-control" term to remind yourself that the insurance company not you, the policy owner, controls it. Watch it!

Decreasing Term Insurance/Mortgage Term Insurance

You can also buy a term insurance policy with a level premium but with a reducing death benefit so that the same premium is sufficient to cover the increasing mortality charges that do go up every year as we get older. This is commonly referred to as *decreasing term insurance*. The insurance companies like to market it as mortgage insurance to make you feel as if you need to buy it. The amount of the death benefit reduces throughout the life of the policy.

When insurance companies put term life insurance in force, they must estimate expenses and the number of people who are going to die. Actual results will inevitably differ from these estimates. If the difference favors the insurance company, mutual insurance companies return that excess to the policy owner in the form of dividends. The insurance company controls the dividend by estimating mortality and expenses either conservatively or aggressively. A mutual insurance company that conservatively estimates mortality and expenses will have higher term insurance costs and higher dividends. The insurer charges more but promises to lower costs by paying dividends if it finds that its estimates have been too conservative.

Alternatively, an insurance company can price aggressively by paring down estimates, calculating as closely as possible, and charging you as little as possible for mortality and expenses. In order to protect itself, the insurer will specify in the contract that if it has charged you significantly less than the mortality and expenses actually incurred, the insurer can raise your rates in the future. Formerly, conservative estimates were the norm, that is, term rates used to be estimated high and the high rates were reduced by returning dividends to the insured. Today, the norm is to rate life insurance policies aggressively and reserve the right to increase costs.

This latter method provides you, the consumer, with a cash flow advantage. It is like receiving your dividends up front. Also, the insurance companies will work to maintain low rates in their term insurance policies and to avoid increasing rates for competitive reasons. The maximum rates listed in the policies set the limits on what the insurance companies can charge you for mortality rates. You will find in today's life insurance policies those maximums will be based upon the 1980 Commissioners Standard Ordinary (1980 CSO) mortality table, which indicates the number of deaths per thousand to be expected in each particular age group. An example of one of these tables is shown in Table 9–1. In all likelihood, you will find that these maximum rates are significantly more than your actual payments to your life insurance company.

TERM PLUS

You have seen the various forms of term-only life insurance. Now consider all other forms of life insurance as "term-plus." They continue to contain the two basic elements of term insurance—mortality and expense charges—but added to them is an investment element, the "plus." Term-plus life insurance includes whole life, universal, variable, and variable universal life insurance. But first, consider whether life insurance may be considered to be an investment.

IS LIFE INSURANCE AN INVESTMENT?

Most of us would agree that term insurance is not an investment in the conventional sense of the word, because an expense is not an investment and mortality costs are not an investment.

investment

An expenditure of money for income or profit or to purchase something of intrinsic value: capital outlay.

The commitment of funds with a view to minimizing risk and safeguarding capital while earning a return; contrasted with speculation.

Webster's Third New International Dictionary

However, based on these definitions, it is clear that the "plus" in term-plus—the funds you put in a policy in excess of mortality and expenses—*is an investment*. The fact that a part of the return on the investment is used to buy life insurance is not dissimilar to the collateral benefits of many investments we make such as home ownership, Broadway plays, horses, and hobby or affinity investments.

TABLE 9-1

1980 Commissioners Standard Ordinary Mortality Table

	Mortality Rate Per 1,000		Expectancy Years	
Age	Male	Female	Male	Female
0	4.18	2.89	70.83	75.83
1	1.07	.87	70.13	75.04
2	.99	.81	69.20	74.11
3	.98	.79	68.27	73.17
4	.95	.77	67.34	72.23
5	.90	.76	66.40	71.28
6	.85	.73	65.46	70.34
7	.80	.72	64.52	69.39
8	.76	.70	63.57	68.44
9	.74	.69	62.62	67.48
10	.73	.68	61.66	66.53
11	.77	.69	60.71	65.58
12	.85	.72	59.75	64.62
13	.99	.75	58.80	63.67
14	1.15	.80	57.86	62.71
15	1.33	.85	56.93	61.76
16	1.51	.90	56.00	60.82
17	1.67	.95	55.09	58.93
18	1.78	.98	54.18	58.93
19	1.86	1.02	53.27	57.98
20	1.90	1.05	52.37	57.98
21	1.91	1.07	51.47	56.10
22	1.89	1.09	50.57	55.16
23	1.86	1.11	49.66	54.22
24	1.82	1.14	48.75	53.28
25	1.77	1.16	28.84	52.34
26	1.73	1.19	46.93	51.40
27	1.71	1.22	46.01	50.46
28	1.70	1.26	45.09	49.52
29	1.71	1.30	44.16	48.59
30	1.73	1.35	43.24	47.65
31	1.78	1.40	42.31	46.71
32	1.83	1.45	41.38	45.78
33	1.91	1.50	40.46	44.84

1980 Commissioners Standard Ordinary
Mortality Table (Continued)

	Mortality Rate Per 1,000		Expectancy Years	
Age	Male	Female	Male	Female
34	2.00	1.58	39.54	43.91
35	2.11	1.65	38.61	42.98
36	2.24	1.76	37.69	42.05
37	2.40	1.89	36.78	41.12
38	2.58	2.04	35.87	40.20
39	2.79	2.22	34.96	39.28
40	3.02	2.42	34.05	38.36
41	3.29	2.64	33.16	37.46
42	3.56	2.87	32.26	36.55
43	3.87	3.09	31.38	35.66
44	4.19	3.32	30.50	34.77
45	4.55	3.56	29.62	33.88
46	4.92	3.80	28.76	33.00
47	5.32	4.05	27.90	32.12
48	5.74	4.33	27.04	31.25
49	6.21	4.63	26.20	30.39
50	6.71	4.96	25.36	29.53
51	7.30	5.31	24.52	28.67
52	7.96	5.70	23.70	27.82
53	8.71	6.15	22.89	26.98
54	9.56	6.61	22.08	26.14
55	10.47	7.09	21.29	25.31
56	11.46	7.57	20.51	24.49
57	12.49	8.03	19.47	23.67
58	13.59	8.47	18.99	22.86
59	14.77	8.94	18.24	22.05
60	16.08	9.47	17.51	22.05
61	17.54	10.13	16.79	20.44
62	19.19	10.96	16.08	19.65
63	21.06	12.02	15.38	18.86
64	23.14	13.25	14.70	18.08
65	25.42	13.25	14.70	18.08
66	27.85	16.00	13.39	16.57

1980 Commissioners Standard Ordinary Mortality Table (Concluded)

Age	Mortality Rate Per 1,000		Expectancy Years	
	Male	Female	Male	Female
67	30.44	17.43	12.76	15.83
68	33.19	18.84	12.14	15.10
69	36.17	20.36	11.54	14.38
70	39.51	22.11	10.96	13.67
71	43.30	24.23	10.39	12.97
72	47.65	26.87	9.84	12.28
73	52.64	30.11	9.30	11.60
74	58.19	33.93	8.79	10.95
75	64.19	38.24	8.31	10.32
76	70.53	42.97	7.84	9.71
77	77.12	48.04	7.40	9.12
78	83.90	53.45	6.97	8.55
79	91.05	59.35	6.57	8.01
80	98.84	65.99	6.18	7.48
81	107.48	73.60	5.80	6.98
82	117.25	82.40	5.44	6.49
83	128.26	92.53	5.09	6.03
84	140.25	103.81	4.77	5.59
85	152.95	116.10	4.46	5.18
86	166.09	129.29	4.18	4.80
87	179.55	143.32	3.91	4.43
88	193.27	158.18	3.66	4.09
89	207.29	173.94	3.41	3.77
90	221.77	190.75	3.18	3.45
91	236.98	208.87	2.94	3.15
92	253.45	228.81	2.70	2.85
93	272.11	251.51	2.44	2.55
94	295.90	279.31	2.17	2.24
95	329.96	317.32	1.87	1.91
96	384.55	375.74	1.54	1.56
97	480.20	474.97	1.20	1.21
98	657.98	655.85	.84	.84
99	1000.00	1000.00	.50	.50

Used with permission of Chicago Title and Trust Co.

The only reason you would put additional money with an insurance company over and above the costs of buying term coverage would be to earn a return. What is unique about the return inside of life insurance is that it can be used to pay the mortality and expense charges that are within the life insurance contract without the return being subject to income taxes. Earnings on your investment in excess of the mortality and expense charge reductions also are not subject to current taxes. The fact that you may purchase a consumable commodity—the mortality and expense charges of a life insurance policy—with pretax earnings is unique to investment type of life insurance. It is a frequently overlooked and underused tax advantage.

Is life insurance a good investment? The answer depends upon your need and desire to have "life insurance." For example, suppose you put $10,000 into a life insurance policy that had a $100,000 death benefit. At the end of the year, you received a report from your insurance company that said that the account balance remaining in the policy was $10,000. It had not grown at all! You might say that was a terrible investment; the $10,000 earned absolutely nothing during that year. The fact that the policy would have paid $110,000 if you died during that year was totally irrelevant. In that case, for that investor, *it was not a good investment because the life insurance was not wanted.*

However, another individual who previously had been paying $1,000 per year for a $100,000 yearly renewable and convertible term policy would realize that he had received $1,000 worth of protection from the insurance company. He had purchased $100,000 worth of life insurance for the year from the tax-free earnings on his $10,000 investment within the policy. He bought a needed commodity with pretax dollars rather than with after-tax dollars. The $1,000 worth of life insurance was equivalent to a 10 percent tax-free return on the $10,000 investment in the contract. If he had purchased straight term insurance, he would have had to earn $1,442 outside of the contract. He could then pay the taxes ($30\% \times 1,442 = \$442$) on his earnings and have enough left to send $1,000 to the insurance company for his term insurance. Buying term insurance with the pretax earnings within the policy saved him $442.

The key fact is, if you want and need life insurance, the extra capital you put in a policy to earn a return for you can be an investment. If you don't want life insurance, then using part or all of your investment return to pay mortality and expense charges is an unnecessary expense.

THE "INVESTMENT" TYPES OF LIFE INSURANCE

This section describes the three main types of investment life insurance—whole life, variable life, and universal life—and the evolution of newer, offshoot types of policies.

The "menu" of life insurance products in Table 9–2 summarizes the generic forms of life insurance, describing the basic features of each policy. The policy that appeals to you will depend on your life insurance needs, your economic situation, and your likes and dislikes in regard to the various types of investments available within an insurance company and an insurance policy. Later, Figure 9–1 presents a life insurance suitability questionnaire to assist you in deciding which policy is best suited to you at the present time.

Refer to Table 9–2 as you fill out the suitability questionnaire. Once this process is complete, you should be able to make a personal choice about what policy or policies suit you best.

The objective of this process is to see that you understand the life insurance products available and are aware of the costs of life insurance. Life insurance is a consumable commodity that is paid for each year. Its cost must be extracted from investment earnings or your payment, depending on the method of payment you have chosen. The election to invest or not to invest additional cash into a life insurance policy is a voluntary decision. The decision should be based upon the availability of investment capital and whether the particular investment medium available within the life insurance contract meets your investment needs, personal goals, and objectives. Once you've made your decision regarding which of the six generic forms of life insurance is appropriate for you, you may then select a contract based upon more quantitative analysis of expenses, mortality charges, investment alternatives, flexibility, contract provisions, company, and service.

TABLE 9-2

The "Menu" of Life Insurance Products

Term Only Contracts

	General Description	Investment Vehicle	Investment Flexibility	Premium Flexibility	Face Amount Flexibility	Appropriate for
Non-guaranteed Term	Lowest cost No control	None	None	None	None	Very limited situations
Yearly Renewable & Convertible Term	Higher cost Greater control	None	None	Increases	None	Limited cash flow Temporary needs Protection now

Term-Plus Investment Contracts

	General Description	Investment Vehicle	Investment Flexibility	Premium Flexibility	Face Amount Flexibility	Appropriate for
Whole Life	Fixed life Dividends provide investment return	General account Primarily bonds & mortgages	None Borrow	None Loans or dividends can reduce premium	None Buy another	In force now Older Substandard insureds

The "Menu" of Life Insurance Products (Concluded)

Term-Plus Investment Contracts *(Concluded)*

	General Description	Investment Vehicle	Investment Flexibility	Premium Flexibility	Face Amount Flexibility	Appropriate for
Variable Life	You direct the investments	Separate accounts Money market stocks & bonds etc.	Maximum (almost) Split it Move it No withdrawals	None Loans can reduce premium	None Buy another	Investors (alternative to "buy term & invest the difference")
Universal Life	Current interest rates	General Account Short-term guaranteed interest	None Borrow or withdraw	Maximum Enough for mortality & expenses up to maximum the law allows	Maximum Increase or decrease it Stay healthy for increases	Those who like only short-term interest rates
Variable Universal Life	Control Disclosure Flexibility	Separate accounts Money market, stocks & bonds Guaranteed interest, etc.	Maximum You split it You move it You withdraw it or borrow it	Maximum Enough for mortality & expenses up to maximum the law allows	Maximum Increase or decrease it Stay healthy for increases	Investors (alternative to "buy term & invest the rest" or "I want it my way!")

Whole Life...A General Account Policy

Prior to 1975, almost all life insurance policies issued by companies in the United States had the investment portion of premiums invested in the general portfolio of the company. The long-term general account portfolio of life insurance companies is composed primarily of bonds and mortgages. The fixed interest rate bonds and mortgages within the insurance company's general account investment portfolio earn the prevailing interest rate at the time they are purchased.

Until 1975, whole life insurance policies whose investment element was in the general account of the insurance company were the dominant investment type of policy available in the United States. Your policy may have been called a family policy, a life paid-up at 65 policy, an endowment policy, a 10- or 20-pay life policy, or even a single pay life policy. The names describe how long you paid the fixed premium required by, and unique to, whole life insurance. Each policy was issued with a fixed face amount and a fixed annual premium. Whole life insurance policies pass investment results through to the policy owner by way of dividends if they are participating policies. These dividends are considered to be a return of premium. The insurance company collects more than is necessary and therefore returns the excess to the policy owner. These dividends are federal income tax-free as long as the total dividends paid to you do not exceed the total premiums you have paid into the policy.

Variable Life Insurance

In 1975, the first variable life insurance policy was introduced. Essentially, the insurance company created this policy by changing the investment available within the contract. In that first variable whole life policy, the insurer removed the long-term bond and mortgage account and replaced it with just two accounts, a common stock account and a money market account. The insurer gave the policy owner the option of using either one or both and the ability to change back and forth between the two. This was the first-generation variable life policy. This policy, just like its predecessor, whole life insurance, had a fixed premium and a fixed face amount. If you wanted more life insurance, you had to buy another contract. If you couldn't pay the premiums when due, the policy would lapse. Relative to the investment performance of whole life, variable whole life has performed admirably, assuming that the policy owner had the assets invested in the common stock account. Ironically, one reason it did so well was because the stock market did so poorly. The stock market languished below the 1,000 point of the Dow Jones Average from 1976 until late 1982—six full years—while people were putting money into the policies and building up their number of shares cheaply. They obtained lots of shares to enjoy the ride up with the stock market since that time.

Universal Life Insurance—The Product That Changed All Life Insurance

In late 1979 and early 1980, universal life insurance was introduced. Universal life was the life insurance companies' direct response to the consumer's demands for the high interest rates of the time. Insurance companies decided to use relatively short-term investments and to promise policy owners a stipulated rate of interest for a one-year period commencing on the date they purchased their policy. The interest rates of the early 1980s were high, money markets were popular, and these policies became popular as well.

The insurance company promised policy owners a stipulated rate of return for a year. The policy owner naturally wanted to be able to verify that he or she was actually receiving the promised rate of return and so did the regulators. As a result, for the first time, the insurance company had to reveal to the policy owner the monies in the life insurance contract that were necessary to pay the expenses and the mortality charges.

Transparent Policies

The day this happened, all life insurance changed. For the first time, a life insurance policy was transparent. You could now see interest earnings and mortality costs. Prior to that time all anyone had ever seen were the results, without a breakdown of exactly what was going on inside of the policy each month and each year. Total disclosure became a reality of life insurance with universal life. The impact of this total disclosure on improving the quality of life insurance products for the consumer has yet to be fully realized by consumers and salespeople.

Not only did universal life bring total disclosure to life insurance, it also brought flexibility to life insurance policies. Whole life dictated a fixed face amount, a fixed annual premium, and a fixed investment vehicle to the policy owner. Variable life had the fixed minimum face amount and fixed premium; however, it gave the policy owner flexibility of investment vehicle. Universal life eliminated the fixed premium and fixed face amount but, for the moment, offered no flexibility of investment vehicle.

The Flexibility of Universal

Universal life provides the policy owner with an annual report in which three items are presented—the insurer's expenses, the mortality costs, and the interest earnings. If the policy owner wants to increase the death benefit, it increases the charges for the mortality and/or the expense to the extent necessary to support the increased death benefit. Reversing that process, if the policy owner wants to reduce the death benefit, the mortality charges are reduced. Thus, universal life offers flexibility of face amount, so that the policy owner can use one policy and increase it or decrease it as his or her life situation dictates as long as the insured remains able to qualify for any increase in coverage.

Universal life also offers flexibility of premium payment. The policy owner can add to the investment in the policy by increasing premium payments. At a minimum, the policy must have sufficient monies in it to cover the mortality and expense charges. The maximum a policy can accept is stipulated in the Internal Revenue Code and regulations. In 1988, Uncle Sam decided that life insurance was too good an investment and limited the tax benefits of life insurance by reducing the maximum you could put into a policy. You may not have thought of life insurance as a good investment, but the IRS thinks it is too good to allow you to put too much into it.

Variable Universal Life Insurance

The next inevitable step in the evolution of the life insurance policy came about in 1985. Universal life, which offered flexibility of premium payment and of face amount but no flexibility of investment, was combined with variable life, which offered flexibility of investment. In these variable universal policies, you are given personal control over the life insurance policy's face amount, amount of premium, and types of investment. You now control all three basic features of your life insurance policy. High policy owner control is synonymous with high quality. Such control makes these policies drastically different from the whole life policy you tend to put in the safe deposit box and forget about—as long as the mandated premiums are paid on time.

Variable universal life insurance gives you a great deal of control. Your management can make these policies perform extremely well or very poorly. You can make decisions not only about the policy's face amount but also on levels of funding within the policy. *Funding level* refers to how much you choose to pay into the contract. You choose where monies paid in are invested in the policy. With flexibility comes responsibility, and opportunity!

Hybrid Policies

A number of hybrid policies have been developed that combine features of the four investment types of policies. For example, policies referred to as *adjustable life policies* are first-generation universal life policies. Universal life, as you can imagine, takes a rather sophisticated computer tracking system to accept varying policy owner premium payments and varying face amounts of life insurance. If a company had not yet obtained the necessary computer expertise, an insurer would issue adjustable life that required less sophisticated computer equipment and technology. This policy requires that you submit a written request for any change in the amount to be paid into a policy. Based on this written request, the company would "adjust" the policy. Paying premiums at the lowest premium level, your policy would be similar to a 10-year term policy. If you paid premiums at the highest premium payment level, your policy would approximate a 10-pay life policy. A

10-pay life policy is a contract in which all of your investment is invested in the contract within 10 years. Thereafter, no additional funds can be accepted by the policy. The written request procedure of adjustable life allows the insurance company to go back into your policy, reprogram what was being recorded, and reissue your policy on the new basis. The computer system servicing the policy does not have to be very sophisticated because the insured's paper request for a change gives time for reprogramming. Insurance companies prefer adjustable policies to universal life because they think that you will be more inclined to keep paying premiums into your policy if you have the semicompulsive encouragement of a premium notice that requires payment or adjustment.

These "adjustable" policies share some of the flexibility of a universal life policy and frequently use the same kind of investment vehicle that enables the insurance company to guarantee you an interest rate for one policy year followed by renewal rates that vary depending on market and insurance company conditions.

Insurance companies, similar to every other financial institution, want investment money coming into the company each and every year. They are positively disposed toward recurring premium policies. Because the adjustable premium policies are less flexible than universal life and require policy owner action to change the billed premium level, adjustable premium policies are more likely to have recurring premiums paid into them than the universal life type of policy. Universal life leaves the payment of premium entirely to the discretion of the policy owner without the necessity of any particular action other than sending, or not sending the money. If you need the encouragement of a billed premium to maintain a healthy investment level in your insurance policies (and many of you do), the rigidity of adjustable life serves a good purpose.

The *interest-sensitive whole life* contract is another of the hybrid policies. This policy takes the fixed face amount and fixed premium level features of whole life and combines them with the investment vehicle used in a universal life policy. If you prefer the annual interest rate guarantee type of investment over the long-term bond and mortgages of whole life insurance, but you still seek a fixed face amount and fixed premium policy, this could be your policy of choice.

Single Premium Life Insurance

Single premium life insurance frequently is structured as an interest-sensitive whole life contract allowing only one premium. As you know, whole life insurance is a fixed premium, fixed face amount contract. Single premium life insurance is a fixed premium, fixed face amount policy but with only one premium allowed. The policy is designed to accept at issue the maximum premium allowable relative to its face amount under the income tax regulation laid out in Section 7702 of the Internal Revenue Code. In other words, the investment in the policy is maximized immediately. Because the investment is maximized, the net amount at risk (life insurance) is minimized. *Net amount at risk* may be defined as that amount that must be paid by the insurance company in the event of the death of the insured that is insurance company money. It is not the return of the policy owner's investment or account value, which is also paid out at death.

Reducing the amount at risk to a minimum also reduces mortality charges to a minimum. Because the policy would accept only one premium, expenses were minimized. The underlying investment, therefore, had as little of its return as possible allocated to mortality and expense charges. By maximizing investment and minimizing life insurance, investors took advantage of the fact that the investment within the insurance policy earned without current taxation and could be recovered via policy loan without taxation. Business boomed for this policy until June 21, 1988, when Uncle Sam instituted the Modified Endowment Contract laws decreasing the amount you could invest in a life insurance policy and still enjoy all the tax benefits. The insurance companies aggressively designed these single premium policies in order to attract investment dollars. They promised consumers a net rate of return on the investment capital after all expenses and mortality charges were paid. In other words, the insurance company would take your money on a single premium policy investment and promise you, for example, 8 percent. The insurance company had determined that it could lend that same money out at 9 percent or 10 percent. The spread between what they were paying you, 8 percent, and what was being paid to the insurance company, 10 percent, would cover mortality and expense charges and provide profit for the insurance company.

Because the net rates of return without current taxation were so competitive with other alternative investments, single premium life policies attracted quite a bit of consumer attention. Even those who had no interest in the life insurance element bought single premium life policies. The fact that you could earn compound interest without current taxation was attractive to many people. You also could borrow those untaxed earnings and spend that money without paying current taxes on what you had borrowed. You probably could borrow the money from your policy at an interest rate of 6 percent and at the same time the insurance company would credit your policy on the amount you had borrowed with an identical 6 percent. Thus, you could borrow and enjoy tax-free income, within limits, for potentially substantial periods of time with little or no effective cost.

Despite the big income tax trap in this (if you terminate the policy in any way other than by dying, all the deferred taxes have to be paid) and despite the fact that not many policy owners took advantage of the loan feature, it was viewed with disfavor by legislators. The ability to borrow without triggering current taxation on gains within a single premium life insurance policy was terminated, effective for policies issued after June 20, 1988. Thereafter, any monies borrowed from single premium life policies or modified endowment contracts as the law refers to them (a whole new class of life insurance policies) issued after June 20, 1988, would trigger current taxation to the extent of any gain in the policy. The borrowing policy owner also would be subject to penalty taxes of 10 percent of the amount included in gross income if that policy owner were less than 59½ years of age. Exceptions to the penalty tax are made in certain circumstances, such as in the event of disability or if there is annuitization of the policy proceeds.

You also can maximize payment into other types of policies, such as universal life, variable universal life, and single premium variable life. Variable universal and universal life policies, of course, are not single premium contracts. However, you can maximize your investment into the policy in a single premium, which means that you have paid as much as the law will allow you to pay into that policy at that particular time. Possibly in the future additional premiums may be paid into such policies and the policies will still remain within the IRC 7702 restrictions on how much investment a policy can accept and remain a life insurance policy.

Since June 21, 1988, single premium and investment-oriented policies, called *modified endowment contracts (MEC)* have lost appeal as retirement vehicles and sources of ready cash as a result of the taxation and penalties on withdrawals or policy loans. If the policy owner takes money from such contracts, he or she must accept the fact that there will be immediate income taxation on the amount borrowed or withdrawn to the extent of gain and, if the policy owner is younger than age 59½, there also will be a 10 percent penalty on the amount included in gross income.

The single premium policy or MEC is still an advantageous vehicle for an insured's beneficiaries. It remains an efficient way to transfer wealth that has enjoyed tax-free compounding to beneficiaries without any income tax liabilities. All life insurance proceeds payable at death are excluded from income taxation under Section 101 of the Internal Revenue Code. However, if you are seeking to gift the life insurance policy on your life out of your estate, any modified endowment contract is likely to create more gift and income tax problems that a non-MEC contract.

Second-to-Die Life Insurance

A strategy now being used with greater frequency is for the estate owner and spouse to minimize estate taxes at the first death of one of the spouses as much as possible. This involves using the marital deduction and the $600,000 exemption to eliminate estate taxes entirely on the estate at the first death. The results of the strategy will be that the surviving spouse will inevitably have to pay estate taxes on all he or she owns at the time of death in excess of $600,000. The tax starts at 37 percent and goes up to 55 percent, so cash from some source will be necessary. In order to ensure that cash is available to pay estate taxes at the second death when no marital deduction is available to protect assets from estate taxes, a *second-to-die policy* (also called a *survivorship life policy*) may be purchased. This type of policy will not pay off at the death of the first of the two to die but rather at the second death. As a result, this type of life insurance requires lower premiums than a regular life insurance policy. It also allows a couple, one of whom may not be in the best of health, to obtain life insurance that will pay off at the second death.

Survivorship life is a single-purpose policy. Its objective is to maximize death benefits at the second death. Its specific purpose is to provide funds to pay estate taxes *for* an estate, rather than *from* an estate.

If the estate owner or the spouse of the estate owner owns this policy, the full face amount of the death benefit will be includable in the estate and therefore could trigger estate taxes as high as 55 percent against the total death benefit. This is hardly an appropriate arrangement. The primary benefit of this policy is to the survivors of the estate owner and spouse. If it is sufficient in amount to pay all taxes, it will allow the beneficiaries to take the full value of the assets willed to them at death, rather than splitting those assets with Uncle Sam. Thus, the beneficiaries of the estate owner and spouse are the obvious and appropriate purchasers and owners of such a policy either directly, or through an irrevocable life insurance trust or a family limited parternship. If these beneficiaries purchase and pay for the policy, the cash to pay the estate taxes will come into their hands at the exact time the taxes are due, at the death of the surviving spouse. The beneficiaries may use the cash from the life insurance proceeds to buy the estate assets, thus providing the estate with cash to pay federal estate taxes. There are whole life, universal life, and variable universal second-to-die policies.

THE "MENU" OF LIFE INSURANCE

The "menu" of life insurance on pages 149 and 150 summarizes the generic forms of life insurance in a matrix that describes the basic features of each policy. The policy that appeals to you will depend upon your life insurance needs, your economic situation, and your likes and dislikes in regard to the various types of investments available within an insurance company and an insurance policy. The suitability questionnaire in Figure 9–1 will assist you in deciding which policy is best suited to you at the present time.

FIGURE 9–1

Life Insurance Policy Suitability & Selection Questionnaire

The Life Insurance Products Menu summarizes the variations in life insurance based upon the six basic generic types of life insurance. After going over the menu complete the following questions indicating your preferences.

Policy Type	Highly Prefer	Prefer	Satisfactory	Acceptable	Unsatis-factory
Nonguaranteed Term					
Renewable & Convertible Term					
Whole Life					
Universal Life					
Variable Life					
Variable Universal Life					

1. Put a check mark under the word that best describes your initial reaction to the type of policy named in the chart above.

2. I wish to put enough money into a life insurance policy to buy the life insurance protection only—no investment.

         Yes   No

3. I At this time, I am able to *consider* investing with an insurance company.

         Yes   No

4. The term policy need not be renewable or convertible as long as it provides uninterrupted life insurance for at least _____ years.

         Yes   No

5. I want the term policy to be renewable and convertible.

         Yes   No

6. I would prefer to have the charges for expenses and term insurance (mortality costs) deducted, pretax, from my policy investment account earnings.

         Yes   No

Life Insurance Policy Suitability & Selection Questionnaire (Continued)

7. I prefer the *whole life* arrangement of paying for life insurance for all of the following reasons:

   _____ Not applicable.

   _____ I like the long-term bond and mortgage, general account investments of whole life insurance.

   _____ I understand that I can only use this account for the life of my policy.

   _____ I desire low volatility.

   _____ I prefer a fixed, contractually guaranteed premium that I must pay or risk losing my policy.

   _____ I desire a policy with cash value guaranteed by an insurance company.

   _____ I am not concerned by possible reductions in dividends.

   _____ I prefer a *low management* type of policy.

   _____ I do not want premium, face amount, or investment flexibility.

8. I prefer the *universal life* arrangement of paying for life insurance for all of the following reasons:

   _____ I prefer having the insurance company specify the interest I will earn each year on the capital invested within my policy.

   _____ The guaranteed interest account is sufficient for my life insurance investment purposes. I do not and will not want or need any other investment alternatives in the future.

   _____ I like being able to see exactly what my investment is earning and the exact charges being made against my policy.

   _____ I like the flexibility of being able to adjust the face amount of the policy.

   _____ I like the flexibility of being able to vary my premium payments.

   _____ I want face amount and premium flexibility but not investment flexibility.

   _____ I like the fact that I can get at my money within this policy by either policy loans or withdrawals.

9. I prefer the *variable whole life* arrangement of paying for life insurance for all the following reasons:

   _____ I like the security of knowing that I only need to pay a fixed premium to maintain my policy regardless of what happens to my policy investments, mortality costs, or expenses.

   _____ I like the fixed premium arrangement.

   _____ I like having the ability to invest in a variety of investment accounts and being able to reposition these investments.

Life Insurance Policy Suitability & Selection Questionnaire (Concluded)

_____ I do not want premium or face amount flexibility, just investment flexibility.

_____ I like the guarantee that my death benefit will never go below the original face amount of the policy as long as I pay the required premium.

_____ It does not concern me that I cannot withdraw money from this type of policy but can only access my money via policy loans.

10. I prefer the *variable universal* arrangement of paying for life insurance for all the following reasons:

_____ I prefer to retain premium, face amount, and investment flexibility.

_____ I welcome the opportunity to exercise management control over premium, face amount, and investments in this policy and to enjoy the living benefits that it offers to enhance my family's/company's security. I am aware of the responsibility that is inherent in such flexibility.

_____ I understand that it is up to *me* to guarantee that my policy stays in force by making sure it always has enough money in it to cover the expenses in the policy each year.

_____ I want to have the opportunity to use the family of mutual funds within a policy to accumulate for family investment objectives without creating income tax liabilities.

_____ I understand that the more money I put into this type of policy the more opportunity I have to earn investment returns not subject to current taxation and that the best way to take advantage of this opportunity is to maximize what I put into it, whereas with other policy designs I often minimized what I put into them.

Review your answers to these questions. They have been designed to make you look at the generic forms of life insurance and to help you determine which you currently prefer. If your choice is yearly renewable and convertible term life insurance, make sure that you also have determined your preference among the investment forms of life investment-oriented policy you may want to convert to in the future.

CHAPTER TEN

Managing Your Life Insurance

You can and should manage your life insurance. You cannot afford to ignore the substantial accumulation of wealth that exists in your life insurance policies as a result of premiums paid and the earnings on investments within the policy. Yet most of you still do just that. It is no longer justified or necessary. You will find today's new life insurance policies are much easier to understand and manage.

The first level of management is the amount of the policy's death benefit. Chapter 8 was designed to assist you in determining a total face amount of life insurance that would be appropriate for you. You may obtain additional assistance in making this determination from a life insurance salesperson, an accountant, an attorney, a bank trust officer, or a financial planner. However, *you* are the final decision maker. Your sense of values will determine an appropriate amount for the beneficiaries that you are seeking to protect. Once the face amount decision has been made, the next decision will be how much you should pay into a life insurance policy.

WHOLE LIFE AND VARIABLE LIFE

If you have chosen a whole life or a variable whole life policy, the insurance company will dictate the amount of premium to be paid each year based on the face amount, the number of years that you have agreed to continue to pay a premium, your age, sex, smoking habits, and your health. These are fixed premium policies. You may elect to pay for the policy with a single premium, with premiums payable each year for the rest of your life, or somewhere between these two extremes. These are known as fixed premium, fixed face amount policies because your decisions regarding face amount and billed premium level are made when the policy is applied for and are not altered by the insurance company thereafter. With these policies, you must apply and qualify for a new policy if you want more life insurance, rather than simply adding additional coverage to the existing contract.

In a whole life contract your investment is fixed also. It is stipulated to be the long-term general account (whole life) or the short-term general account (interest-sensitive whole life) of the insurance company from which you have purchased the policy. There are no future investment choices to be made. If you wanted to direct the capital in that policy to some alternative investment, your only choice would be to borrow or withdraw funds from the policy and put them to work outside of the contract.

With variable whole life insurance, your level of premium payment and face amount is fixed as of the application date, but the funds may be invested in any of the accounts the insurance company makes available to you within the policy. Thus, the variable contract comes with a fixed premium and face amount but with a variable investment vehicle, whereas whole life has a fixed face amount, premium, and investment vehicle.

"VANISHING PREMIUM" OR PAID UP?

If your insurance company tells you your policy is "paid-up" it should mean that it is paid up by the terms of the contract (20-pay life, life paid up at age 65, or reduced paid-up insurance) and *cannot* accept any more premium payments. The policy will pay the death benefit, and the policy owner can put it in the safe deposit box and ignore it. The insurance company is contractually guaranteeing the payment of the death claim.

Vanishing premium, on the other hand, is a term used by marketers, salespeople, and other intermediaries to indicate that "they think," or the policy illustrations show, that the use of the dividends or excess interest they expect to be generated by the policy cash values will be sufficient to pay the mortality and expenses they expect to be charged in the policy at some future date. It is a way to get you to buy "on the cheap." You are told you will have to pay only 4, 7, 10, or 12 premiums and your policy will take care of itself (the premium will vanish) after that. Don't you believe it! Just imagine when some of the worst of the vanishing premium estimates were made: the early eighties when the prime rate hit 21.5 percent. Those estimates used the high interest rates of those days and projected that the rates would remain that high.

Those vanishing estimates are not coming to pass, and some policies whose premiums did indeed vanish (excess interest or dividends were sufficient for a time to pay the contractually required premiums) are reappearing because at today's lower interest rates, the policies just are not capable of generating sufficient return. Don't buy into vanishing and short-pay scenarios presented by an intermediary without knowing, and agreeing with, all of the assumptions that make up the calculation. Don't expect a bond fund to stray far for long from what it has historically been able to provide in return: about 5.2 percent gross. Don't expect a three- to five-year treasury security (about what you can expect in a universal life policy) to stray far from what it has historically been able to generate (about 4 percent to 5 percent). Yes, the insurance industry led you to believe it could do better than that; shame on it! If you go on believing it now, shame on you. Factor into your planning that there could come a day when your whole life policy would pay no dividend or your universal life policy could pay no excess interest.

TERM INSURANCE

Term insurance probably requires the least amount of management on the part of the policy owner. The policy owner stipulates the face amount, then submits to a physical examination and questions regarding occupation, avocations, health habits, smoking, and so on. Based on the insurance company's determination of the risk involved, the policy owner is asked to pay a stipulated premium for a stipulated period. In the case of annual renewable and convertible term insurance, the annual premium is sufficient to cover the mortality and expenses required by the policy for one year. As Table 9–2's menu of life insurance in Chapter 9 shows, there are varying types of term insurance. The short-term objective of those who buy term insurance is to pay the least possible amount of cash out-of-pocket for such protection. Table 10–1 illustrates some term insurance costs based on rates for a male nonsmoker purchasing a $250,000 face amount policy. It shows the approximate amount you would pay on a per thousand dollar basis into such policies. These rates are for planning purposes only, because life insurance rates change rapidly and can vary significantly based on your health and the amount of insurance you choose to purchase. Insurance companies frequently give discounts to purchasers of larger policies, which means that the per thousand cost comes down at higher levels of policy face amount.

In Chapter 8, you saw that once the need for life insurance was identified, the first order of business was to put a life insurance policy in force. Take your beneficiaries off the hook by putting the insurance company on the hook. Yearly renewable and convertible term insurance is the most expeditious way of doing this with the least amount of commitment on your part. Use renewable and convertible term insurance and make sure that you understand the privileges granted you within the contract for the premium you pay. Does the insurer allow you to change your term insurance policy to any of the other varieties of life insurance—is the policy convertible? Does the particular company from whom you are buying the term policy have a variety of life insurance types to which you may wish to convert? In most cases, when you convert your term policy into another type of contract, you will get credit for the premium you have paid for the term insurance in the year of conversion. As a result, you have nothing to lose by putting the term policy in force immediately and making the management decisions concerning the long-term financing of that policy at a more leisurely pace.

TABLE 10–1

Representative Term Insurance Rates, Cost per Year per $1,000
Male Nonsmoker Rates, $250,000 Face Amount

Age	Policy 1	Policy 2	Policy 3	Policy 4	Maximum Mortality Charges*
25	.49	.88	1.07	1.14	1.77
30	.49	.88	1.14	1.14	1.73
35	.49	.92	1.20	1.24	2.11
40	.52	1.13	1.34	1.43	3.02
45	.77	1.72	1.98	2.09	4.55
50	1.20	3.16	3.16	3.52	6.71
55	1.75	4.37	4.31	5.01	10.47
60	2.68	6.63	7.66	8.43	16.08
65	4.27	12.17	12.08	14.34	25.42
70	5.90	N/A	25.92	23.25	39.51
75	14.72	N/A	55.39	41.79	64.19

Policy 1. Nonguaranteed Term—3 year coverage limit.

Policy 2. United Services Automobile Association (USAA) direct-purchase annual renewable term—no commission product—add $30 per year policy fee.

Policy 3. Commercial Insurance Company Term Rates (1989)—add $30 per year policy fee.

Policy 4. Mortality/term insurance charges inside a universal or variable universal life insurance policy.

*Maximum mortality charges—1980 Commissioners Standard Ordinary Mortality Table.

Table 10–1 shows representative term rates for four different products: the first column shows a very limited nonconvertible, nonrenewable three-year term product, the second column shows a low-load yearly renewable term product; the third column, a commercial insurance company term rate; and the fourth column the term rates within a universal or variable universal policy. The fifth column shows the maximum rates an insurer can charge. These are the 1980 Commissioners Standard Ordinary Mortality Table Rates (1980 CSO).

As a life insurance buyer and policy owner, your second management decision basically is which of the term rates shown in Table 10–1 you should pay, and how you wish to pay them.

Policy 1: Nonguaranteed Term

If you elect Policy 1 in Table 10–1, the nonguaranteed term life insurance policy, make sure that the period of time for which the protection is offered is identical to the period of time for which you want and need the life insurance coverage. Although this is the lowest cost term insurance, understand that the risk that you face with this type of policy is that you lose control over this policy when the term of coverage ends. Your insurance objectives and your health may have changed by that time. The continuation of that policy might be valuable for you, but you would not be able to continue it. Murphy's Law tends to come into play in such situations. It is referred to as "cheap" term on the menu because you do not control it, the insurance company does. Company control allows the company to charge less for the coverage initially.

Policy 2: Low-Load Term

It is possible to purchase life insurance without going through a commissioned agent. In some eastern states, such as New York, you may buy life insurance from the bank. You may also go to an insurance company in San Antonio, Texas, called United Services Automobile Association (USAA) and purchase insurance directly over the phone without the involvement of a commissioned agent. Policy 2 of Table 10–1 gives some representative rates for USAA policies for a male nonsmoker at the $250,000 face amount level. With any insurance company, you may be able to get lower rates than are shown in this column by purchasing higher face amount policies.

Can you accomplish your purchase without the assistance of an agent? USAA life allows you to convert this policy to other forms of life insurance available from USAA Life. Does the insurer have the alternative policies that you may want? These are important questions that should affect your purchase decision.

A word about "no-load" insurance is in order. First, in its pure form, it does not exist. An insurance company may or may not pay commissioned salespeople, or it may pay them a little ("low-load"), but every insurance company does have marketing costs and purchasers pay these costs. A wise purchaser determines exactly how much is saved by buying a product touted as "no-load" or "low-load." There is no such thing as a no-load plumber, doctor, dentist, accountant, or store owner. You can't buy no-load cars, suits, food, medicines, or anything else. You are not in a no-load business or your family would not be eating, let alone buying life insurance. Consumers pay people to help them with their life insurance purchases. The key is not "to pay or not to pay"; the key is to receive full value for what you are paying. If you do pay an agent or any other intermediary to assist you with your life insurance purchase, service and continuing management ensure that you select carefully and that your chosen helper deserves your business and puts your best interests first.

Policy 3: Commercial Term

Policy 3 in Table 10–1 shows representative rates for term insurance available from commercial life insurance companies that pay commissions to agents. You purchase this type of policy if it is convenient and if the assistance and advice from the agent who will earn the commissions will be of value to you. The agent should provide sufficient "value added" to the policy to make any additional amounts that you may pay for the policy worthwhile. You should evaluate the agent's ability to do so based on recommendations from your other financial advisors and the individual agent's background, education, and activities. Above all, you should sense in the agent a personal concern for your well-being. Dismiss that agent if you ever sense that commission earnings are more important than are your personal objectives. There are too many good insurance sales representatives available for you to do business with one who isn't attentive and professional.

When you shop for term insurance remember that the mortality costs, which compose the major portion of your payments into these policies (the balance being expenses), go up every year as you get older. The insurers issue policies in different ways to pass this inevitably increasing cost on to you at varying rates. The insurer may raise the premium every year or average it over a given span of years. The insurer may keep the cost constant but take away some of your insurance protection, as in decreasing term insurance, which frequently is referred to as *mortgage insurance*. Unfortunately, "low-balling" is used too commonly in the industry. A company may promise low rates in a marketing letter, but after you buy you may find that rates increase rapidly in future premiums.

Be careful of the quote services that promise to find you low rates. If they are licensed insurance sales organizations, they earn a commission if you buy from them so they do not particularly care whether all facets of a policy fit your needs. Indeed it is unlikely they will know or ask about your needs; they sell you whatever you perceive as the cheapest policy. A quick sale is a profitable one for them. A quick sale may be an unwise and expensive one for you.

If the company is a fee-only quote provider, its only real interest is collecting the fee. Charging $50 to mail out computer printouts is profitable business for them but possibly a waste of money for you.

In most cases, you can get the same information plus explanations and assistance from your life insurance professional. Save your $50, and buy or don't buy at your discretion. Don't be afraid of insurance salespeople! Fire the bad ones . . . buy from those who put your needs first and serve you well.

In your term policy, check for guaranteed renewability that enables you to keep the policy in force for as long as you want. Compare forecaster renewal rates for the period of time during which you plan on continuing the policy. Avoid "reentry" term policies that give you favorable rates *only* if you can pass another medical examination. Do not be too concerned about the level of the guaranteed maximum term premiums the insurance company can charge you. These rates are the company's rates as filed with state regulators of insurance. Competition in the field will never allow the rates to go exceptionally high unless some catastrophic epidemic drives the rates up for all insurance companies. The factors that force term rates up will affect the whole industry, so that if rates *do* go to the maximums, they will probably go up across the board, affecting all companies.

Policy 4: Term Insurance Inside Universal and Variable Universal Policies

Universal and variable universal life insurance policies are investment-type policies that identify the exact amount of money allocated to their term insurance costs. You will note in Table 10–1 that they typically run somewhat higher than the previous, stand-alone, three types of term life insurance. One reason for this is that investment-type policies are more likely to result in the insurance company paying a death claim than the stand-alone term varieties, 99 percent of which are terminated by policy owners prior to death.

Term Insurance Costs

Every life insurance policy includes a charge to policy owners for mortality costs and expenses. Some policies stipulate exactly how much you have been charged each year for these elements, and some do not. The policies that itemize all costs and benefits within the contract are the straight term policies, and the universal and variable universal life policies.

After-Tax Term
When you choose a term policy from among Policy 1, 2, or 3 of Table 10–1, you are electing to pay a premium for a straight term insurance policy based on the death benefit offered. For any of these contracts you will be paying for the policy with your "after-tax earnings." You will have to earn enough money to pay income tax on the earnings and have enough left over to pay premiums to the insurance company. For example, if you are a male, age 45, and a nonsmoker, you could buy $250,000 worth of life insurance from USAA life at the rate of $1.72 per thousand (as quoted in Table 10–1). Your premium for the $250,000 worth of insurance would be approximately $430 (250 × $1.72). In order for you to have $430 to send to the insurance company, you would have to earn $614 [$430 divided by one minus your marginal tax bracket (1 − 30 percent), or $430 divided by 0.70]. Having earned $614, you would send 30 percent of that to Uncle Sam in taxes—$184—and you would have $430 left to send to the insurance company. You had to earn $614 in order to have $430

left, after taxes, to pay for your life insurance. That is how you buy life insurance with after-tax earnings. In order to pay $1.72 per thousand, you had to earn $2.46 per thousand.

Pre-Tax Term or Minimizing Term Costs by Cutting Out Uncle Sam

Why would you want to pay $2.09 per thousand, the cost per thousand indicated in Policy 4 of Table 10–1, as the term cost in a universal or variable universal life policy, rather than the $1.72 per thousand to USAA used in the previous example? The reason is that the $2.09 may be paid with pre-tax earnings on your investment within the contract. You have to earn only $2.09 to pay the insurance company $2.09, versus the $2.46 you would have to earn to pay $1.72 for the straight term policy—which creates a savings of 37 cents per $1,000, or 15 percent! The question is, "Do you have after-tax capital available to reposition into an insurance policy in order to enjoy tax-free earnings to pay term premiums?"

FUNDING LEVELS IN UNIVERSAL AND VARIABLE UNIVERSAL POLICIES

Once the decision has been made to buy life insurance with pre-tax dollars earned on an investment account, the decisions of *how much* to invest, and *where* to invest, remain. If you have decided on conventional whole life that invests in long-term bonds and mortgages, or the interest-sensitive variety that invests in short-term money markets types of investments, both the "amount to invest" and the "where to invest" decisions have been made. The company tells you how much to pay based on the face amount and the type of policy in which you invest. There is little flexibility of premium payment after that. Similarly, with variable whole life, you agree at contract inception to a set premium and face amount, but you retain management control and flexibility over where the money is to be invested in the contract.

On the other hand, funding level decisions with variable universal life are important not only on the day you decide on a specific face amount of life insurance and put the policy in force, but continue to be an important decision throughout the life of the contract. The ability to vary premium payments gives you important investment opportunities. To take advantage of this opportunity it may help you to think of your funding strategy as one of the following: (1) parity funding, (2) adequate funding, (3) underfunding, (4) minimum funding, (5) investment funding, (6) maximum funding. A description of each strategy follows.

Parity Funding Level

Parity is the quality or state of being equal. You know that the primary objective of the life insurance policy is to provide insurance protection on your life in the amount you deem necessary. You want to pay for this insurance in the most efficient way. The parity funding level in a life insurance policy is the point at which the amount of capital invested inside the policy will earn enough nontaxable return in the year in question to pay all of the mortality and expense charges within the policy in that year. There is "parity" between policy earnings and policy costs. Such a strategy ensures that you will be paying for your life insurance with the pre-tax earnings on the after-tax capital you have invested in your insurance policy. As long as the mortality and expense charges are fair, adequate, and competitive, you will have accomplished your primary objective of providing life insurance coverage at the least possible cost by paying that cost with earnings not subject to income tax.

To determine parity funding level, you need to know the amount of the expenses and the mortality charges to be charged within your policy for the year. This information is readily available in universal and variable universal policies. Whole life and variable whole life policies, however, do not divulge the amount of these costs. Variable universal policies provide a way for *you* to manage your investment based on costs that are stipulated for you.

Parity Funding

Current Investment Results	Equal	Expenses Plus Mortality Charges

---

The parity funding level is determined by dividing the amount of the expenses and mortality charges for the year by the return expected or guaranteed for that year. If your mortality and expenses are to be $400 this year and your return is 8 percent, you will need $5,000 in your policy to reach parity funding level. That is, $5,000 earning 8 percent will generate $400 of pre-tax interest, which is sufficient to cover $400 worth of expenses and mortality charges.

The next decision is to determine where to invest the capital among the choices offered within the policy. The universal life policy will offer only one choice, guaranteed interest, whereas the variable universal will offer multiple choices. The first investment objective within the policy would be to seek an investment account that would produce the type of investment results that are needed to service the policy's expense and mortality charges. The need is for monthly income to cover monthly costs. An investment vehicle that is appropriate to serve that particular need would be the guaranteed principal, guaranteed interest account (note that it is a general account, not a separate account), a money market account, or some other account that generates dependable monthly income. A variable universal policy normally offers at least one account suitable for paying the mortality and expense charges in addition to other accounts that can be used for your other investment objectives.

Adequate Funding

Parity funding was defined as a strategy whereby investment proceeds in the policy generate enough investment return to pay all mortality and expense charges incurred in the policy in the year in question. Use of the adequate funding level is for those who do not have, or do not wish to invest, sufficient capital within a policy to reach parity funding level immediately. *Adequate funding* is a level of payment designed to allow you to arrive at parity funding at some particular point in time.

"Adequate" is an amount of money that covers all current expenses and mortality charges and also makes a significant investment into the policy. For example, if approximately $6,000 in capital is needed to reach parity funding and you don't have $6,000 to put into the policy immediately, you may decide

---

Adequate Funding

Current Premium
  Plus
Investment Results

          Exceed

                  Expenses Plus
                  Mortality Charges

---

on an investment of $100 per month, or $1,200 a year. At this rate of funding you may find that, based upon projected mortality costs, expenses, and interest earnings, you will arrive at parity funding in approximately five years. Periodically, at least yearly, you can check your policy to see how it is progressing, and adjust the funding level to your current situation and objectives.

Underfunding

Underfunding of universal and variable universal life policies occurs when the mortality and expense charges exceed the combined total of the investment earnings in the policy and the current year's payment into the policy. For example, when you examine your policy, you may find that expenses incurred for the year were $50 and mortality costs were $450, totaling $500 in costs for that particular year. After further examination, you find that interest earnings in your policy amounted to only $100 and, on inspecting your checkbook, you find that you have paid only $100 into the policy during the year. Your contribution and the interest earnings totaled $200, whereas expenses totaled $500. In order to cover the $500 due, the policy was forced to take a $300 bite out of principal—the capital previously accumulated in the policy. At the end of the year, you will find approximately $300 less capital in the policy than you had when you began the year. If you ignore this process, you will find in the coming year that you will have still less capital to earn interest. If you don't increase your contributions, you'll find at the end of that year another decrease in capital that will exceed the decrease of the previous year.

The situation gets worse as the mortality charges in the policy increase as you get older. The expense charges also may be increased to some contractual maximum, and the interest earnings in the policy could be decreased because of changes in the prevailing level of interest rates. If all four events occur at the same time (capital down, interest rates down, expenses up, and mortality costs up), your policy would consume its principal at an even more rapid pace. As the capital base in your policy approaches zero, the insurance company will let you know that it will terminate the policy unless you start making larger payments into your policy. Underfunded policies eat up principal within the contract at an ever-increasing rate—don't let this happen to you!

When universal life policies first appeared in 1979 and 1980, interest rates were high. Funding levels were chosen during those periods assuming that those inordinately high interest rates were going to stay at that level. Many of these policies are underfunded, and indeed many of them actually have been involuntarily terminated. Angry policy owners do not understand why their policies are being terminated, which has resulted in consumer complaints to state insurance commissioners.

In many cases, even insurance salespeople who were selling these policies were not sure what they were selling. In competitive situations, an agent could sell you the same amount of coverage at a "cheaper" rate. This smaller premium represented a lower investment and lower investment returns.

Lower investment returns meant lower tax-free interest and thus a less efficient policy. Underfunding is the poorest of strategies in a universal or variable universal life policy. It is wiser to

---

Underfunding

		Expenses Plus
		Mortality Charges
	Are Less Than	
Current Premium		
Plus		
Investment Results		

Minimum Funding

Current Premium		Expenses
Plus	Are Equal To	Plus
Investment Results		Mortality Charges

---

buy a yearly renewable and convertible term policy with after-tax dollars. Minimum funding should be the lowest funding level into a universal or variable universal policy.

Minimum Funding Level

The *minimum funding level* for these types of policies should be the level at which the interest earnings in the policy and the policy owner's contribution to the policy are no less than the amount of the mortality and expense charges in the policy in that particular year. Such a funding level will ensure that the capital accumulated within your contract will stay at a constant level for the year and not be depleted by policy costs.

It's an advantage to own a policy in which you can adjust the premium level back to that of a straight term policy during those times when you do not have extra money to invest in the policy, but try hard not to pay so little in that your policy is forced to deplete its capital.

Investment Funding

If you have reached the parity funding level and policy earnings are sufficient to cover all policy expenses, why would you choose to invest even more capital to "investment fund"? You would do that to earn more for you, for your emergency fund, your college education funds, and your eventual retirement, taking advantage of the protection from income taxes provided by your policy. Assume that you have purchased a variable universal policy life policy and start out in a strategy of adequate funding. This strategy may be interspersed periodically in years of stress with years of minimum funding. One day you attain parity funding, the point at which expenses and mortality charges are entirely covered by policy earnings. If you have been using the guaranteed-principal, guaranteed-interest account to provide the earnings to cover funding your costs as we have suggested, you still have the family of separate account mutual funds available for your use. These separate accounts differ from commercially available mutual funds because of the fact that earnings, capital gains, dividends, and interest earnings within these accounts create no current income tax liability. You enjoy tax-free compounding in your IRA investments and qualified retirement plan investments, and this advantage is available to you within your life insurance policy as well.

Many of you participate in successful mutual funds and use them appropriately to build family wealth. Such mutual funds outside of the life insurance policy require the payment of taxes each year on any earnings and capital gains realized. In your profitable years you will be required to send to Uncle Sam almost one-third of realized capital gains, dividends, and interest earnings in any mutual fund that is subject to current taxation.

Examine Schedule B in your itemized income tax return. Are the positive results of your various mutual fund investments recorded there? Determine how much you actually had to pay in taxes for those positive investment results.

During the year, if you decide to sell one of your mutual funds and reinvest the money from that sale in a different mutual fund, the transaction will result in current taxation on the capital gains realized by the sale. The sale of the investment in one fund of a family of funds and the repositioning of those assets

---

Investment Funding

Current Premium
  Plus
Investment Results

                        Greatly
                        Exceed

                                            Expenses Plus
                                            Mortality Charges

into another of that family's mutual funds will cause taxation on any capital gains realized from the sale. This taxation reduces your net returns. This taxation does not occur in your IRAs, retirement plans, annuities, or life insurance.

The gains will be reinvested intact into the funds and taxation will be deferred until some future time. If you are using a life insurance policy and the policy pays off as a death benefit, the gains will escape income tax entirely.

If you own a variable universal policy, taxable mutual funds are obsolete for you until that policy has reached its maximum funding level, assuming the policy offers separate accounts competitive in performance to your taxable mutual fund choices. Assuming you can get comparable investment performance within your policy, you are wasting money listing your positive mutual fund results on Schedule B of your income tax return and paying up to a third of those increased values to Uncle Sam.

Maximum Funding

The *maximum funding level* is based on the policy death benefit, your age, and sex. It is the point at which no additional funds can be added to the policy based on the controlling income tax provisions in Internal Revenue Code Section 7702. Your insurance company will tell you what the amount is for you. According to the tax code, funding above this level causes the policy to cease to be a life insurance policy, resulting in immediate taxation of all deferred earnings. Your insurance company should not accept money that would cause your policy to go above maximum funding.

To determine whether a maximum funding strategy would be advantageous for you, you must first determine exactly

---

Maximum Funding

Current Premium	Equals	The Maximum
		The Law
		Will Allow

what additional expenses, if any, will be incurred when you
send in additional investment dollars. The first thing you
will find is that these additional investment dollars will be
diminished by state premium taxes. State premium taxes are
charged by your state of residence on every premium that is
paid into a life insurance policy. The additional investment we
are discussing is considered a premium payment under the
state regulations.

Table 10–2 lists the state premium taxes as charged by the
individual states. You may be one of the fortunate people who
lives in the State of New York and find that only 0.80 percent
of your investments will go to state premium taxes. In this
case, a $100 premium would incur only an 80-cent tax. If the
insurance company makes no additional charges against your

TABLE 10–2

State of Residence Premium Taxes

State	Premium Tax	State	Premium Tax	State	Premium Tax
AL	3.300	KY	3.000	OH	2.500
AK	2.700	LA	2.750	OK	2.250
AZ	2.000	ME	2.000	OR	2.250
AR	2.500	MD	2.000	PA	2.000
CA	2.350	MA	2.000	PR	4.000
CO	2.250	MI	1.330	RI	2.000
CT	2.000	MN	2.000	SC	0.750
DE	2.000	MS	3.000	SD	2.500
DC	2.000	MO	2.000	TN	2.000
FL	1.750	MT	2.750	TX	2.400
GA	2.250	NE	1.000	UT	2.250
GU	1.000	NV	3.500	VT	2.000
HI	2.750	NH	2.000	VI	5.000
ID	3.000	NJ	2.100	VA	2.250
IL	2.000	NM	3.000	WA	2.000
IN	2.000	NY	0.880	WV	3.000
IA	2.000	NC	2.023	WI	2.000
KS	2.000	ND	2.000	WY	1.600

$100 investment, you will find $99.20 going to work for you in your accumulation account. In this case, this charge will probably be lower than most low-load mutual funds. On the other hand, residents of the Virgin Islands have a state premium tax of 5 percent. This means an investment into the mutual fund of $100 is going to be diminished by $5; only $95 will be invested. Determine these costs *before* you buy a policy.

One of the advantages the variable universal product offers compared with the straight universal product is that the variable universal product, in addition to the additional investment options, is a registered product, subject to the regulations under the Investment Acts of 1938, 1939, and 1940. Registered products must provide a prospectus providing total disclosure and defining certain limitations on expenses. This prospectus will be invaluable to you in determining the charges that you will incur within your policy and also the type of investment results that you may expect on the various investment alternatives. Registered products also provide annual and semiannual reports. Typically, these reports will compare the investments to some readily available baseline so that you can evaluate performance. The prospectus and annual policy reports will describe the funds, stating their objectives and investment philosophies. Your objective in selecting such a policy is to find one with a family of funds in which the investment manager's objectives are in concert with your own, that has acceptable investment risks, and whose long-term returns are satisfactory to you.

These separate account funds levy charges for management, which will be taken from the fund's total return, just as in mutual funds. Normally the reports you get will be based on a net return after these expenses. Although it may seem that low fund management expenses would result in a higher net return to you, remember that you cannot buy good managers if you skimp on management fees. The value you receive for the fees is substantially more important than just low fees.

If you have quality mutual funds within your life insurance policy that are comparable in performance and expenses to the field of taxable mutual funds, use them to the maximum extent possible prior to using taxable mutual funds.

THE INCOME TAX BENEFITS OF LIFE INSURANCE

Death Benefits—Income Tax-Free

The primary advantage of life insurance is that if you contribute a small sum when the life insurance "hat" is passed, and subsequently you die, the whole hat will be given to your beneficiaries. This is good not only for beneficiaries but also for society, because these beneficiaries then do not become economically dependent on the rest of society. The death benefits of life insurance policies therefore have been blessed by the U.S. Congress with certain protections from income taxation. It doesn't matter whether the death benefit comes from "net amount at risk," from the policy owner's investment in the contract, or from the positive investment results; it is all tax-free income under Section 101 of the Internal Revenue Code. There are ways to mismanage your policy with the result that the death benefit would become taxable

---

Income Tax Benefits of a Life Insurance Contract

- Death benefits from a life insurance contract are excluded from the beneficiary's income. Death benefits include the net amount at risk and policy owner equity within the contract, plus earnings.

- The annual increase in value (inside buildup) is not subject to current taxation and escapes taxation entirely at death.

- The income tax basis of your policy includes amounts expended for life insurance and expenses.

- In life insurance policies other than "modified endowment" contracts, withdrawals up to policy owner basis are the first amounts to be paid out and are received without income tax liability. Policy loans currently are not taxable except in "modified endowment" policies.

- Neither policy withdrawals nor loans are subject to early withdrawal penalties for those younger than 59½ in policies that are not modified endowment contracts (MECs).

---

income, such as selling your policy to another for valuable consideration. Don't make any changes in ownership of your policy without considering it carefully with your income tax advisors.

Current Earnings and Gains
Not Currently Taxed

While a policy is in force, all interest earned, dividends earned, and/or capital gains realized on the policy investments are not subject to current income tax. The taxation is deferred until the gains are taken from the policy by the policy owner by withdrawal. Remember: Surrendering a policy (cashing it in) is a withdrawal. All investment type life insurance policies enjoy tax deferral on this "inside buildup" and a possibility of total tax-exemption on investment returns within the contract, which occurs when the proceeds are paid out as death benefits.

Policy Tax Basis Includes Amounts Paid
for Life Insurance and Expenses

Your income tax cost basis in your life insurance policy that you recover tax-free includes all the life insurance costs that the policy has charged during the time the policy has been in force. Policy mortality and expense costs increase your cost basis and thus are recovered tax-free if you surrender your policy. This means you have never had to pay income taxes on the earnings in your policy that were spent to provide you with life insurance while it was in force.

Tax-Free Use of Untaxed
Earnings and Gains

A fourth income tax benefit of life insurance depends on whether you incur taxation as a result of *using* the values accumulated within the life insurance policy while it is still in force. As long as your policy is not an MEC, you can use its values by (1) withdrawing, (2) borrowing against them from the insurance company, or (3) pledging the policy as collateral for a loan. If you withdraw from your life insurance policy an amount equal to what you invested in the policy, you will not pay any income taxes on those funds. Uncle Sam considers the transaction a straight return of your original investment and none of it is considered investment earnings. If you withdraw an amount exceeding the investment in the contract, the amount withdrawn beyond this basis will be subject to ordinary income tax. As a result, you normally would withdraw from a policy no more than what you had put into it, and if you wanted to use additional funds that had accumulated in the policy, you would borrow against the policy or collateralize the policy in order to get at those funds without being taxed on them. Prior to June 21, 1988, this could be done on almost any life insurance policy, but since that date it is applicable only to non-MEC policies.

The income tax benefits of life insurance are provided for a purpose. They encourage people to buy life insurance policies that provide for family and business security. In 1986 Uncle Sam came down hard on all tax shelters. Life insurance appeared to be about the safest tax-advantaged investment that remained available. Insurance companies recognized this, and carefully designed their policies to maximize investment opportunity and minimize life insurance expenses in order to get the consumer's investment business. Insurance companies made policy loans attractive by charging a low rate of interest equal to the policy owner's earnings on funds inside of the policy that were collateralized by the loan. You could borrow money from an insurance company at 6 percent and the company would still credit you with 6 percent on the amount borrowed. Thus, you would have little concern about the amount or duration of a policy loan. Policy loans are entirely a policy owner decision. This feature means that you can compound tax-deferred/tax-free and spend without current taxation—quite a deal!

MODIFIED ENDOWMENT INSURANCE–TAMRA

Single premium life policies are the most investment-oriented life insurance policies. In effect they become maximum funded policies with the first—and only—premium. Prior to June 21, 1988, these policies combined (1) high returns, (2) tax deferral or tax avoidance on those returns, and (3) the ability to access those returns without current taxation. In 1988, Congress decided this was too much of a good thing. The result was that in November of 1988, the Technical and Miscellaneous Revenue Act of 1988 (TAMRA) was signed into law. This new law defined a new class of life insurance policies that Uncle Sam considered too investment-oriented, named modified endowment contracts (MEC), and removed the tax-free accessibility to the cash in these policies. Any policy issued after June 20, 1988, that falls into the classification of a modified endowment contract cannot provide the policy owner with the privilege of withdrawing from, borrowing from, or collateralizing the values accrued within the policy without incurring immediate taxation on policy gains that are withdrawn, borrowed, or collateralized.

Indeed, if the policy owner is under age 59½, not only do income taxes become due on the amount of gain accessed in the contract, but also a 10 percent penalty would be applicable to the amount included in gross income as a result of the withdrawal, borrowing, or collateralization. Exceptions to this penalty are if the funds are withdrawn as a result of disability or over a period of time related to the policy owner's lifetime (annuitized).

How to Avoid "Modified Endowment" Status

Assume that you, the policy owner, want all of the income tax benefits of life insurance, and in particular you want the ability to make withdrawals up to your basis or loans on your policy without being exposed to ordinary income tax or penalties. In order to accomplish this with a policy issued after June 20, 1988, you may invest no more into your policy during the first seven policy years than an amount determined by the government-mandated test called the "seven-pay test."

The seven-pay test has nothing to do with you having to pay seven premiums or your paying seven equal premiums. It concerns only the limitation on the amount of money you can pay into your policy within the first seven years of its existence, as summarized in Figure 10–1. For example, if the insurance company offering you a life insurance policy informs you (and the insurance company *should* provide you with the information) that the seven-pay test allows no more than $1,000 per policy year, you could put no more than $1,000 into the policy in the first year. Regardless of whether you put in the full $1,000 in year one—or something less than that, for example $200—the total maximum that can be put into the policy during the second year cannot exceed an amount that would bring your total two-year contributions to $2,000. For the first seven policy years, the cumulative maximum you could contribute to the policy would be $7,000. At that point your policy would have completed the testing period, it would not be considered an MEC, and your accessibility to policy values by way of loans and withdrawals up to basis would not incur taxation or penalties.

The amount of your contributions to your policy are also controlled by the other provisions of Internal Revenue Code Section 7702. Indeed, often you will find these other provisions are more restrictive in the fifth through seventh policy years than the seven-pay test restrictions, and you will not be able to contribute even as much as the seven-pay test indicates. Your insurance company should inform you if your contributions exceed those allowed by the IRS provisions. You, however, will want to keep track of the seven-pay test maximum limits of your policy and keep your investment below them. Most insurance companies offer tracking assistance. Find out how your insurance company does it.

FIGURE 10–1

The "Seven-Pay" Test Assuming a $1,000 Seven-Pay Maximum Premium

| Year 1 Room for up to $1,000 | Year 2 Room for up to $2,000 | Year 3 Room for up to $3,000 | Year 4 Room for up to $4,000 | Year 5 Room for up to $5,000 | Year 6 Room for up to $6,000 | Year 7 Room for up to $7,000 | Seven-pay testing period over unless policy is materially changed |

Material Change to a Policy Issued Before June 21, 1988

The TAMRA provisions also put restrictions on policies purchased before June 21, 1988, if they are materially changed. The "material change" provision could cause problems. Other than death benefit and future policy value increases resulting naturally from the payment of premiums that comply with the seven-pay test in the first seven contract years, and benefit increases resulting from investment and/or interest earnings on those premiums, *any change in a policy is likely to be deemed a material change.*

A material change will result in the policy being considered a "new" contract entered into after June 20, 1988, and subject to the seven-pay test as of the date the material change takes effect and for seven years thereafter. If your policy fails the test at any time during those seven years, it will become an MEC; once a policy is deemed an MEC it always will be a considered one. Policies that can pass the seven-pay test are *not* modified endowments and retain *all* the tax benefits of life insurance. Be careful in making changes to your policies and know how such changes will affect your investment limitations.

When to Ignore the Seven-Pay Test Limits

You can still buy a single premium policy, an investment-oriented policy, or a policy referred to by Uncle Sam as an MEC. Such policies still enjoy the tax-free death benefit of the total proceeds to be paid by the contract and the tax deferral on the inside buildup or earnings within the policy as a result of interest, dividends, and/or capital gains. What's new for these policies is that now (subsequent to June 20, 1988) if you borrow, withdraw from, or collateralize this policy, you will have to pay income taxes (on that amount) to the extent that you have gain in your policy plus a 10 percent penalty on any amount included in income as a result of withdrawing, borrowing, or collateralizing your policy (exceptions being disability or annuity payouts). If the inability to withdraw from or borrow against the money within your policy without current taxation is *not* important to you, the change in the law is irrelevant and you may continue to use these policies to accomplish your objectives. In the past, more than 90 percent of the purchasers of single-premium policies have not borrowed from them. For those who do not use the money in their policy or those who will never want to change the cost basis in the policy during its life, the new rules will have no impact.

If you are not sure whether it will be necessary for you to access the money within your policy in the future, we recommend that you comply with the seven-pay test regulations. It is not hard to do and does not restrict your ability to invest in your policy all that much. Retaining the flexibility of a non-MEC policy is worth it. Make sure that your policy is not deemed an MEC so that you may retain the tax and penalty-free access to your cash. If you may be subject to estate taxes, keep in mind that a reason that you might want to withdraw or borrow from your policy would be to reduce its gift tax value prior to giving the policy away to move it out of your estate. You would be unhappy with an MEC under these circumstances.

Try the following. Using your own age, consult Table 10–3. Look at the figures provided alongside of your approximate age. A 40-year-old, for example, could invest $209 per $1,000 into a single premium life insurance policy and enjoy only the first three

TABLE 10–3

Life Insurance Premium Choices
Male Nonsmoker Rates, Annual Premium
per $1,000 Face Amount

Age	Term Insurance	Target Universal Life	Whole Life	Seven-Pay	Maximum Single
30	1.30	7.20	$ 11	$ 29	$135
40	1.49	11.40	15	42	209
50	3.34	18.70	22	60	314
60	8.75	31.50	36	83	446
70	28.26	51.10	70	114	592
75	*	64.20	102	135	665

Note: These are approximations and appropriate for illustration purposes only. For precise numbers for you and the policy you are considering, contact your insurance company.

*Seldom available.

income tax benefits of the life insurance policy. Thus, $209 per $1,000 would mean a $20,900 investment into a $100,000 policy. That would be the only premium you would pay into that contract, and the funds would compound within that contract without current taxation for the rest of your life. At your death all of the death benefit, which may or may not include extra death benefits caused by the compound earnings within the policy, would be payable to your named beneficiary and there would be no income tax liability. However, should you borrow from, collateralize, or withdraw from this policy, you would be taxed on the amount borrowed, withdrawn, or collateralized to the extent of gain in the contract. You also would incur the 10 percent penalty if you are younger than 59½ years of age. These same tax regulations would apply to any policy that was above the seven-pay test maximum of $42 per $1,000, right up to the $210 per $1,000 maximum. If you paid only $43 per $1,000 into the policy (note that the seven-pay test maximum in Table 10–3 is $42), the policy would be considered a modified endowment. However, if you limited yourself to paying no more than $42 per $1,000 per year into this policy for the first seven years, you would retain the ability to borrow on the policy without paying taxes or penalties on withdrawals, policy loans, or collateralizations.

DEATH BENEFIT OPTIONS

When you apply for a universal or variable universal life policy, the application asks whether you want your death benefit to be payable on Option A or Option B. (In some cases these may be labeled Option 1 or Option 2.) It is important for you to select the proper option if you expect to maintain management control over the amount of life insurance your policy provides.

Option A/Option 1

Under Option A you stipulate to the insurance company the total amount of the death benefit that is to be payable to your beneficiaries—for example, $200,000. If you stipulate Option A (or Option 1), your chosen level of premium payments and the investment results in your policy will have no impact on your death benefit. If you have elected $200,000 as your death benefit under an Option A policy, that's exactly what your beneficiaries will receive. If you had paid $50,000 worth of premiums and had investment results that doubled that amount, your account value would be $100,000. The insurance company would still pay off a total of $200,000, $100,00 of which would be your account value and $100,000 insurance company money. Option A minimizes life insurance costs, because every time your account value increases either with premium payments or positive investment results, the life insurance or the amount at risk (the amount of insurance company money that is to be paid to your beneficiaries in the event of your death) is reduced. When the amount at risk is reduced, your mortality charges are reduced.

With Option A, you lose control over the amount at risk; it goes down as your account value goes up. Also, good investment returns and capital you have accumulated in your policy become irrelevant when you die: Good or bad, a lot or a little, $200,000 is the total payment. Say, for example, that you possess a $10,000 certificate of deposit (CD) and a $200,00 life insurance policy and you decide that the $10,000 would earn more inside of the policy than inside the CD. You transfer $10,000 into the life insurance policy, but you die immediately thereafter. The insurance policy pays $200,000. The day before, while the CD was still in the bank, you had a $200,000 life insurance policy and a $10,000 CD. Had you died at that point, your beneficiary would have received both the $200,000 and the $10,000 CD. But the instant the insurance company received your CD for deposit into an Option A policy, the insurer reduced the amount of the "net amount at risk," the life insurance, the amount of the insurance company's money the company was providing by an amount equal to what they had received from you. Poor timing could make this a poor investment. For this reason, during your accumulation years you should avoid an Option A policy unless you have a specific reason for selecting this option. Figure 10–2 summarizes this scenario.

The *face amount* is the death benefit and includes the value of the investment account. For example: The face amount/death benefit is $200,000 on Option A. The *policy account value* is $100,000 and the *amount at risk* is $100,000. The death benefit will be $200,000.

FIGURE 10–2

Option A/Option 1

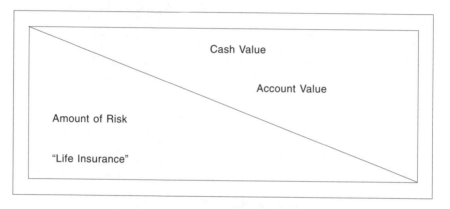

Option B/Option 2

When you elect Option B for your variable universal life insurance policy, you direct the insurance company to pay the stipulated benefit from *its* money, not yours. Instead of having the $200,000 death benefit included in the investment account, you ask that your investment account be paid in addition to the amount at risk of $200,000. By electing Option B in the previous example, when the individual transferred the $10,000 into his investment account, that investment account would increase by $10,000. In the event of death, the life insurance, $200,000, (the amount at risk), *and* the investment account ($110,000) would be paid to the beneficiary for a total of $310,000. Figure 10–3 illustrates this circumstance.

The *death benefit* is the face amount plus the value of the investment account. For example: The amount at risk is $200,000, the investment account is $100,000, and the total death benefit is $300,000.

True, mortality charges under Option B will be higher than under Option A. This is because more life insurance company money (life insurance) will be paid out; thus, higher mortality costs will be charged.

However, you maintain control over your death benefit with Option B. If you want the insurance company to reduce the amount

FIGURE 10–3

Option 2/Option B

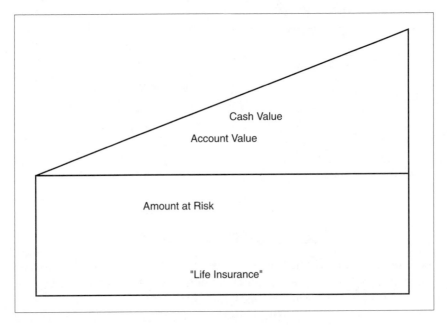

at risk, you may direct the insurance company to reduce the face amount of your policy to *your* predetermined level. The insurer will do so and thereby reduce your mortality costs.

Be cautious if you ask for any reductions in the death benefit of your life insurance policy, particularly during the first 15 years of the policy's life. Uncle Sam has stipulated the maximum amount of premium or investment that you may have in a particular life insurance policy and that amount is related to the death benefit under the contract. If you have a substantial investment and you direct the insurance company to reduce your death benefit, you may find that the company can do so only if it gives you back some of the cash within your policy. This is referred to as *force out*. Force out means that there is too much cash in relation to the face amount of your policy. The insurance company is forced to take money out of the policy and return it to you to remain in compliance with the definition of life insurance in IRC 7702. Money forced out in this manner will trigger ordinary income tax on the amount forced out to the extent of gain in the policy, in addition to possible 10 percent penalties.

The optimal solution: Use Option B in your contracts, avoid a reduction of face amount during the first 15 years of your policy life (do so only *after* ascertaining that it will not create tax problems), and thereafter do so only with a great deal of caution. Consider the potential income tax implications of your changes. Work closely with your insurance company and other advisors in order to avoid income tax surprises.

USING THE MONEY IN YOUR POLICY: WITHDRAWALS OR POLICY LOANS

The rule of thumb when you need cash from your policy is to use a policy loan in lieu of a withdrawal. This recommendation is based on the assumption that the variable universal policy you own is working for you and that you are satisfied with the investment results within the policy. However, you may have a temporary need for cash. A temporary need for cash infers that you probably will return those funds to the policy at some future date. The question is, will those funds be subject to the state premium tax and front-end loads (expenses) when they are put back into the policy? The return of withdrawn funds will be subject to the state premium tax and possibly premium loads because they will be considered to be new premiums. However, if you borrow from your policy and pay off your policy loan, that is not a premium and is not subject to state premium tax or front-end premium loads. As a result, a policy loan usually is preferable to a policy withdrawal in order to avoid the reimposition of state premium taxes and front-end loads.

When you borrow from your policy, you probably will pay the insurance company 1 or 2 percent more than the insurer pays you on the amount you borrow for the time you have the money out. This cost is likely to be much less than the reimposition of state premium taxes and front-end loads. A withdrawal typically is more expensive than a loan. In order to determine which would be most advantageous, balance the net cost of the policy loan against the state premium tax and front-end loads that would be incurred if you were to withdraw and pay back that withdrawal at a future date.

What to Do

If you choose what I consider to be the most manageable of the manageable life insurance policies—the variable universal contract—can you determine the amount at risk that you require, purchase a variable universal life insurance policy using Option B, and at least adequately fund your contract? Strive to get to parity funding level as soon as possible. Use the guaranteed-principal, guaranteed-interest account to pay all of your mortality and expense charges. Use the equity separate accounts (mutual funds) to help you accomplish your other financial objectives such as accumulating for college education or retirement funds.

Near-Term, Specific-Purpose Money

The guaranteed-interest, guaranteed-principal account can be used as an emergency fund or a place to accumulate funds for some important purpose that will occur within a year or two. The funds in excess of your surrender fees can be available to you by means of a policy loan in most cases within 10 days of your request. In the typical variable universal policies, you will find separate accounts that will also be appropriate for near-term investment objectives, such as the money market fund or even an intermediate-term bond fund with short maturity date securities. Match the fund objectives to your objectives. The capital you invest should earn competitive interest rates without current taxation and still be available for your use for any number of near-term purposes such as the down payment on a home or the purchase of an automobile. In these days of nondeductible consumer loans, it makes good sense to prefund auto payments. Make car payments in advance into your policy where they compound without current taxation and then borrow from the policy when you want to buy the car. You can pay this loan off by continuing to make car payments into your policy. Cash will then compound without taxation and be available in the account when your car needs to be replaced. This strategy eliminates automobile loans, which generate nondeductible interest. It turns the situation around, generating compound interest that is not taxable to you. Remember, invest no more than the amount allowed by the seven-pay test.

College Education, Retirement, and/or Net Worth Buildup

Where and how do you accumulate funds for those college educations that will arrive in 7, 10, or 15 years? What about retirement? How can you increase your net worth so that you and your family are more secure? One way is to use dollar–cost averaging within your variable universal life (VUL) policy. With dollar cost averaging you invest a set amount at specified intervals of time. Table 10–4 presents a five-period dollar–cost averaging strategy using $100 per period with dramatic decreases and increases in unit value during the accumulation period.

Dollar–Cost Averaging Insurance Investments

Dollar–cost averaging enables you to invest in volatile investments, such as common stocks, and take advantage of the volatility. This strategy is not likely to generate instant investment returns, but you are likely to grow rich *slowly* if you practice it consistently over long periods of time.

TABLE 10–4

Effects of Dollar–Cost Averaging

Month	1	2	3	4	5	Totals
Investment	$100	$100	$100	$100	$100	$500
Share value at purchase	$100	$50	$25	$50	$100	
Shares purchased	1	2	4	2	1	10
Sell all shares at the end of the fifth month						

10 shares @ $100 market price	=	$1,1000
less investment	–	500
Gain on investment	$	500

The various separate accounts offered by your variable universal policies are perfectly suited for dollar–cost averaging strategies. Your insurance company can bill you monthly and you may direct regular payments among the various mutual funds. No income taxes are charged against your accumulated funds. You may make the payments to a common fund, rather than earmarking funds separately for each child. People who allocate investments to individual children often find themselves with one child who has a large education fund and no desire to continue schooling, and another child who has a small education fund but a great desire to attend college. It can, and does, create problems. The strategy of accumulating unallocated education funds makes it much easier for a family to use the money where and when it is needed and, if it is not needed, to retain it for retirement security—all without current income taxation. This is a better alternative than Uniform Gift to Minors Accounts (UGMAs). Also, keep in mind that life insurance account values currently are not charged against you when you seek financial aid for your college student.

If you do adopt a strategy of dollar–cost averaging, your investment results will start out slowly and unimpressively. In fact, the more unimpressive the better because it may mean that the fund you have chosen currently is not popular or stocks are out of favor and therefore you are accumulating units at a low cost. One thing is certain about the securities market; it goes up and it goes down. A well-diversified, well-managed equity mutual fund that is out of favor eventually will come back in favor *if* you allow time—and this is a big and important *if*. Well-managed funds will one day come into favor. With consistent investing, you will accumulate a block of investment capital that *you* will define one day as significant. At that time you may decide that you do not wish to risk losing what you have accumulated. If so, sell off the volatile mutual fund in your policy at one of the "in-favor" times and move the funds to a less volatile or lower risk account within the policy, but continue dollar–cost averaging into the more volatile accounts. When your gains are significant to you, *take them!*

This strategy could be referred to as "nibble and nab"— nibble at the stock market via dollar–cost averaging and nab your earnings when you consider them significant for your purposes. Doing this in your policy incurs no income taxation. Doing this in your taxable mutual funds can incur considerable income taxation. Couldn't you end up with better returns if you just dumped the money into the market and held onto investment for a long period of time? The answer would probably be yes as long as you never sold because of market concerns or some crisis in your life . . . not many of us can do that.

Is this the fastest and best way to invest and accumulate? Dollar–cost averaging can be the best way to invest if it enables you to do what you otherwise would not have been able to do.

It will be necessary for you to accumulate capital for your own retirement in order to supplement whatever income may be provided to you through your employer-provided plan, social security, or other government programs for which you qualify. Retirement is a long-term accumulation objective. Inflation is one of the most substantial risks affecting the sufficiency of your retirement accumulations. Inflation constantly erodes the adequacy of your income. Prices rise over time, and if your income stays at a fixed level, you will find yourself an unhappy and destitute retiree.

Remember Chapter 8's description of the Rule of 72. Divide the interest rate you are earning on an account into 72 to find out about how long it will take that account to double. For example, if the account is earning 5 percent, it will double in about 14 years: $72 \div 5 = 14.4$.

Keep in mind that this is also the half life of money. If inflation is 5 percent during your retirement, 14 years after you retire your fixed income retirement dollar will purchase one-half of what it did when you retired. Your retirement income would have to double for you to retain the same standard of living. You have to deal with this risk directly in your investment and accumulation strategy. This strategy will inevitably include the ownership of a diverse portfolio of common stocks. Your VUL insurance policy gives you the opportunity to accumulate, own, and buy and sell stock funds among the family of separate accounts offered within your insurance policy, and to do it all without having your returns diminished by current income taxes.

There are insurance contract tracking services that try to guide investors into stock funds during market rises and out of them during market dips. There are asset allocation accounts offered by life insurance companies that will allocate funds depending on your objectives and willingness to accept risk.

In short, a quality VUL policy that can do all that we have described should eventually be a core holding in most family situations. It should be used to the maximum extent that the economic circumstances of the family allow.

In order to monitor your strategy and to keep track of your funding level, fill in the blanks of the Funding Finder Worksheet in Figure 10–4.

FUNDING FINDER WORKSHEET

When you consider the purchase of a VUL policy, make sure that the numbers for the four top boxes in the figure are based on reasonable assumptions that have been explained to you and that you understand and accept.

FIGURE 10–4

Funding Finder Worksheet For Universal and
Variable Universal Life Insurance

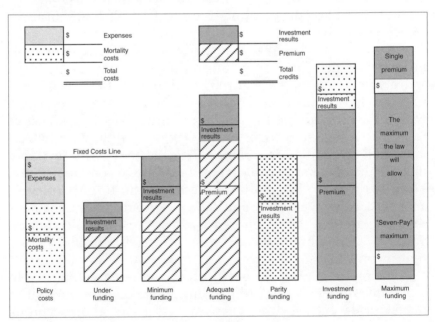

Once you have purchased one of these policies, you will receive an annual report that contains the actual results for your policy for the past policy year. Extract the four numbers for the top blanks from that annual report and place them on the Funding Finder Worksheet.

Fill in numbers for expenses, mortality costs, investment results, and premium paid. Next, determine whether your premium and/or investment results for the year are less than, equal to, or exceed the amount of expenses and mortality costs. Once you have determined their relationship to policy cost, fill in the appropriate lower column with your numbers. This will show you the funding strategy you have been using for the past year. Then, take control! Decide what funding strategy you will adopt for the coming year based on your needs, resources, and objectives. I will be cheering for you to move to the right.

VARIABLE UNIVERSAL LIFE: THE "SWISS ARMY KNIFE" OF FINANCIAL PRODUCTS

The VUL policy is not just a hot product. It is the result of the evolution of the life insurance contract. This is a life insurance contract that provides term insurance and tax-sheltered investments. It is unique in that it has empowered you, the policy owner. This is not a paternalistic contract that dictates how much you must pay into it for a particular face amount and then tells you that the insurance company will manage the investment portion in the single general account (that is accessible to the creditors of the insurance company).

This contract asks you for instructions. A VUL policy asks how much you wish to put in, within practical and legal limitations. It asks you where you wish to have it invested among multiple investment opportunities, including the general account and an ever-increasing number of separate accounts (not subject to the creditors of the insurance company). It reduces risk for you through diversification and control. It enables you to vary the death benefit in accordance with your varying needs.

A VUL policy is not necessarily an easy thing to grasp, considering that a lot of what has been said about life insurance for the last 150 years, even from the insurance industry itself, is that life insurance is a poor place to invest. The marketing terms and strategies used by both agents and companies alike have been ways of saying that absolute nirvana in life insurance is not having to put any more money into the contract. All the familiar phrases— *minimum deposit, paid-up, short pay, 4-pay, 7-pay, 12-pay, vanishing premiums,* and so on—relate to the cessation of the premium stream. In short, prior to variable universal life, insurers acknowledged by their words and actions that no sane person would put more money into a life insurance policy than was absolutely necessary to maintain it in force.

Commonly Raised Issues about Variable Universal Life Insurance

How Much Can a Policy Holder Invest in His or Her Policy?
There has been a paradigm shift, a sea change. The new world of life insurance is "How much can a policy holder put into his or her life insurance policy and still enjoy all of its income tax benefits?"

A VUL policy is basically term life insurance and a group of separate accounts similar to a family of mutual funds that are available within the contract to help you meet your investment objectives.

Why Is It So Good?
The primary attraction of a VUL policy is that you don't have to pay income taxes on what goes on inside this family of mutual funds. Dividends and realized capital gains are not taxed currently.

Why Do You Resist It?
People are gun-shy about the VUL policy because they just don't believe it and want to dismiss it or are worried about one of the other components of the *life insurance policy recipe,* as summarized in Figure 10–5.

Are the Expenses Too High?
You need to be aware of the expenses and the mortality costs inside of variable universal life. Uneducated consumers want the

FIGURE 10–5

The Life Insurance Policy Recipe

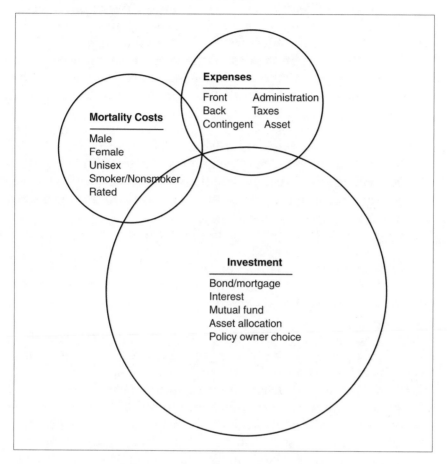

term costs to be as low as the low-ball, loss-leader, under-reserved, discounted "Yugo" term policy that they read about in some insurance company promotions. They want the insurance companies to price the product as if it were going to stay in force only a few years and, in all likelihood, not result in a death claim like the typical "cheap term." In reality, the VUL product *is* likely to last a lifetime and result in a death claim.

These people would prefer the insurance company to lose money. By now, you would think that people would realize that companies that lose money are companies that are going to fail. These failing companies have been particularly bad for their policy owners' economic health. If someone wants a Yugo policy, he or she should buy a Yugo, and not a VUL policy. You would be surprised how many Mercedes drivers buy Yugo term policies.

The bottom line on the cost of the term life insurance is that it will cost more than that type of term insurance that doesn't stay in force long enough to result in a death claim, but market forces will push the costs to stay competitive. It stands to reason that if a company raises its costs beyond what is reasonable in the marketplace, new business will cease. The healthy people that they insure will move to other companies, whereas the unhealthy insureds will be forced to remain and result in earlier death claims. This isn't good long-term strategy for a company nor for the intermediaries who sell its products.

Expenses and mortality costs (the term insurance element) inside of comparable variable universal life insurance policies should be competitive. However, unless these costs are way out of line, they are not what drive the policy. The investment capital will drive the policy.

If One Buys a Tax Shelter, Shouldn't One Use It?

Notice in Figure 10–5 that the investment circle is significantly larger than the smaller mortality circle and the smallest expense circle. The actual relationship in the size of those circles in your VUL policy is up to you! If you choose to put little or no money into the policy, you chose to buy and pay for a tax-shelter but have decided not to use it. You have decided not to put in investment capital on which tax-sheltered returns can be earned. That's not a problem with the policy, it's a problem with your implementation of the strategy. Of course, you could be going through a time when no investment capital is available and then you simply take advantage of the policy flexibility, maintaining the death benefit and holding the policy for investment purposes in the future. This is a valuable and important feature of this policy.

On the other hand, if you have filled the policy up to the maximum amount the policy can hold and still retain all of the income tax benefits, it will not be long before the expenses and mortality costs in any credible policy will pale in comparison to the income tax-sheltered growth delivered by the separate accounts in the policy.

Many people consider only the tax-deferred/tax-free compounding as the driver of policy profits. They forget about the fact that when they move money around between the policy accounts they incur no transaction costs or capital gains taxes on the profitable investments within the policy. The capital gains tax savings actually have proven to be the most significant savings policy owners enjoy. Compare this to accumulating capital within a taxable family of mutual funds and paying taxes as the investor sells one profitable fund in order to safeguard his or her gains. Almost one third of the hard-earned profits will go to Uncle Sam. We all have seen people refuse to sell at times when their personal situation dictates that they should sell, simply because of the taxes that would result.

Capital gains taxes are not an issue within a VUL insurance policy. You do not pay capital gains taxes as you sell one fund within your policy and move that money into another fund in the same policy. Thus, the capital gains tax savings alone within these policies can exceed the expected lifetime costs within the policy.

What Else Can This Product Do That Other Products Can't?

How about protecting assets within the policy from the claims of creditors? In most states you will find that life insurance death benefits and account values enjoy some degree of protection from the claims of creditors. Because the rules in the various states differ and are subject to change, you will want to have a lawyer who practices in your state bring you up-to-date.

Generally speaking, the protection will not work if the assets have been put into the policy with the intention of defrauding creditors. Creditor protection is a significant benefit in this litigious society.

How Can You Turn Tax-Deferred Compounding into Tax-Free Compounding?

Avoiding tax permanently is easy: Die with the policy in force. All of the proceeds paid to your beneficiaries as life insurance death benefits, under Section 101 of the Internal Revenue Code, are free of income taxes.

Why Use Variable Universal Life?
The following summarizes why VUL policies are so attractive:

- Flexibility of death benefit, funding level, and investment.
- Tax-deferred/tax-free compounding.
- Availability of separate investment accounts (like mutual funds).
- Ability to buy and sell separate accounts without transaction costs or taxation.
- Ability to withdraw your investment (cost basis) at any time without taxation or penalties.
- With proper planning, death benefits can be free of all taxes—income, gift, inheritance, and estate.
- Tax-free earnings within the policy pay for life insurance and other insurance benefits.
- Not subject to probate.
- Protection from creditors in many states.
- A financial tool that *protects* via insurance, *educates* via investment choices, *enhances family wealth* via accumulation without taxation and, eventually, *distributes* family wealth *tax-free* to heirs.

CHAPTER ELEVEN

Annuities

The *annuity contract* could be defined as a life insurance policy without the mortality charges because there is no "net amount at risk"—no life insurance. The basic elements of the contract are (1) the tax-deferred investment accounts and (2) the expenses associated with the contract. The primary objective of the annuity contract is to pay investment returns *to the annuitant*, not to pay tax-free death benefits to others. You use an annuity either to accumulate money to be used at some future date, usually in retirement, or to provide for the systematic payment of monies that you have accumulated during a limited period or throughout your lifetime. The three primary distinctions between the annuity contract and the life insurance contract are (1) the annuity contract has no significant mortality charges, (2) annuities have no "net amount at risk," and (3) the annuity contract is *not* paid tax-free to a nonspousal beneficiary at the annuitant's death.

The tax-deferred annuity contract loses all of its deferral if it has not been used up prior to the annuitant's death. It can be passed to a nonspousal beneficiary, but any income tax liabilities in the contract go with it and become income tax liabilities for the beneficiary of the contract. The spouse of the annuitant may be able to continue the contract and continue to enjoy tax-deferred earnings, but nonspouse beneficiaries are forced to begin distribution and thus pay taxes.

Note in Figure 11–1, the annuity decision tree, that the right side of the diagram is labeled "Deferred Annuity" and the left side, "Immediate Annuity."

People usually think of annuities only as "payout" annuities because of their ability to pay out a systematic monthly income as retirement income to an annuitant. In fact, the term *annuity* is

FIGURE 11–1

Annuity Decision Tree

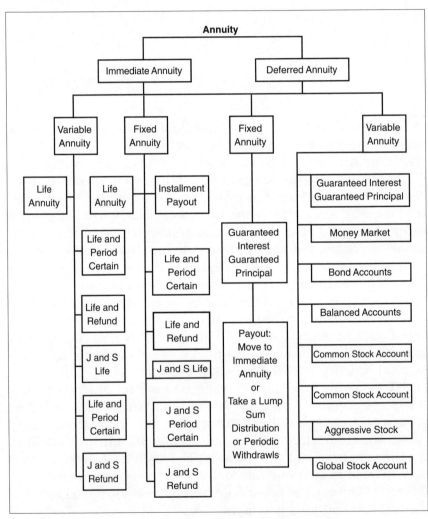

defined as "an amount payable yearly or at other regular intervals for a certain or uncertain period." It defines the *annuitant* as one who receives benefits or payments from an annuity or who is entitled to receive such benefits. Employers frequently pay pension and retirement benefits as an annuity. They offer the retiree varying monthly incomes depending on the guarantees made about what will happen to the payment should the annuitant die. Because this is the most common use of annuities, it is easy to understand why some people only think of them in terms of employer-supplied retirement income.

The other side of annuities, however, is their ability to act as vehicles to accumulate capital for future use without current income taxation of interest, dividends, or capital gains within the annuity contract. More and more individuals are purchasing annuities as a way to accumulate capital to be used in the future to supplement their pension and social security incomes.

An annuity contract is not a particular investment in and of itself. The annuity contract is, so to speak, a wrapper around investments. You may wrap an annuity contract around many types of investments, varying from very conservative investments, such as guaranteed-principal, guaranteed-interest accounts, to relatively aggressive investments, such as aggressive stock accounts, high-yield bond accounts, or anything in between. *Variable annuities* contain families of separate accounts, similar to mutual funds. How you allocate your money among the various funds (separate accounts) will determine whether your annuity contract is conservative or aggressive. An annuity contract is not inherently risky or safe, aggressive or conservative. You tailor it to your purposes. The primary functions of annuities are assisting you to accumulate and spend your retirement capital.

PAYOUT/IMMEDIATE ANNUITIES

Annuities for Fixed Periods or Fixed Amounts

The payment of the fixed-period/fixed-amount immediate annuity is a periodic check issued to the annuitant, in a fixed amount for the duration of the payout period. One way the duration of the payout period may be determined is by stipulating to the insurance company the period of time during which you wish to receive the checks. For example, you may request that checks be sent monthly for the next 10 years. At the end of that time, the payments would terminate. Based upon the amount of money available, prevailing levels of interest rates and the period of time you select, the insurance company will determine the amount of your periodic check. Alternatively, you could request checks of a specific amount such as $1,000 per month for as long as you have funds available from the accumulated value in your annuity contract. In this case, the company would determine for how many months it would be able to pay the $1,000 per month, based upon the same factors.

Annuities for Life

As you look at the decision tree under "Immediate Annuity" in Figure 11–1, you will find that the first decision you must make when purchasing an annuity is whether it is to be fixed or variable.

You might be concerned that your money will run out before you do—that your capital will be exhausted before you die. If so, you could ask the insurance company to have the monthly checks continue for the rest of your life. This seems reassuring, but what if you die after just one check has been paid? The checks do indeed terminate at death, and any capital remaining in the annuity contract would be forfeited to the insurance company. In this case you, the annuitant, take that risk. You usually will receive a greater income than someone who demanded more in the way of guarantees from the insurance company than those promised by the life annuity. Alternatively, you could order the insurance company to make payments for life but to continue those payments for some stipulated period of time if you should die early. For example, you could insist that the insurance company make payments for your life with a minimum period of at least 10, 15, or 20 years, or until you or your beneficiary had received back at least the entire amount that you had originally invested in the contract with the insurance company. The latter is referred to as a *refund annuity*.

Insurance companies can guarantee payments for the lives of two people. These are referred to as *joint and survivor annuities* and are used most frequently by married couples. Joint and survivor annuities also can be issued with minimum guarantee periods such as the 10-, 15-, or 20-year–certain variety, or the refund-certain variety. These annuities also can be issued with a higher amount of income while the two parties are living and a reduced amount after the death of the first, such as joint and 75 percent, 66.6 percent, or 50 percent to the survivor.

Should You "Annuitize"?

Annuitizing may be defined as contracting for a series of payments from your annuity. There are three risks involved. The first was just discussed—the risk that you die too early and/or select the wrong guarantee and do not receive back from the insurance company what you could have, had you not accepted the monthly payout arrangement. The second risk is that once you have informed the insurance company which payout you will accept, there is no turning back. Once the insurer has issued the contract and you have cashed the first check, your checks will keep coming in exactly as you originally requested. If that proves to be inappropriate or indeed disastrous to you personally as a result of some change in your economic status, the typical annuity contract cannot be changed.

In response to consumers' concerns over this lack of liquidity and flexibility, insurers are bringing new types of immediate annuities to market that provide some flexibility through "market value adjustments." Insurers do this by constructing two annuities and combining them for you. One annuity is for a fixed period of time and the capital in it is available to you if you are willing to accept the current adjusted market value. The second annuity that is a true life (or joint and survivorship, and so on) annuity starts at your age 85 and goes for life.

Innovations in annuity products are constantly made to give you improved accessibility to your capital sum even after annuitization. Check for new products being designed as you shop around.

The third risk in a fixed immediate annuity is that the amount of the check will be the same each month for the duration of the annuity period. If prices increase at 5 percent per year, the dollars that you receive from your annuity, although fixed in amount of dollars, will purchase 5 percent less each year. This decrease in your purchasing power will mean a reduction in your standard of living each year that you live. You may receive a check that purchased $1,000 worth of goods in 1989, but 21 years later in the year 2010 that same check will purchase a 1989 equivalent of only $340.56 worth of goods, assuming 5 percent inflation. Your standard of living would have been cut to one-third of what it was when you retired. This is a major risk for retirees and is the reason that *variable* immediate annuities will become more popular.

Many employer-provided retirement plans do not give you the choice of whether to annuitize, but merely the opportunity to choose among the various types of fixed annuity guarantees. Your employer will determine the income generated by the various alternatives for you. It will be up to you to adapt those alternatives to your personal situation and to select the one best suited to your family's needs. It is often easier to select which annuities are not appropriate than which one is best for you. Do your decision making backwards—cross out the selections you do not like. For example, if you were in poor health, you would not elect a life annuity without a guarantee period. If fact, you probably would choose the longest guarantee period to provide the longest payout period available. If you were sick but your spouse were healthy, a joint and 100 percent survivor annuity would be an obvious choice. Each situation is different. Your choice must be based on the facts and circumstances as they stand on the day your decision must be made. This is a decision you want to do a good deal of thinking about ahead of time but hold your irrevocable decision to the last possible moment.

Annuitize or Take a Lump Sum from Your Employer Plan?

Whether to annuitize your employer's retirement benefit depends upon what you are going to do with it. If you suspect you will blow it, annuitize. If you are going to roll it over into your own IRA to be used for future income, then it is worth considering (if your employer gives you the choice).

How do you decide whether to annuitize, take a lump sum rollover into a personal IRA account, or take a cash disbursement?

The first step is to determine the amount of the payout, what the lump sum cash disbursement could be used for, and how much would be left to invest, net after taxes. If you don't have a particular opportunity to exploit with this money (and it had better be a good one), roll it into an individual IRA account. Using a rollover IRA you could conserve the principal from which you could draw interest earnings, but you would not have to annuitize. You could compare the income that would be generated from the earnings in the IRA funds to the income offered under the payout annuity arrangements offered by your employer. The younger you are, the more likely you are to find that the earnings in an IRA account could be equivalent to the monthly income offered by the employer on an annuitized basis. The amount of income generated on the annuitized basis should exceed what you are able to receive in an arrangement where you use only the interest on your capital sum, not the principal. The annuity, after all, is making payments to you of both principal and interest. If there is little difference in income, the fact that the rollover IRA, not annuitized, conserves your principal and your flexibility for the future makes it the more attractive alternative. You are not locked in to any particular monthly payment, you have access to your principal, and you may change your mind in the future.

Why would you annuitize? You might be forced to do so if it were the only way to provide sufficient income for your family's survival. It might not be possible for you to conserve principal in a rollover IRA. Fixed annuities do guarantee income for life, but they also put your income at risk of being eroded by inflation, having the principal forfeited to an insurance company because of premature death, and eliminating the possibility of changing the contract to suit your needs (which may change) in the future.

Suppose you do use the IRA rollover strategy and try to survive by withdrawing just the earnings from your IRA account. You may find that after a year or two, the earnings are not providing enough income. You may, at that time, have to go back and consider the annuity option again. As a result of being

older, it is highly likely that the income available when you annuitize will be higher than it would have been when you originally
retired. Annuities are based on your life expectancy, so the
insurance company is able to pay you more as you get older. When
you deal with immediate annuities, the consequences of waiting—as long as you are careful to conserve principal—are not
detrimental. It pays to compare when you purchase a lifetime
income. Ask a number of the highest quality insurance companies what they will pay you based on the immediate annuity
and the guarantees that you require in that immediate annuity.
There can be substantial differences in what various companies
will offer, and you might even be able to do better than what your
employer is offering you. Your immediate annuity action letter,
presented in Figure 11–2, will help you to get the information you
need to make a decision.

The decision to annuitize a capital sum can be an emotional
one. Seek the counsel of a trusted and objective financial advisor, financial planner, your CPA, attorney, the trust officer at the
bank, and the professional insurance company salesperson who
can help you come up with the numbers. These people can examine your situation and suggest alternatives that you may not have
considered.

Variable Immediate Annuities

The decision tree also has a "variable immediate annuity" branch.
The variable immediate annuity is intended to overcome the objec-
tion to the decrease in purchasing power that is the inherent risk
in a fixed annuity as a result of inflation. Anyone dependent on
a fixed annuity income for a lifetime can look forward to an ever-
decreasing standard of living in an inflationary economy. The idea
behind a variable annuity is to invest the capital sum of the annuity in a portfolio of common stocks, anticipating that inflation will
cause the common stocks to appreciate and that appreciation will
allow for increasing income to the annuitant. To date, there has
not been a great deal of demand for variable immediate annuities. The first risk inherent in the variable immediate annuity is
that the income can go down. You do not know which way the
stock market will go. You cannot be sure that the annuity will

FIGURE 11–2

Immediate Annuity Action Letter

Dear_____:

I am considering the purchase of an immediate annuity contract. I am interested in purchasing a single premium, immediate *fixed/variable* annuity contract. I am a male/female born _____. I also would like a quote on a male/female born _____ for my spouse.

In addition to these quotes, I would like a quote on a joint life annuity for a male/female born _____ and a male/female born _____. We are residents of the state of _____ and our personal marginal state and federal income tax bracket is ____ percent. Please base your quotes on a single consideration of $_____ and/or a monthly income of $_____ per month. The monies that I would be investing in this immediate annuity contract are coming from my personal funds/IRA funds/TSA funds/lump sum distribution from my employer's qualified retirement plan or _____.

For quote purposes, please assume the insurance company would receive these proceeds by _____ (date). I would ask that my monthly payments begin _____ (date).

(This date should be at least one month after the date that the insurance company receives the proceeds.)

Please provide me with quotes from _____ [number of] insurance companies and send all of the financial ratings available on each insurance company that is providing a quote.

Please mail the information to me at the following address. I will call you with my questions after I have had a chance to review the information. If you have any questions, please call me at _____.

Thank you very much for your assistance.

Sincerely,

Name
Address
Phone Number

produce increased income as inflation increases because high inflation does not necessarily mean a rising stock market and increasing variable immediate annuity income. Secondly, variable annuities do not satisfy the demand for maximum consistent monthly income that most people who annuitize are seeking. For example, I put a variable immediate annuity in force with a portion of a relative's retirement capital. The contract was established in 1972 to pay $100 per month based on the performance of the underlying stock account. Payments were disappointing during the first 10 years of the policy's existence, getting as low as $72 per month. The annuitant was not thrilled with what I had done; however, by the time she died in 1986, payments had risen to as high as $262 per month. Unfortunately, by that time she could not enjoy the increase as much as she could have in her younger years. For these reasons, not many variable immediate annuities are sold. But this is changing quickly as people read about people living to 120 and hearing serious researchers talk about today's babies having a life expectancy of 140 years. For people who are exposed to the risk of living too long, variable immediate annuities are likely to turn out to be a wise choice for at least a part of their retirement capital.

You can expect increased interest in variable immediate annuities for part of your retirement capital. Perhaps you have friends and relatives who retired in the 1960s and are being blessed with good health and/or long life. Although these people retired "very comfortably" financially 30 years ago, they may now have to worry about money. Property taxes, property upkeep, and medical costs along with reduced income from investments are changing people from gentlemen and gentlewomen into poor old men and poor old women, not because they invested or saved unwisely but because of the economics of today.

People retiring today with large IRA accounts will, if they are single, find the accounts empty at age 85 because of the government force-out provisions. The minimum distribution requirements that start for you at age 70½ will empty your account as shown in Figure 11–3. If people retiring are married, the accounts will be empty by their early 90s when many of the retirees still will have 10, 15, or even 20 years of expensive living to look forward to.

A partial solution to this problem is a single or joint life immediate variable annuity with an IRA or qualified plan money by the year you attain age 70½. That is your last chance, so con-

FIGURE 11–3

IRA Minimum Distribution Graph
Single, Non–Recalculated (in thousands)

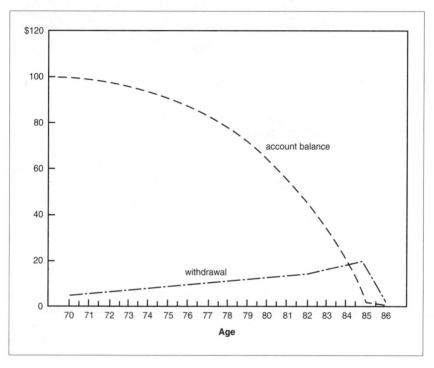

sider this alternative carefully. You must make your decision regarding the minimum distribution of these funds by that age, and you are stuck with that decision for the rest of your life according to Uncle Sam.

Immediate Annuity Action Letter

Now that you have a basic understanding of accumulation and immediate annuity contracts, it's time to go shopping. The appropriate annuity depends on your objectives and those of your spouse, in addition to your health situation and the capital available. With all of this in mind, you need to know the actual dollar amounts the annuity could provide to you in your situation. This information is easy to obtain by adapting the action letter (Figure 11–2) to your personal situation and sending it to the insurance companies from whom you would consider purchasing an annuity contract. Based upon the information you provide, they will be happy to give you a quote to provide you, free of charge, information regarding what their contracts will do for you. Don't hesitate to ask all of your questions; you need to understand what features and costs you are considering.

The information you gather as a result of sending the action letter will assist you in making a decision regarding your employer-provided retirement plan options. It also will give you the information you need in order to purchase an immediate annuity. Discuss the plans that seem to meet your family objectives with your financial advisors and a quality insurance professional. Because interest rates change frequently, the quotes that you receive will only be valid for a short period of time. Last month's quote— or even last week's—may no longer be good today.

An immediate fixed annuity contract is relatively simple because it is so inflexible. It promises you only the amount of the check that you are going to receive, how often you are going to receive it, and for how long. Therefore, you will be looking for the maximum amount of income based on the guarantees that you require from an insurance company that you are sure is going to last as long as you do.

ACCUMULATION/DEFERRED ANNUITIES

Do you like the investment results of some of the investments you have right now? Would you like those investment results even more if you did not have to pay income tax on them currently but could defer taxes until some future date? If the answer to both questions is yes, it is highly likely that there is a deferred annuity that will mirror the investment results that you are obtaining in that taxable investment.

Fixed Deferred Annuities

When people first think of deferred annuities as an accumulation vehicle, they usually think of fixed interest. They often use the product as a CD alternative and many banks sell them as such. However, you should know that a fixed income alternative is available in many variable deferred annuities. Most variable deferred annuity contracts have a guaranteed interest, guaranteed principal account within them so that the risk-averse buyer could allocate all money in the contract to that account. We will refer to this as the "safe haven" account; the one you need not be concerned will drop in value. Although it cannot grow like the varible accounts, there are times when most people like to safeguard capital in this type of account. The degree of risk that you take as an annuitant depends on the account or accounts that you choose to use within your contract. Using a fixed annuity contract limits you to fixed interest investments just because that is the only choice offered. Your investment decisions through the years will be limited to and based on the length of interest rate guarantee you desire. If you knew which way interest rates would go in the future, you could become very wealthy by accurately forecasting interest rates for others. You also could choose the interest rate guarantee period that would be most beneficial to you. If interest rates are at their peak and inevitably are going to go down, then you would like to lock in the high interest rates for the longest period available. Alternatively, if interest rates are at a low point and are inevitably going to go up, you would seek to have a short guarantee period so that as soon as it expired, you could renew the contract at a higher interest rate.

However, you cannot know the future levels of interest rates, and errors can be costly. An incorrect decision can leave you with little flexibility and returns that do not offset inflation. Fixed deferred annuities are a single-pocket, single-dimension, interest rate–sensitive investment. As such, they are appropriate for a limited amount of your portfolio, but not your *total* portfolio and not all the time. You lack control and you lack the ability to diversify your investments in such a contract. Also, the general creditors of the insurance company have a claim against your assets if the company goes broke. People have lost money in fixed annuities. I am not a fan of fixed deferred annuities. One buys them based on greed for the highest interest rate available and then, stuck in the contract, is surprised and disappointed when interest rates decline. Don't let this happen to you. Remember: You've been warned.

Variable Deferred Annuities

Your alternative is a variable deferred annuity. As shown in Figure 11–1's decision tree, a number of investment accounts are available in variable deferred annuities. The advantage of the variable deferred annuity is that you can use the various accounts available in the contract to diversify your investments. You can move assets from the stock account to the guaranteed interest account when the stock market is up, thereby locking in your capital gains, and you can do it without having to be bothered with income tax considerations. There is no question about it— you can build wealth faster if you don't have to share it with Uncle Sam.

The variable deferred annuity offers you the advantages (compared to a fixed deferred annuity) of investment control, ability to diversify, and the ability to use the fixed account for some or all of your capital if you wish to emulate the fixed annuity. Keep in mind that the interest the insurance company pays in the fixed account of your variable deferred annuity must compete with the earnings available to you in the other investment alternatives within the policy so that you can expect more realistic and sustainable interest rates in the variable deferred annuity. Also keep in mind that if you should ever fear for the solvency of the insurance company that holds your variable deferred annuity, you can exit (watching for restrictions) the fixed general account investment and move to the separate account investments. The former are subject to the general creditors of the insurance company, and you would not have access to that money if the state seized your insurer. The latter (the separate accounts) are not subject to company creditors, and assets within them have been available to contract owners even after companies have been taken over by the state regulators.

The other side of this coin is that losses inside of annuity contracts cannot be deducted currently, which makes them inappropriate investment vehicles for those long-term investments that have a higher probability of resulting in losses. Your high-risk investments that could result in an actual capital loss belong outside of annuity contracts because the major benefit of such investments may be the deductibility of the losses.

Deferred Annuities versus Nondeductible IRAs

Use a deferred annuity instead of a nondeductible IRA. Mind you, a tax-deductible contribution to an IRA account that can easily be included inside of a tax-deferred annuity is something that I *always* recommend. However, you also should avoid a nondeductible IRA contribution. If you can't deduct your IRA contribution, don't make one. The only advantage of a nondeductible IRA contribution is the deferral of taxes on capital gains or profits available as a result of it being an IRA contract. That same deferral is available in a regular deferred annuity contract or a life insurance policy. The advantages of the regular deferred annuity contract as opposed to the IRA are these:

- There are no government restrictions on the amount that you can put in the contract.
- You need not file an IRS Form 8606 with your tax return.
- You need not follow the incredible instructions provided in IRS Publication 590 on how to pay taxes on your nondeductible IRA contributions when combined with your qualified IRA.
- The nonqualified annuity does not have substantial IRS penalties for errors, as do nondeductible IRA accounts.

The penalties for errors in nondeductible IRAs are overstatement of amount put in–$100; failure to file form 8606 every year–$50 per time (even if you have no requirement to file income tax), plus taxation of your total distributions *including* non-deductible contributions. There are no redeeming features in a nonqualified IRA that can make up for the IRS hassle factor involved in those investments because you can obtain the benefits in a nonqualified deferred annuity or a life insurance policy without the hassle.

Withdrawals before Age 59½

The deferred annuity, used as an accumulation vehicle, is protected from current income taxation because Uncle Sam assumes these accumulations are for your retirement security. Currently, the federal government is not interested in providing you with tax benefits for money that you take from your annuity contract prior to the age 59½. In fact, if you make withdrawals prior to that age, not only will you have to pay taxes on the amount withdrawn to the extent of earnings in the contract but you also will have to pay a 10 percent penalty on amounts included in your gross income. After age 59½, withdrawals are subject to income tax but not the 10 percent penalty. The pre-age 59½ exceptions to the penalty are distributions as a result of your death, disability, or distributions taken under one of the life income arrangements.

A Deferred Annuity as a Tax-Sheltered Checkbook

Make sure that your nonqualified deferred annuity contract does not force you into annuitization until as late as possible, preferably age 85. During the deferral period, after age 59½ you can use your annuity contract like you would use a tax-sheltered checkbook. You can take funds from the contract as you need them, accepting the tax liability. Don't take funds in those years when you don't need the income, thus deferring the income tax liability. A deferred annuity contract managed in this fashion gives you a great deal of flexibility for planning withdrawals consistent with your needs and income tax planning. Remember that annuities holding qualified plan money must start to pay out by age 70½, so in those contracts you will have to make your annuitization decision by that age. Consider carefully the variable immediate annuity alternative.

Not annuitizing enables you to retain the advantage of controlling your income tax liability through continued deferral and periodic withdrawals from your annuity contract. It also gives you continued flexibility over the investment of the capital held within your annuity contract, and you do not risk forfeiture of any capital to the insurance company in the event of death, as you do under "payout" annuity arrangements.

The disadvantages of the continued deferral and periodic withdrawal strategy is that the income available to you may not be as great (if you are not diminishing principal) as it would be if you annuitized. In addition, under the withdrawal method, all that you take out of your post-August 14th, 1982, annuity will be taxable income until you have withdrawn all interest in the contract. Before August 14th, 1982, annuity investments usually can be withdrawn principal first (no tax) and interest last (taxable).

Under the annuitization method, each payment that you take is part principal and part interest. Frequently the tax-free return of the principal portion of your annuitized monthly income will be between 40 percent and 60 percent of the total check that you receive. The annuitization method, therefore, is not only likely to generate more income than the interest-only method at higher ages, but half of that income is likely to be exempt from income tax. It can give you greater after-tax income to spend. However, after you have recovered an amount equal to your cost basis (the amount you invested) under the exclusion allowance, 100 percent of all future payments will be taxable.

Financial Strength of the Insurance Company

The financial strength of the insurance company from whom you buy your annuity is important. If you are going to succeed financially, the insurance company must also. Demand quality. Deal with well-known household names in the insurance industry that have been keeping their promises to policy owners throughout a significant number of years. (The quality of insurance companies is discussed further in Chapter 12.) One way for you to obtain information in regard to a particular company is from the various rating services' reports. Note that a summary of the most current ratings are requested in the action letter.

Deferred Annuity Action Letter

A deferred/accumulation annuity is a more complex purchase than a fixed annuity because the contract can be far more flexible. Generally speaking, if you are going to invest in a deferred annuity, you should seek flexibility. The most successful deferred annuity contracts are typically those that remain in existence for a long period of time. Your needs and attitudes inevitably will change over time, so you will want a contract that is adaptable to such change. If the annuity contract is not flexible, it is likely that you will terminate it, trade it for a variable annuity contract, or put it in a drawer. Any one of these three options might result in fees, penalties, potential tax liability, and the losses that occur because of inattention. The deferred annuity action letter in Figure 11–4 will help you indicate to the insurance company your specifications for a deferred annuity quote based on your personal situation and requirements.

This action letter specifically does not ask for illustrations regarding how your money might compound based on some particular investment or interest rate. The return from your annuity investment will be based on interest rates and investment returns over a long period of time, as well as minimization of expenses. Your product evaluation should be directed toward the specific information regarding all expenses and charges that may be incurred under a particular contract, as well as the investment and interest rate track record.

The Buyers' Checklist

I'm not what you would call *objective* about what I recommend you own. More than 30 years of selling, writing, and talking about these products has made me more opinionated than one ought to be. Keep that in mind as I proceed to "should" you, which I should not do, because I don't know anything about your personal situation. Nevertheless, my recommendations give you a place to start, and even when you disagree with me it will help you toward your own buying decision.

Should 1: Buy "Variable" Deferred Annuities

You should buy a variable deferred annuity. You should not buy a fixed annuity. You should not purchase any annuity that has only one investment alternative. You should not buy a single premium annuity, and you should not buy a contractual premium annuity that would cause forfeitures should you have to stop investing. You should buy a flexible premium variable annuity with a good selection of nicely performing, separate accounts.

Why do I make these recommendations? Because in my experience inflexible, insurance company–controlled products do not serve people as well as flexible contract owner-controlled products. Ask anyone who owns one of those old single premium,

FIGURE 11-4

Deferred/Accumulation Annuity Action Letter

Dear_____ :

I am considering investing in a deferred annuity. I would prefer an annuity contract that allows me the flexibility of investing at my personal convenience when funds became available for investment. I would prefer not to purchase a contract that makes investment in the contract mandatory over some predetermined time. I prefer not to accept the restrictions imposed by a single premium deferred annuity contract unless such a contract would offer superior returns or features different than those available from a flexible premium annuity contract. For quote purposes, please use $_____ as my initial investment into the contract.

Please provide an explanation of any and all charges that will be made against my investment and the net amount that will go to work for me in the annuity contract. Also, please indicate any surrender charges or contingent withdrawal fees that I could be exposed to should I cash in the annuity contract and the time period during which these charges are applicable.

I am in favor of variable annuity contracts as long as there is a safe-haven account available within the contracts. Please indicate which account is a safe haven account and what guarantees of principal and interest are available within that account. I would also like to know whether there are any restrictions on my movement into and/or out of any accounts during the life of the annuity contract. Please provide me with the prospectus and all other information that is available regarding all of the accounts within the contract.

I prefer an annuity contract from a quality company with low expense and sales charges. I would prefer surrender charges to front-end sales charges so that all of my money would go to work for me immediately and so that, if I maintain my contract until after the surrender charge period, I may never have to pay such sales charges. I would like maximum flexibility; a good safe-haven account providing interest and principal guarantees; and well-performing, alternative mutual fund types of accounts. I seek flexibility and convenience of investment and frequent and convenient reporting regarding account balances. I would like to be able to switch among the various accounts at my convenience, preferably by telephone.

At this time, it is my intention to defer the annuity for as long a period as possible, so please let me know at what age the insurance company insists that I begin to take funds. I would like to avoid forced annuitization for as long as possible. Please state explicitly any penalties I could be exposed to if I choose never to annuitize my contract. Please send the information to me at the address indicated below. Call me if there is anything else you need to know in order to provide me with this information.

Thank you for your assistance.

Sincerely,

fixed-interest only annuities how happy they are stuck in the product. In the variable deferred annuity you can stay in the fixed
account if you wish and can earn interest just as you would in
the fixed annuity, but you have a choice. If the manager of the
fixed general account won't pay you sufficient interest, you can
switch to one of the separate accounts. The general account
manager must compete with the separate account managers for
your money, which is healthy.

Should 2: Choose a Financially Strong Company
You should choose a company that will last as long as you do—
select nothing less than investment grade companies, preferably
with improving ratings. Be suspicious of inordinately high
interest rates and "bonus" rates.

A few war stories will illustrate the reason for my bias. From
1979 to 1983 the Baldwin-United companies, National Investors
and University Life, sold more than 3 billion fixed annuities. They
were touted as offering risk-free, promising interest rates of up
to 15 percent to the annuitants and paying commissions to agents
of 5 percent. Total promised payout in year one was 20 percent!
The companies then invested the money illegally in the stock of
their own subsidiaries. In May 1983, the Arkansas and Indiana
insurance commissioners put the companies into receivership.
For more than three and one-half years the case dragged
through the courts while policy owners suffered. Some people
who really do not understand what the policy owners suffered
through those years say the policy owners were made whole when
Metropolitan Life assumed the contracts.

Another company, Executive Life, in 1980 and in 1981 started
buying up high yield (junk) bonds so that, of the $16 billion in
Executive Life's portfolio, more than 50 percent was invested in
junk bonds. By 1990, when Executive Life was put into receivership, its assets were down to $10 billion and its highly touted $2
billion cash reserve had flown out the door in the run on the company. Many people who bought Executive Life contracts
because of the promise of inordinately high interest rates still suffer today because they fell for the highest interest rate and did
not look behind that number. Companies do not pay you high
interest rates because they love you. They have to pay you high

interest rates in order to get you to lend them the money so they can lend it to someone else who needs money and is willing to pay about 2 percent more than the insurers are paying you.

So, who can help you dodge these bullets of insolvency? First, understand that the primary risk is in the general account of the insurance company, which is subject to the claims of the creditors of the insurance company, not the separate accounts, which are not subject to the claims of the company's creditors. That, in itself, is a good argument for variable annuities in which you can choose whether to use the general account or the separate accounts. Keep in mind that the separate accounts have been protected in the rehabilitation process of all insurance companies.

Your allies in trying to locate good life insurance companies are the National Association of Insurance Commissioners (NAIC), the various rating services (A.M. Best, S&P, Moody's, Duff and Phelps, Weiss), and the services that provide statistical information such as Ward's Insurance Results. Also, a professor from Indiana publishes a monthly paper discussing insurance industry trends, called *The Insurance Forum.* You will find the information on the regulators, rating services, and *The Insurance Forum* in the last chapter.

Once you identify a contract with acceptable expenses and an acceptable portfolio of investment accounts (including an account that will provide a safe haven, that is guaranteeing principal and interest), what you do with it will determine its long-term performance. Basically you are seeking flexibility, good reporting, and ease of management.

Should 3: Use Nonqualified Deferred Annuities, Not Nondeductible IRAs

Use deferred annuity contracts in situations where you want deferral of taxation on investment earnings and the safety and security offered by the quality insurance company backing your contract. Consider a deferred annuity contract for the investment of personal funds in lieu of an investment in a nondeductible IRA. Because the appeal of a nondeductible IRA is the deferral of taxation and this benefit is available within the deferred annuity contract, why should you limit yourself to the nonqualified IRA rules? With the nondeductible IRA, you are limited to a maximum of $2,000 per year, current reporting, confusing tax calculations at eventual payout, forced payouts, and penalties if you happen to err. Alternatively, the nonqualified annuity contract gives you the same tax deferral, has no maximum limit, does not require current reporting, has straightforward tax calculations at eventual payout, a longer deferral period potential, and no penalties.

Should 4: Annuity Assets Are to Be Spent During the Lifetime of You and Your Spouse

Make sure that your qualified annuity contracts (those from your IRAs, retirement plan rollovers, and such) are arranged so that if you are survived by your spouse, the spouse will be allowed to continue the deferred annuity and manage it just as you had during your life. Deferred annuity contracts are not as efficient as life insurance policies in accomplishing the transfer of wealth to a nonspouse beneficiary. The annuity contract, although deferring taxation on earnings within the contract until future use, never escapes that pent-up income tax liability. If the beneficiary of an annuity contract is not your spouse, the income tax liabilities within the contract become the beneficiary's tax liabilities. Income taxes will have to be paid as the funds are paid out. The beneficiary who is a nonspouse is not allowed to continue the deferral but must establish a payout arrangement with the insurance company within one year of the death of the survivor of the annuitant. The income tax liabilities will have to be paid based on the payout arrangement your beneficiary selects: annuity, lump sum, or during five years. Compare this to a life insurance policy in which a death benefit is substantially greater than your investment within the life insurance policy (the net amount at risk) and is passed to the beneficiary without any income tax liability. The difference in the tax treatments of annuities and insurance policies requires you to define your objectives carefully in order to determine which will serve you and your family best.

NONQUALIFIED ANNUITIES—INCOME TAXATION

Nonqualified annuities are contracts that you personally purchase with your after-tax income or capital. Your investment in these contracts constitutes your cost basis. You and/or your beneficiary eventually will get this cost basis back out of your annuity contract without taxation. Assuming you do not annuitize an annuity contract—that is, turn it into a series of payments throughout a stipulated period of time—periodic withdrawals from these contracts will be considered interest earnings first and thus be subject to income tax as you make withdrawals. When interest earnings have been entirely withdrawn and taxed as ordinary income at the time of withdrawal, the remaining funds (constituting your basis) will be withdrawn without taxation. The exception to this rule is any annuity contract issued prior to August 14th, 1982, which is taxed in just the opposite fashion. Withdrawals are considered to be principal first, then interest.

Annuities are subject to the penalty tax on withdrawals of income before age 59½. The penalty tax will be waived if the owner of the annuity contract is 59½ or older, dies, becomes disabled, as well as if the annuity contract is being used relative to the periodic payments required under a personal injury suit. The penalty also will be waived if the benefits are annuitized and paid out as a series of substantially equal payments throughout the life of the annuitant or the joint lives of the annuitant and the primary beneficiary.

Make sure that you keep any annuity contracts created before August 15, 1982, separate from those purchased after that date so that you may continue to take advantage of this ability to withdraw your basis first.

ANNUITY TAXATION AT DEATH

Income taxation of annuity proceeds in the event of the death of an annuitant depends on whether income has commenced and whether the beneficiary receiving the proceeds of the annuity is the annuitant's spouse. Follow the summary of taxation appearing in Figure 11–5 as you read on. Assume that payments have not yet begun and the annuitant dies leaving the proceeds of the annuity to the surviving spouse. The spouse should have the option of continuing the annuity and enjoying continued tax-deferral on earnings if the contract provides for this contingency. On the other hand, if the annuitant has started to receive the benefits and dies leaving the annuity proceeds to the surviving spouse, the benefits must

FIGURE 11–5

Annuity Taxation

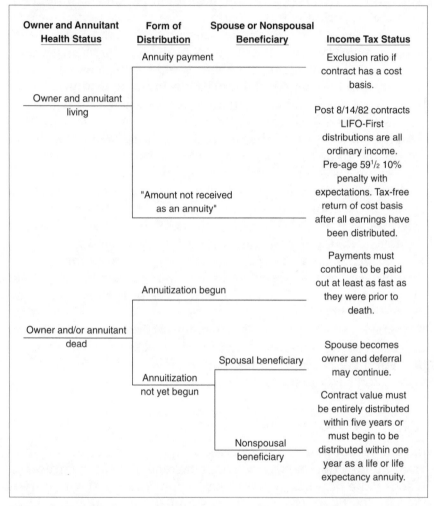

© 1995 by Ben G. Baldwin.

be distributed at least as rapidly as the method that was in effect at the time of the annuitant's death, and taxation will continue to apply to those proceeds.

If a nonspousal beneficiary receives the proceeds and the annuitant's death occurs prior to distribution of any income, that nonspousal beneficiary may elect a lump sum distribution without penalty but with full taxation on the accrued interest or gain within the contract. Alternatively, the nonspousal beneficiary may elect a series of payments to be made during a period of time not to exceed the beneficiary's life expectancy beginning within one year of the annuitant's death. A nonspousal beneficiary has no option to continue the contract. The payment is not subject to 10 percent penalty tax because it is as a result of the annuitant's death. If the annuity income had started prior to the annuitant's death, the proceeds would have to continue to come out of the annuity at least as rapidly as the method that was in effect before the annuitant's death, with the normal taxation continuing.

Exclusion Ratio

Taxation of annuitized nonqualified annuity contracts is based on an exclusion ratio. Because you have directed the insurance company to distribute both principal and interest from the contract in a series of equal periodic payments, your cost basis (your original after-tax investment in the contract) is paid out tax-free as a portion of each of those payments. The proportion of the annuity income that is tax-free is determined in accordance with Section 72 of the Internal Revenue Code as the income tax exclusion ratio. It often represents 40 percent to 50 percent of the total periodic payment being received.

Fixed Immediate Nonqualified Annuity Exclusion Ratio

The exclusion ratio for an immediate nonqualified fixed annuity is determined by dividing the *investment* in the contract by the *expected return* as of the annuity starting date, the day the income stream commences. You might invest $60,000 in an annuity and expect $100,000 as the payout. Therefore, 60 percent of each payment would be nontaxable return of capital, whereas the balance would be taxable interest.

Investment $60,000 / Expected return of $100,000 =
60% Exclusion ratio

Exclusion ratio × Payment received =
Amount excluded from taxation
60% × $1,000 = $600

that will be received not subject to income taxes until such time as you have received your entire cost basis.

Variable Immediate Nonqualified Annuity Exclusion Ratio

The exclusion ratio for a variable immediate annuity is determined in a similar fashion; however, you run into the complication of not knowing your "expected return" because your income will vary based on the actual performance of stock investments supporting the annuity payments. Payments will vary and are likely to be more or less with each check. What you can agree with Uncle Sam about this contract is how long you are expected to live. You agree by using the life expectancy tables Uncle Sam provides, and Uncle Sam says you can recover your investment (cost basis) throughout your life expectancy. The procedure is to take your life expectancy in years and divide it into your cost basis to determine "how much" rather than what percent you can recover tax-free each year. If you ever have a particularly bad year and receive an amount of income less than the amount you can recover tax-free, you are allowed to continue your recoveries until such time that 100 percent of your investment in the contract has been recovered.

If you outlive the annuity tables, there may come a time when you have received your entire cost basis back from your annuity contract. When that time arrives, all subsequent payments will be subject to ordinary income tax in their entirety. This foolish rule was incorporated in the Tax Reform Act of 1986 and applies to annuities that had not been annuitized as of January 1, 1987. Annuity contracts that had been annuitized before that date enjoy the exclusion ratio for the rest of the annuitant's life and may continue to exclude the same percentage even after the annuitant's entire cost basis has been recovered. The new rule adds an additional income tax burden for senior citizens in their mid-eighties.

It would be interesting to learn how much revenue the government expects to receive from this additional tax on senior citizens who may have been living on a fixed income from an immediate fixed annuity for a substantial period of time. Not only has inflation eaten away at their standard of living but Uncle Sam is now going to increase their taxes also.

Qualified Annuity Income Taxation

Qualified annuities are purchased with funds generated from qualified retirement plans. Contributions to qualified plans generally are not subject to current taxation when they are contributed to the plan. IRAs that qualify for an income tax deduction are qualified plans as are simplified employee pension plans (SEPs), tax-sheltered or tax-deferred annuities (TSAs), 401(k) plans, profit-sharing plans, pension plans, and the like. These qualified plans are unique because, in addition to enjoying the deferral on the earnings within the plans that you enjoy within your nonqualified annuities, you and your employer also may make capital investments into these plans without you paying taxes on the amount of investment in the year of contribution. Because you have never paid taxes on the amount contributed to the plan, you do not establish a cost basis. Therefore, in many instances, there is nothing to return to you that is not taxable from the tax-deductible qualified plans.

Payments from such contracts are subject to ordinary income tax at the time received. The following is an example of the benefit of deductible contributions to your qualified plans. If you are in the 30 percent marginal tax bracket and you qualify for one of these plans, a $100 contribution would reduce your income taxes by $30. The $30 reduction on your income tax, and a $100 investment into the plan, means that your investment has cost you $70. For that $70, you will have $100 on your net worth statement. That is a $30 gain on a $70 investment, which translates to a 42.8 percent initial rate of return. This return does not even count any actual investment return that your $100 is earning inside of the plan, which also is sheltered from current taxation.

Your employer may encourage you to invest in these plans by offering to match, for example, 50 percent of your contribution. If so, rather than gaining $100 on your net worth statement for a $70 investment, your $100 would appear on the net worth statement along with $50 of your employer's money, giving you a $150 total on your $70 investment, or an $80 gain on a $70 investment. This is a return of 114 percent. That is quite a benefit and one that you should not pass up. Uncle Sam will, however, do all in his power to prevent you from using these monies indiscriminately prior to age 59½.

If you would like to retire someday at 100 percent of your standard of living, you will have to take advantage of social security, your employer's qualified retirement plans, and save 20 percent of your gross income each and every year. It's a tough task. There is no better way to begin this personal accumulation pattern than by participating at the maximum level possible in the employer-provided plan that allows you to invest with pre-tax dollars.

One unique feature of qualified plans is that you are required to begin payouts from these plans in the year in which you attain age 70½. With nonqualified annuities you do not have to start withdrawals at age 70½. Your basic objective with non-qualified annuities could be to continue deferral of annuitization as long as possible in order to maintain flexibility and to continue the tax-deferred compounding on the earnings within the contract.

In order to comply with Uncle Sam's distribution rules for qualified money, it is not necessary for you to annuitize your contract. For example, based on a single life, the minimum distribution requirement at age 70½ is one-sixteenth of your balance on the previous December 31. One-sixteenth is only 6.25 percent of that balance, and hopefully 6.25 percent is less than what you are earning within your contract. Thus, even if you pull out the 6.25 percent, the principal balance on the following December 31 is likely to be higher than it was on the December 31 prior to your 70½ birthday. The next year you will have to withdraw about 7 percent, and by the time you attain age 75, about 8 percent. As a result, even when you comply with the requirements to take distributions each year after you attain 70½, you still can maintain your annuity, make the required withdrawals, earn a substantial return not subject to ordinary income tax, and ideally not diminish the principal within your account during the early years.

The case is even better for those with qualified plans who elect to make withdrawals from their plans on a joint and last survivor basis because the table for this type of distribution requires that an even smaller amount be distributed. For example, if you are age 70½ and your spouse is age 68, only 4.65 percent of your account must be withdrawn. In the following year, it would be approximately 4.83 percent and at age 75, the required distribution amount would be about 5.8 percent. Not until you are age 85 would the amount required for distribution exceed 10 percent. Failure to make the required withdrawals will expose you to substantial penalties from Uncle Sam, so make sure you check with your tax advisor and take what you must.

For planning purposes you may use Figure 10-5 if you are making withdrawals on a single basis or Figure 10-6 if you are making withdrawals with a joint beneficiary. Determine the amount in your qualified plan contract or contracts on December 31 of the year preceding the year you reach age 70½. Find the factor (called a "multiple" in the table) based on your age if based on a single life (Table 11–1) or based on your own and your joint beneficiary's age (Table 11–2). Divide the amount in your accounts on the previous December 31 by the factor in the table. That is the minimum amount you must withdraw in that year, all of which will be taxed as ordinary income.

For example, say you are a single individual calculating minimum distribution requirements for the year that you attain age 70½. You will find the factor to be 16 by age 70. This would mean you must divide your account value on December 31 of the

TABLE 11–1

Ordinary Life Annuities Expected Return Multiples for a Single Life

Age	Multiple
70	16.0
75	12.5
80	9.5
85	6.9
90	5.0
95	3.7
100	2.7
115	.5

TABLE 11–2

Ordinary Joint Life and Last Survivor Annuities Expected
Return Multiples for Two Lives

First Annuitant Age	Second Annuitant Age				
	70	72	75	80	85
60	26.2	25.8	25.3	24.8	24.5
65	23.1	22.5	21.8	21.0	20.5
68	21.5	20.8	19.9	18.9	18.3
70	20.6	19.8	18.8	17.6	16.9
73	19.4	18.5	17.3	15.9	15.0
78	18.0	16.9	15.4	13.5	12.3
83	17.1	15.9	14.2	11.9	10.2

previous year by 16 and take that amount out by April 1 of the following year. If your account value was $100,000 you would have to take out $6,250 ($100,000 divided by 16). If you are 70½ and your wife is 68 years old, the factor would be 21.5 and the minimum withdrawal amount would be $4,625 ($100,000 divided by 21.5). If you do wait until after January 1 of the year following the year in which you attain age 70½ to take a distribution, you will have to take two distributions in that tax year, which could increase your income tax liability if the combined withdrawals moved you into a higher tax bracket.

There are also two different methods you can use to calculate each year's withdrawal: the *annual reduction method* or the *annual recalculation method*.

Annual Reduction Method

Using this method you reduce your life expectancy by one year each year. For example, if you started out using 20.6 years, the next year you would merely subtract one year and use that number as your divisor. You divide your retirement plan balances by your life expectancy. Specifically, your calculation in the year you attained age 70½ would be as follows. Add up *all* of your qualified plan balances as of December 31 of the year prior to the year you became age 70½. It certainly will simplify your life if you have consolidated all of those small IRA accounts and your qualified plan amounts into one place by this point in your life.

Divide the total of all retirement account balances by your life expectancy or joint life expectancy factor, whichever you have selected. If it happens to be 20.6, dividing by that number will tell you your minimum distribution requirement for that calendar year. It would be wise to take the distribution out during that calendar year, even in the first year, if you wish to avoid a double withdrawal in the following year. If you have chosen the annual reduction method you will take the balance on the *next* December 31st and divide it by 19.6 to determine that year's minimum distribution requirement for the second year. Do likewise in each succeeding year (18.6, 17.6, and so on).

Annual Recalculation Method

With the recalculation method, you use the IRS table factor for your ages each year rather than just subtracting one year from the previous year's life expectancy. Thus, instead of going from 20.6 to 19.6 as you do in the reduction method, you would go from 20.6 to 19.8 as indicated by the table for the life expectancy of two 71-year-olds. As you can see this method reduces the amount you have to take out and thus allows you to leave more in your plans to continue to enjoy tax-deferred compounding.

However, there can be an income tax disadvantage in this recalculation method for those without a spouse beneficiary. If you die during the payout period, it affects how your beneficiaries are taxed. Uncle Sam in his infinite wisdom says that under the recalculation method your life expectancy is now zero in the year *after* your death! Thus, your spouse will now have to do the recalculations on a single life basis and cause the distributions to be much larger than would have been the case had you selected the annual reduction method, which could be continued at the same pace after your death.

Nonspousal beneficiaries must take total distribution and pay all income taxes due in that year... no more tax deferral for them! However, if you had chosen the annual reduction method, they could continue the payment schedule you had set up or take it faster, but no slower. The deferral to April 1 of the following year is available only for the first year distributions. In all succeeding years, distributions must be made within the calendar year. Be cautious in your minimum distribution planning! To take less than the minimum exposes you to a 50 percent penalty on the amount you should have withdrawn but did not.

LUMP SUM DISTRIBUTION TO A ROLLOVER IRA RETIREMENT STRATEGY

The rollover IRA is gaining popularity as an option for the disposition of retirement plan funds. One of the main reasons is because it puts the retiree in control of the funds instead of the ex-employer. It also avoids current income taxation in the rollover process and provides for the continuation of tax-deferred earnings. These funds have been accumulated over a lifetime of work and are likely to be considered core assets that should be managed most carefully.

Prior to age 70½, if you live on only the income from the capital you have in your rollover IRA and do not invade principal, you will have more money to support you beyond age 70½. If you are able to live on less than the income generated within the IRA, you will see your capital increase. You will be better off each year. Your capital base, with positive investment results, should increase each year so there will be more capital available to generate income. If you are in this happy state of affairs, you should be looking for a way to make reinvested earnings work as hard as possible for you in offsetting the risks of inflation. One way to do this is to dollar–cost average the earnings from a guaranteed-principal, guaranteed-interest account into one of the common stock accounts in the family of funds available within your rollover IRA contract. This provides for some diversification and, given time and patience, positive investment results. When the money dollar–cost averaged into the equity accounts becomes significant, earnings may be swept back to the safe-haven account in which you hold your core assets. This builds up your core account, which then generates more interest that can be used to increase the amounts being dollar–cost averaged into the stock account. The more earnings you receive, the more earnings you generate!

Many conservative investors find this a comfortable method of managing their rollover funds. It enables them to enter the stock market when they would not have been able to do so otherwise, and thereby earn greater returns than they could with just compound interest. It increases diversification and allows the retiree to maintain control.

TRADING LIFE INSURANCE AND ANNUITY CONTRACTS: THE 1035 TAX-FREE EXCHANGE

Throughout this book we have recommended flexibility as a feature of the life insurance and annuity contracts that you use to enhance your own and your family's financial security. Change is inevitable for all of us. If the contract you have purchased is adaptable to your economic circumstances as they change and develop, it is more likely you will be happy with it.

However, you may find yourself owning a life insurance or annuity policy that is no longer suitable and so inflexible it cannot adapt. If so, don't just surrender that contract. Income taxes and penalties may result when you surrender an annuity burdening you with unnecessary expenses. Section 1035 of the Internal Revenue Code allows you to make tax-free exchanges of a life insurance policy for another life insurance policy, a life insurance policy for an annuity contract, or an annuity contract for another annuity contract. You simply trade annuity contracts. You cannot trade an annuity contract into a life insurance policy without taxation.

Caution: Your old annuity contract may have some unique advantages because of terms the government okayed when you purchased it, so do not use the 1035 exchange without careful consideration with your advisors. For example:

Variable annuity contracts purchased before October 21, 1979 are eligible for a step up in basis if the owner dies prior to the annuity starting date.
IRC Sec. 72; Revenue Ruling 79-335, 1979-2 CB 292

An annuity issued prior to August 14, 1982 taxes withdrawals as cost basis first (not taxable) and gain next (taxable).
IRC Sec. 72(q) (2).

To effect a 1035 tax-free exchange, you assign your company A contract to company B and direct company B, in writing, to put the company A contract proceeds into the company B annuity. If done properly, you should not have to pay income tax on the transaction. You may, however, have to pay surrender charges to company A and acquisition charges to company B. If these are acceptable and the alternative contract is better suited to your needs, then proceed.

The advantage of the tax-free exchange is that you will not have to pay any taxes on the gains earned in the original contract at the time of the exchange. What if there are no gains in the original contract? Indeed, what if there is a loss? Surrendering the contract does not allow you to take a deduction for that loss on your income tax return. Losses as a result of surrendering life insurance or annuity contracts are not deductible. The reason you have a loss in the old contract is because your cost basis (your investment) exceeds the capital accumulated in the contract. The advantage of doing a 1035 tax-free exchange in this case is that you would be rolling that high cost basis into the new contract. The higher your cost basis in your new contract, the more you will be able to take out of that contract in living benefits without taxation in the future. Old contracts that have not performed adequately can still be valuable to you in this way. In short, regardless of the gain or loss in your old contracts, the 1035 tax-free exchange is likely to be to your economic advantage.

The 1035 tax-free exchange also is advantageous if you own a life insurance policy and, at some point in the future, determine that it is no longer needed or appropriate. You can reclaim the money that you have put into your contract (your basis) out of your life insurance policy by making a withdrawal if the policy permits. Then, via a 1035 exchange of that policy into an annuity contract, you can avoid current taxation on the gain. From that point forward, the investment return within the annuity contract will not be subject to the mortality charges of the life insurance policy, and your tax-deferral will continue. Your cost basis in the life contract includes your previously paid life insurance costs and expenses!

Many old annuity contracts were less flexible and provided lower investment returns to contract holders than do those being issued today. If you find yourself with such a contract, you may opt for a 1035 exchange into an annuity contract that would better suit your present needs and provide you with greater investment returns and more flexibility.

PURCHASE CONSIDERATIONS FOR ANNUITIES

Company Rating

The insurance company's industry rating is all-important if your choice is a fixed annuity. Your only investment in such a contract is in the general account of the insurance company and you have no choice. If your company becomes questionable, you may have problems exiting the company. You may be exposed to a surrender charge. You will not want to just cash it in because that immediately triggers taxation and penalties if you are under 59½. Exercising your right to trade your contract in to another company (the 1035 tax-free exchange) takes time, which you may not have. For these reasons, I worry about fixed annuities and the higher interest rate they offer you and the higher commission they pay the agent. Because of my concern, I'm going to recommend that you deal with investment-grade companies, those in the top level of "secure" as shown in Table 12–1 in Chapter 12, with an up trend (ratings have been improving not deteriorating) as your minimum criterion for a fixed annuity.

For a variable annuity with a fixed account choice (general account), you still will want a strong company, but the ratings are not quite as important because you, the contract owner, have choice and control. Should you become concerned about the company, avoid the general account selection and move the funds you have in the general account into the separate accounts as quickly as your contract will let you. Expect some restrictions on your funds' movement out of the general account fixed interest investment into competing separate accounts. These restrictions are important to protect the general account from suffering capital losses because people withdraw quickly in times of rapid changes in interest rates. It is prudent and appropriate for the company to implement such restrictions, so you need to know the rules regarding your ability to move out of the general account.

Expenses in Fixed Annuities and the Fixed Alternative in Variable Annuities

The insurance company makes its money the same way banks do, on the spread. That is, if an insurer promises you a 6 percent return, it will plan to lend the money you invest to others at 7½ percent or thereabouts and make a 1½ percent profit (the spread).

The 1½ percent to 2 percent spread will reimburse the company for its expenses over time and provide its profit margin.

You also should check on front loads in fixed annuities as well as surrender charges that may start at contract start date and end after a specific time or may start when you put money in the contract and then come off after that money has been in the contract a certain number of years (known as a *rolling surrender charge*).

Ideally, you will never pay a surrender charge. You will buy only contracts that you know you will not need to access in a fashion that would incur that cost. You will, however, want to know under what circumstances you can get at your money without paying a surrender charge, that is, your withdrawal privileges. The most typical is the 10 percent free corridor, meaning that you can get at 10 percent of your annuity value or your amount invested at any time without incurring the surrender charge. Know what it is before you purchase . . . the charges vary.

Expenses of Separate Accounts in Variable Annuities: Administrative Expense

Insurance companies typically will make a charge of about one-half of 1 percent to cover administrative expenses of running their family of separate accounts. They also may charge a contract fee of $30 to $60 per year if your account is under a stated amount because it is too small to be profitable to the company.

Mortality and Expense (M&E) charges

Insurance expenses, which are often referred to as the M&E charges (mortality and expense charges against the investment subaccounts), are charged in variable annuities. The reason for the emphasis on "against the investment subaccounts" is that many writers say or imply (when criticizing the expenses within variable annuities in comparison to conventional fixed annuities) that the charges unique to the subaccounts (such as the M&E charges and the investment management expenses) are also deducted from the general account (the guaranteed interest account commonly found in life insurance company variable deferred annuities). The guaranteed interest account within the variable annuity works in the same manner that it does in a fixed annuity, that is, its expenses are "spread-based." The insurance company examines the marketplace for current interest rates; figures out what it has to deduct for commissions, expenses (including M&E) and profit; and then reports a net interest rate to the contract owner. This is what is credited to the contract owner, undiminished by any other charges.

M&E charges are meant to compensate the insurance company for all the guarantees that it places within the annuity contract. They will ensure the return of investment in variable annuities at death regardless of investment performance and other guarantees such as a maximums on expenses, guaranteed annuity rates, and minimum guaranteed interest rate in the general account investment alternative. Because insurers typically do not charge an up-front fee to the purchaser, the M&E charges are the primary way insurance companies make money on variable annuities and recover the commission paid up front to salespeople. There is a trend toward paying trail commissions on these products. Trail commission is compensation paid to the salesperson who sold your contract, for providing continuing service on your contract. The increased cost will be justified if the assistance provided helps you manage your contract.

A Lipper study of returns of the entire universe of mutual funds and variable annuities concluded that mutual funds typically outperform variable annuities by about 70 basis points, which is a little less than the cost of all the features available within the annuity. Do the features in the contract that make you less likely to redeem an annuity over your taxable mutual funds allow the managers to invest in a fashion that enables them to make up some of the M&E costs? Are the tax benefits of an annuity sufficient to overcome the extra cost of the annuity?

Separate Account Expenses

Management fees and operating expenses charges apply to the separate accounts. These expenses are charged against your separate accounts (mutual funds) to pay the fund managers and the operating expenses of the fund. It may not include the brokerage costs.

You can see from these charges that bond funds within a high-expense variable annuity will not be able to do much for you, because their long-term rate of return could be diminished too much by the expenses. It is important to be aware of these expenses as you invest in these products. You are looking for an acceptable *net* after-expense rate of return. If you have a general account investment within your variable annuity, the interest quoted normally is *net*, not gross.

Watch for annuity state premium taxes when you annuitize in the states shown in Table 11–3.

CONCLUSION

Annuities are not strictly payout vehicles demanding equal periodic payments to an annuitant who stands the risk of forfeiting a substantial amount of his or her investment to an insurance company if he or she does not live long enough. That situation is easily avoided. Annuities today can be extremely efficient asset

TABLE 11–3

State Premium Taxes at Annuitization

State	Nonqualified	Qualified	State	Nonqualified	Qualified
California	2.35%	.5 %	Pennsylvania	0	0
District of Columbia	2.25%	2.25%	Puerto Rico	1.00%	1.00%
Kansas	2.00%	0	South Dakota	1.25%	0
Kentucky	2.00%	2.00%	West Virginia	1.00%	1.00%
Maine	2.00%	0	Wyoming	1.00%	0
Nevada	3.50%	0	Virgin Islands	5.00%	5.00%

accumulation vehicles that will serve you well in retirement. Use the checklist in Figure 11–6 to shop around. You should look for convenience and flexibility. Examine carefully the expenses in the contract, the contract limitations, the variety of accounts, the service, the reporting, management, and (by all means) the company.

FIGURE 11–6

Annuity Purchase Checklist

Fixed Annuity		Variable Annuity (Preferred)
(Most important)	*COMPANY RATING*	(Important)
%	NAIC - RBC%	%
(125% plus)		(125% plus)
Level *Trend*		*Level* *Trend*
	A.M. Best	
	S & P	
	Moody's	
	D & P	
	Weiss	
	Other	
(Prefer above level 7 and up trends rather than down trends)		
	General Account	
(Most important)	*INTEREST RATE*	(Important)
%	Current	%
Months	Guarantee Period	Months
%	Minimum Guarantee	%
%	Bail-Out Interest Rate	%
%	Cost of Bail-Out %	%
	Interest Rate Track Record	
	Crediting Method	
(None)	*SEPARATE ACCOUNTS*	_____(Total Number)
	Variety and Track Record (see prospectus)	_____
	PREMIUM TYPE	
	Single	
	Contractual	
	Flexible	

Annuity Purchase Checklist (Concluded)

		EXPENSES		
	%	Front Load		%
	%	Surrender Charge		%
	Years	Years Surrender Applies		Years
Yes/No		Rolling Surrender Charge	Yes/No	
$		Annual Contract	$	
	%	Charge		%

WITHDRAWAL PACKAGES

10% Free Corridor

Separate Account Charges   (see your prospectus)

Not applicable

FUND EXPENSE   (note for each fund)

Name of Account

_____

_____

_____

_____

_____

Not applicable   Mortality & Expense Risk

(M&E)   %

Administration Expenses   %

Total Expense   %

Other Free Corridors

Death

Disability

Terminal Illness

Nursing Home Confinement

CHAPTER TWELVE

Insurance Company, Product, and Agent Selection

Prior to the mid-1970s, few financial professionals or consumers worried about the financial integrity of insurance companies. Street talk regarding a company's products, services and stability would serve as a good indicator for most people.

We have learned that such confidence was unjustified. Many readers will remember the Equity Funding fiasco in which insurance company staff people actually manufactured phony policies for nonexistent insureds. The fraud was finally exposed by an alert reporter. Then came the Baldwin-United failure (no relation to the author!), in which the consumer was promised "too good to be true" interest rates and salespeople received "too good to be true" commissions. Many have been shocked that insurance companies can fail, shocked at their failure to provide service, product failures, abandonment of products, and, yes, the economic collapse of the company itself. On April 11, 1991, Executive Life of California was placed in conservatorship by the insurance commissioner of the state and the world learned a new lesson. Even when you are dealing with large insurance companies, company selection is important to your economic health. When you consider that there are over 1,800 life insurance companies to choose from and 125 of them do 85 percent of the business, you can understand why a substantial reduction in the number of companies is inevitable. Within the last five years more than 500 companies have disappeared due to failure, merger, and purchase by bigger companies.

How do you protect yourself against potential insurance company failure? Deal only with the biggest and the best—those who have been in business for many years. Avoid those whose portfolios are obviously taking exceptional risk in order to earn higher yields and/or avoid the general accounts of insurance companies entirely by using their separate accounts. A number of public sources of information seek to protect you against insurance company insolvency by providing assistance to help you know about your chosen insurance company.

STATE REGULATION

Insurance companies primarily are regulated by the individual states. Assuming the insurance companies that you have chosen are licensed to do business within your resident state, you have the one level of protection. You may assume that your state insurance department has examined the company and its products and found them to be in compliance with state regulations. Unfortunately, this first level of protection isn't always reliable. Despite state regulations, insurance companies have failed and caused economic harm to their clients. William H. Smythe, executive director of the National Association of Insurance Commissioners (NAIC) securities valuation office in New York, once said, "We regulators don't have the authority to tell guys how to run their businesses. We almost have to wait for a disaster to happen, when it comes down to it."

The state does, however, collect information about companies doing business within the state that can be of value. Items such as the company's annual Convention Statements and Schedule M should be available upon request and will give you the information the company is providing to the regulators regarding its financial condition and the assumptions used in their illustrations. If you have a concern about an insurance company, call your state insurance commissioner's office and ask questions. Your call may trigger action that saves you and perhaps someone else from economic harm, so do not be reluctant to make it.

The states vary in the quality and quantity of their regulation. New York State is noted for being the toughest within the industry. Many people say that New York is too conservative and difficult, but a restrictive approach can be an advantage to you as you try to pick an insurance company that will be a survivor in these volatile times. Ask if the company in question is licensed to do business in New York. If it is and it has agreed to follow New York rules wherever they do business, you have the first level of assurance from the New York regulators in addition to those of your own state. A relatively small minority of the companies you have to choose from are licensed in New York.

NATIONAL ASSOCIATION OF INSURANCE COMMISSIONERS (NAIC)

Each state has a commissioner of insurance. The commissioners gather together to work out mutual problems in the National Association of Commissioners. They have proposed model legislation to try to deal more effectively with the solvency of insurance companies.

A most important model law that the commissioners have proposed and passed in many states is the Risk-Based Capital (RBC) Model Law. It is intended to replace what was considered to be the arbitrary and ineffective minimum capital requirements that were found in many states.

RISK-BASED CAPITAL (RBC)

A recent standard set up by these regulators was a definition of a company's "total adjusted capital," a company's assets minus liabilities (net worth) with some adjustments. This enables all companies to report to the NAIC their adjusted capital in a standardized manner that will allow the commissioners to compare the capital the company does have in reserve to the capital the NAIC has determined the company needs to have in reserve.

The "amount they need" standard is risk-based capital (RBC), which is determined by a complex formula that primarily is determined (two-thirds weighting) by the company's asset risk. Higher amounts of capital are required in reserve for assets that the company owns that are considered more volatile or risky. For example, a company needs 100 times more capital to hold common stocks than it does to hold AAA government bonds. You can see that the NAIC values low-volatility, low-risk assets more than it values "return."

Other factors that influence the amount of a company's NAIC-determined risk-based capital amount are interest rate risk, business risk, and insurance risk. (You need 233 times the amount of capital to write noncancelable premium business than you need for life insurance.)

The company's reported total adjusted capital (what the company has) is then compared to the NAIC-determined risk-based capital (what the NAIC formula says the company should have) by dividing what they have by what they should have and coming up with a ratio called the *risk-based capital ratio*. If the ratio is 125 percent or more, NAIC is happy. However, if it is less than 125 percent, certain regulatory requirements are automatically required as listed here:

Ratio	Red Flag Zone—Regulatory Action
124% or less and trend is negative	File RBC Plan and projections for approval
Less than 100%	Company Action Zone—Submit Plan
Less than 75%	Regulatory Action Zone—Corrective Order
Less than 50% Receivership	Authorized Control Zone—Regulatory (optional)
Less than 35%	Mandatory Control Zone—Receivership within 90 Days

The National Association of Insurance Commissioners, through the risk-based capital model legislation is telling insurance companies that they must reduce risk (and thus return) in their general accounts.

Guess what? The model law says the numbers are confidential . . . you can't know them, and agents can't talk about them. A gag rule prohibits "any insurer, agent, broker, or other person engaged in any manner in the insurance business from disseminating . . . directly or indirectly any RBC data." This is all regulatory silliness because you can easily find out your company's RBC ratio. *The Insurance Forum, The Wall Street Journal, USA Today,* and so on are not "in the insurance business" so they can pass along the information that the regulators have made you interested in by making it "confidential." Of 3,624 insurance companies of all types reporting in 1994, only 140 were below the 125 percent level.

You will find that there may not be much correlation between a company's RBC ratio and its financial ratings by the following rating services. The better rating services go beyond the numbers in the risk-based capital ratio when evaluating companies so you should use the RBC ratio only in conjunction with the ratings provided by the credible rating services.

THE RATING SERVICES

The rating services listed in Table 12–1 have enjoyed substantial growth and attention during the last 10 years as the financial vulnerability of insurance companies has been dramatically demonstrated by the failure of companies like Executive Life, Mutual Benefit Life, Capitol Life, and Confederation Life. As you review the discussion that follows regarding the ratings that have been assigned to companies and what they mean, keep in mind that no single rating service has a particularly good track record for giving you significant warning of the imminent failure of any company.

One way to overcome this weakness in the rating system is to know not only the current ratings but know whether the ratings for that company are going up or down. Make sure you understand the reasons for any movement down the rating scales.

A. M. Best Company

One source of public information is the A. M. Best Company of Oldwick, New Jersey, one of the oldest insurance industry rating services. This company provides information regarding an insurance company's financial condition, a synopsis of its history, and information on its management, operating commitments, and the states in which it may write business. A. M. Best Company

TABLE 12-1

Comparison of Insurance Rating Services

	A. M. Best	Moody's	Standard & Poor's CPA	S&P Qualified	Duff & Phelps	Weiss
Secure	A++, A+ Superior A	Aaa, Aa1, Aa2,Aa3 A1,S2,A3	AAA, AA+, AA AA-, A+,A, A-	AAA, AA BBBq A BBB BBq	AAA, AA+ AA	A+, A, A- B+, B, B-
	A- Excellent B++, B+ Very good	Baa1, Baa2, Baa3 Ba1, Ba2, Ba3	BBB+, BBB,BBB-		AA-, A+, A, A-, BBB+, BBB, BBB-	B, B-, C++, C, C-
Vulnerable	B, B- Adequate C++ C+ Fair C, C- Marginal D Very vulnerable E Under state supervision F In liquidation	B1,B2,B3 Caa, Ca, C	BB+, BB, BB- B+, B, B- CCC R	BB B CCC Bq	B+, B,B- CCC DD	D+,D,D- E+ E,E- F

also grants its own ratings to companies, designed to reflect strength and weaknesses in four areas: underwriting, expense control, reserve adequacy, and investments.

In most cases you would be wise to place your trust in companies rated A or better by A. M. Best. Some critics question the integrity and value of the Best ratings, claiming that the information on which the ratings are based may be too old and that insurance companies have the ability to pressure Best for better ratings. Best, of course, vigorously defends its integrity and objectivity. For you, Best is only one source of information regarding the ability of an insurance company to make good on its promises. The A. M. Best Company may be contacted directly at Ambest Road, Oldwick, New Jersey 08858.

Figure 12–1, provided by Best, shows the meaning of the A.M. Best rating classifications. You will find the Best reports in your local library. Use only the most current book. Many insurance companies and agents also can provide summaries of the Best reports regarding the companies they are recommending to you.

Standard & Poor's

Standard & Poor's has a service that rates a modest number of companies on their *claims paying ability (CPA)*. Major employers trying to find a source for guaranteed interest contracts for their retirement plans would use this service to evaluate the financial strength of competing insurance companies. An insurance company wishing to be rated by Standard & Poor's Corporation pays about $20,000 to obtain a rating. If the company is dissatisfied with the rating S&P has given them, it has the option of instructing S&P not to publish it. Approximately 256 life and health insurance companies have purchased a CPA rating. The S&P ratings may be modified by the addition of a plus or minus sign, and are interpreted as shown in Figure 12–2 provided by S&P.

Note that a company could have an A+ rating from S&P and be in the fifth level of their ratings. You easily could be misled if you assumed that this A+ rating was a Best's second rating. If you use these ratings in your decision making, know what they mean and how they vary.

FIGURE 12–1

Best's Rating Classifications

Secure Ratings

AA+ and A+ (Superior)

Assigned to companies that, in our opinion, have demonstrated superior overall performance when compared to the standards established by the A.M. Best Company. A++ and A+ companies have a very strong ability to meet their obligations to policy holders over a long period of time.

A and A– (Excellent)

Assigned to companies that, in our opinion, have demonstrated excellent overall performance when compared to the standards established by the A.M. Best Company. A and A– companies have a strong ability to meet their obligations to policy holders over a long period of time.

B++ and B+ (Very Good)

Assigned to companies that, in our opinion, have achieved good overall performance when compared to the standards established by the A. M. Best Company. B++ and B– companies have a good ability to meet their obligations to policy holders over a long period of time.

Vulnerable Ratings

B and B– (Adequate)

Assigned to companies that, in our opinion, have demonstrated adequate overall performance when compared to the standards established by the A.M. Best Company. B and B– companies generally have an adequate ability to meet their obligations to policy holders, but their financial strength is vulnerable to unfavorable changes in underwriting or economic conditions.

C++ and C+ (Fair)

Assigned to companies that, in our opinion, have demonstrated fair overall performance when compared to the standards established by the A.M. Best Company. C++ and C+ companies generally have a current ability to meet their obligations to policy holders, but their financial strength is vulnerable to unfavorable changes in underwriting or economic conditions.

C and C– (Marginal)

Assigned to companies that, in our opinion, have demonstrated marginal overall performance when compared to the standards established by the A.M. Best Company. C and C– companies have a current ability to meet their

Best's Rating Classifications (Concluded)

obligations to policy holders, but their financial strength is very vulnerable to unfavorable changes in underwriting or economic conditions.

D (Very Vulnerable)
Assigned to companies that, in our opinion, have demonstrated poor overall performance when compared to the standards established by the A.M. Best Company. D companies have a current ability to meet their obligations to policy holders, but their financial strength is extremely vulnerable to unfavorable changes in underwriting or economic conditions.

E (Under State Supervision)
Assigned to companies that are placed by a state insurance regulatory authority under any form of supervision, control or restraint, such as conservatorship or rehabilitation, but does not include liquidation. May be assigned to a company under a cease and desist order issued by a regulator from a state other than its state of domicile.

F (In Liquidation)
Assigned to companies that have been placed under an order of liquidation by a court of law or whose owners have voluntarily agreed to liquidate. Note: Companies that voluntarily liquidate or dissolve their charters are generally not insolvent.

Used with permission of A. M. Best Company.

Standard & Poor's Quantitative Analysis Service

This new service is based solely on quantitative analysis of public information. To obtain these ratings on the approximately 810 companies for which S&P has prepared ratings, call 212–208–1527; call 800–997–9191 for a faxed report. The spread of ratings among the 810 companies rated in August 1995 was as follows.

Secure	AAA	47	4.4%	
	AA	150	14.1%	"A" 32.3%
	A	147	13.8%	
	BBB	369	34.6%	
Vulnerable	BB	226	21.2%	
	B	106	9.9%	
	CCC	21	2.0%	

FIGURE 12–2

Ratings by Standard & Poor's Corporation

Secure Claims-Paying Ability Ratings:

AAA	*Superior* financial security on an absolute and relative basis. Capacity to meet policy holder obligations is overwhelming under a variety of economic and underwriting conditions.
AA+ AA AA–	*Excellent* financial security. Capacity to meet policy holder obligations is strong under a variety of economic and underwriting conditions.
A+ A	*Good* financial security, but capacity to meet policy holder obligations is somewhat susceptible to adverse economic and underwriting conditions.
BBB+ BBB BBB–	*Adequate* financial security, but capacity to meet policy holder obligations is susceptible to adverse economic and underwriting conditions.

Vulnerable Claims-Paying Ability Ratings:

BB+ BB BB–	Financial security *may be adequate,* but capacity to meet policy holder obligations, particularly with respect to long-term or "long-tail" policies is vulnerable to adverse economic and underwriting conditions.
B+ B B–	*Vulnerable* financial security. Currently able to meet policy holder obligations, but capacity to meet policy holder obligations is particularly vulnerable to adverse conditions and underwriting conditions.
CCC	*Extremely vulnerable* financial security. Continued capacity to meet policy holder obligations is highly questionable unless favorable economic and underwriting conditions prevail.
R	*Regulatory action.* As of the date indicated, the insurer is under supervision of insurance regulators following rehabilitation, receivership, liquidation, or any other action that reflects regulatory concern about the insurer's financial condition. Information on this status is provided by the National Association of Insurance Commissioners and other regulatory bodies. Although believed to be accurate, this information is not guaranteed. The R rating does not apply to insurers subject only to nonfinancial actions such as market conduct violations.

Qualified Solvency Ratings:

BBBq	Statistical tests indicate adequate or better financial security.
Bbq	Statistical tests indicate that financial security *may be adequate.*
Bq	Statistical tests indicate *vulnerable* financial security.

Used with permission of Standard and Poor's; taken from *Standard and Poor's Insurance Ratings Focus,* Vol. 4, Number 2, April-June 1995.

Moody's

Moody's concentrates more heavily on the quality of the company's investment portfolio. This company is located at 99 Church Street, New York, New York 10007. Moody's ratings, like S&P's, generally are not available unless the insurance company chooses to make them available to you. Figure 12–3 describes Moody's ratings.

Duff & Phelps

Duff & Phelps (55 East Monroe Street, Chicago, IL 60603) provides an overall approach in its credit ratings and has a reputation of quality and integrity. The Duff & Phelps ratings apply to corporate debt, preferred stock, real estate, asset-backed financing, and the insurance company's claims-paying ability. Its evaluation process includes an insurance company management interview, quantitative analysis, and a view of the company's future. The ratings, not shown at the request of Duff & Phelps, are updated quarterly in an effort to make the material more timely. The D&P ratings probably will be obtainable from the insurance companies that have contracted for their services and are listed in the Morningstar reports on variable annuities and variable life insurance.

Weiss Ratings, Inc.

The Weiss ratings provide financial safety ratings based primarily on publicly filed information, as gathered and published by the National Association of Insurance Commissioners (NAIC). Ratings are published quarterly every year, based on official data filed by each company. Weiss also sends surveys to every company each year to facilitate inclusion of additional information beyond the NAIC statistics. The majority of companies return the surveys with requested information. Unlike other rating agencies, Weiss is not paid by the companies that are rated. Income is generated by the sale of ratings, reports and adjunct materials directly to consumers.

The March/April 1995 issue of *The Insurance Forum* reported the spread of Weiss Ratings on 1,482 life and health insurance companies were:

	Companies	%
A+, A, A–	66	45.0%
B+, B, B–	309	20.9%
C+, C, C–	583	39.3%
D+, D, D–	434	29.3%
E+, E, E–	90	6.1%

When you compare this bell-shaped curve to the percentages in the A category from S&P (97.7%), Moody's (90.9%) and A.M. Best (65.1%), it is obvious that Weiss is a tougher grader, which Weiss says reflects its independence from insurance companies. These ratings are decribed in Figure 12–4.

Rating Services Miss Confederation Life

Confederation Life was seized by the regulators on August 12, 1994. The rating services generally did not see the failure coming. A.M. Best first downgraded the company from A+ to A June 21, 1993, then to A– April 14, 1994, and to B++ on August 4, 1994. Standard & Poors lowered Confederation Life's rating to "A+ on credit watch with negative implications" on April 14, 1994. Duff & Phelps rated the company "AA– Rating watch-down" on the same day. Weiss Ratings, Inc., downgraded the company's U.S. affiliates from C to C– on June 2, 1994. All these dates are too close to the failure dates of August 12, 1994, for policy owners to have taken action to protect themselves.

The message in this scenario is that you should place more importance in the *direction* of the ratings than the *level* of the ratings in evaluating companies.

Company Annual Reports

A review of the company's financial statements and annual report also is in order. These annual reports are readily available from each insurance company and you definitely should ask for them. At least read the president's letter. It should help you determine what is going well for the company and what is going poorly. Obviously, you want products and services that are doing well because they will receive the resources and attention of the company. Poorly performing products and services are likely to

FIGURE 12–3

Ratings by Moody's Investors Service

	Strong Companies:
Aaa	*Exceptional.* Insurance companies rated Aaa offer exceptional security. Although the financial strength of these companies is likely to change, such changes as can be visualized are most unlikely to impair their fundamentally strong position.
Aa	*Excellent.* Insurance companies rated Aa offer excellent financial security. Together with the Aaa group they constitute what are generally known as high-grade companies. They are rated lower than Aaa companies because long-term risks appear somewhat larger.
A	*Good.* Insurance companies rated A offer good financial security. However, elements may be present that suggest a susceptibility to impairment sometime in the future.
Baa	*Adequate.* Insurance companies rated Baa offer adequate financial security. However, certain protective elements may be lacking or may be characteristically unreliable over any great length of time.
	Weak Companies:
Ba	*Questionable.* Insurance companies rated Ba offer questionable financial security. Often the ability of these companies to meet senior policy holder claims and obligations may be moderate and thereby not well safeguarded in the future.
B	*Poor.* Insurance companies rated B offer poor financial security. Assurance of punctual payment of senior policy holder obligations over any long period of time is small.
Caa	*Very poor.* Insurance companies rated Caa offer very poor financial security. They may be in default on their senior policy holder obligations or there may be present elements of danger with respect to punctual payment of senior policy holder claims and obligations.
Ca	*Extremely poor.* Insurance companies rated Ca offer extremely poor financial security. Such companies are often in default on their policy holder obligations or have other marked shortcomings.
C	*Lowest.* Insurance companies rated C are the lowest rated class of insurance company and can be regarded as having extremely poor prospects of ever offering financial security.

Note: Moody's applies numerical modifiers to refer to the ranking within generic rating groups from Aa to B—1 being the highest and 3 being the lowest. Ratings can be letters without modifiers.

Used with permission of Moody's Investors Service.

FIGURE 12–4

Ratings by Weiss Ratings, Inc.

A+   *Excellent.* This company offers excellent financial security. It has
A   maintained a conservative stance in its investment strategies,
A–   business operations, and underwriting commitments. Although the
          financial position of any company is subject to change, we believe
          that this company has the resources necessary to deal with severe
          economic conditions.

B+   *Good.* This company offers good financial security and has the
B   resources to deal with a variety of adverse economic conditions.
B–   However, in the event of a *severe* recession or major financial crisis,
          we feel this assessment should be reviewed to make sure that the
          firm is still maintaining adequate financial strength.

C+   *Fair.* This company offers fair financial security and is currently
C   stable. But during an economic downturn or other financial
C–   pressures, we feel it may encounter difficulties in maintaining its
          financial stability.

D+   *Weak.* This company currently demonstrates what we consider to be
D   significant weaknesses that could negatively impact policy holders. In
D–   an unfavorable economic environment, these weaknesses could be
          magnified.

E+   *Very Weak.* This company currently demonstrates what we consider
E   to be significant weaknesses and has also failed some of the basic
E–   tests that we use to identify fiscal stability. Therefore, even in a
          favorable economic environment, it is our opinion that policy holders
          could incur significant risks.

F   *Failed.* Company is under the supervision of state insurance
          commissioners.

U   *Unrated Companies.* This company is unrated for one or more of the
          following reasons: (1) total assets are less than $1 million, (2)
          premium income for the current year was less than $100,000, or (3)
          the company functions almost exclusively as a holding company
          rather than as an underwriter.

Note: An S preceding the rating designates small companies—those with less than $25 million in capital and surplus. The S designation is not used for companies with more than $500 million in admitted assets, irrespective of the amount of capital and surplus.

Used with permission of Weiss Ratings, Inc.

receive less enthusiastic attention or be cut from the company's product line. Scan the remainder of the report for information pertinent to the sector of the company in which you are interested. Do not miss the footnotes—often, the most important warnings appear in footnotes.

Caution: The bottom line is that you can't know everything. The information you obtain will inevitably be dated. If an insurance company is trying to fool you and the regulators, it is likely that you will find out too late. For this reason, you should continue to use the separate account products and to work with the biggest and the best insurance companies. A company whose primary focus is not insurance will find it very easy to rid itself of an underperforming insurance subsidiary.

If your agent leaves the insurance business, you are referred to as an "orphan" until a new agent is assigned to you. If the company you have your policy with is sold or ceases to exist, you also become an orphan. Both situations are likely to be detrimental to your economic health, so choose both agent and company with care.

STATE GUARANTEE ASSOCIATIONS

There are state guarantee associations in all 50 states. When an insurance company fails, the association will make an assessment against all insurance companies doing business in the state to minimize the losses of the policy owners. When Baldwin-United (whose primary business was piano making) failed in 1983, the life insurance industry and regulators worked diligently for five years to contain the damage. Those who owned Baldwin-United contracts endured five years of uncertainty about their investments. They finally did receive a settlement that generally covered the principal the insureds had invested but not the exorbitant interest rates they had been promised. You certainly couldn't say that they did not suffer a loss!

Companies that promise unachievable interest rates take business away from honest companies, and then leave a mess when they fail, such as Executive Life, Mutual Benefit, and Confederation Life. Informed taxpayers are objecting to these practices in the banking and savings & loan industries. Eventually, the same reaction will occur in the insurance industry. Responsible insurance companies cannot, and eventually will not, absorb insurance company failures at the expense of their own contract owners and stockholders. You, the consumer, must consider carefully the creditworthiness of the general accounts of the insurance companies into which you are entrusting your funds. In short: Don't bet on state guarantee funds, mergers, acquisitions, and reorganizations in the insurance industry to bail you out of a failing company.

The typical guarantee covers up to $100,000 in annuity benefits and $300,000 in all lines, life, health, and annuities. Insurance contracts are *not* actually guaranteed by the state and in many states it is against the law for an agent to even mention the guarantee association. In others, agents must get a signed statement at time of application that the purchaser understands that the contract is not backed by the "full faith and credit" of the state. There is **no state** money in the state guarantee association to serve as a guarantee of annuity benefits. All funding comes from the insurance companies doing business in the state.

JOSEPH M. BELTH

Joseph M. Belth, Ph.D., is a retired professor of insurance from Indiana University and the publisher of a monthly publication called *The Insurance Forum*. He has been referred to as the Ralph Nader of the insurance industry. He exhibits a bulldog-like tenacity in his pursuit of financial information on insurance companies in order to keep consumers and financial professionals informed. He is not the least bit hesitant to point out the companies that he believes are involved in questionable practices. His monthly publication can be obtained by writing to: *The Insurance Forum*, P.O. Box 245, Ellettsville, IN 47429.

Within *The Insurance Forum*, it has been Dr. Belth's practice to publish a list of insurance companies with their risk-based capital ratio and financial ratings from A.M. Best, S&P, Moody's, D&P, and Weiss. You may request his most current list by mailing your request along with a stamped, self-addressed envelope to the address just given.

Professor Belth is a controversial source of information. He has the courage to express his opinions in no uncertain terms, and consequently many take issue with him. However, he does give the background data that leads him to his conclusions. This helps you understand the issues and risks involved so that you can make more informed purchase decisions. Table 12–2 was prepared by *The Insurance Forum* to help everyone understand where companies rank based on all the popular rating services.

TABLE 12-2

RATING CATEGORIES*

	Ratings				
Rank	**S&P**	**Moody's**	**D&P**	**Weisst**	**Best**
1	AAA	Aaa	AAA	A+	A++
2	AA+	Aa1	AA+	A	A+
3	AA	Aa2	AA	A–	A
4	AA–	Aa3	AA–	B+	A–
5	A+	A1	A+	B	B++
6	A–	A2	A	B—	B+
7	A–	A3	A–	C+	B
8	BBB+	Baa1	BBB+	C	B–
9	BBB	Baa2	BBB	C–	C++
10	BBB–	Baa3	BBB–	D+	C+
11	BB+	Ba1	BB+	D	C
12	BB	Bs2	BB	D–	C–
13	BB–	Ba3	BB–	E+	D
14	B+	B1	B+	E	E
15	B	B2	B	E–	F
16	B–	B3	B–	F	
17	CCC	Caa	CCC		
18	R	Ca	DD		
19		C			

*The rating categories in a given rank are not equivalent to one another. See the descriptions of the rating categories from the rating companies.

†Weiss uses the letter S immediately preceding the rating to designate "smaller companies."

OTHER FACTORS IN CHOOSING THE INSURER, PRODUCT, AND AGENT

Product Impact on Company Selection

Another important factor in company selection is the product line offered by the company you are considering. Some multiline companies will provide for both the property and casualty needs of individuals and companies, as well as the life, annuity, and health insurance needs. However, it is unusual for one insurance professional to have expertise in all of these fields though there are, of course, exceptions. There are many partnerships of property/casualty and life agents who combine their expertise to serve their clients. Most insurance companies are oriented toward property/casualty or toward life, annuity, and health. One rule of thumb to remember is that the company you choose should have a sufficiently diverse product line so that if one of its products is legislated out of existence, the company does not fail with it, leaving you "orphaned." Diversification of product lines provides a degree of safety and flexibility for insurance companies just as it does for individuals.

You want to avoid the risk that the insurance product you select may fail to perform as promised. This can happen not only as the result of insurance company insolvency but also because the product becomes unprofitable and the company decides to divest itself of the unprofitable unit.

Company Selection Involves Intermediary Selection

Whoever you use to help you obtain an insurance company contract can greatly influence your product selection and satisfaction. You should learn to distinguish the "client-oriented" salesperson from the "product" salesperson. The product salesperson develops an expertise and an efficient marketing plan for a specific "hot product." Product specialists can be used to your advantage because of their comprehensive knowledge of that specific product. However, it could be to your disadvantage if the "hot product" is sold to you as a solution for a problem you don't have. For example, a single premium life policy is not appropriate for every insured. In 1986-87, such policies were sold indiscriminately by "hot product" salespeople who marketed them more for the salespeople's personal wealth enhancement than for the benefit of their clients.

On the other hand, highly technical products such as pension plans, profit-sharing plans, 401(k)s, and other qualified plans may be more efficiently handled and serviced by product specialists. Frequently, a client-oriented generalist works jointly with a product specialist to make sure you get adequate service and technical assistance with specialized products.

You need to understand the type of person with whom you are working so that you can determine his or her role in your risk management process. The choice is yours. Don't think that hiring a qualified, empathetic salesperson is an admission of naiveté as the press may have you believe. Can you do it alone? If so, can you do it better than if you had hired the proper salesperson? Exactly what would the salesperson cost you?

Know what *you* are paying the salesperson. How much of the money transferred to the insurance company was allocated to pay the salesperson? In these days of contingent deferred sales load products, you often will find that the salesperson receives more commission dollars than are actually subtracted from your funds in the first year. This is because the insurance company advances the pay to the salesperson and plans on recouping this expense from profits on your product throughout the years you keep your business with the company. If you keep the business with the insurer long enough, it is all recouped and you will be charged no contingent deferred sales charge after that point. However, if you take your business away from the insurer too soon and it is unable to recoup these expenses, it will charge you a contingent deferred sales charge or back-end load. It is really a rather fair and economical way to pay for the services of good salespeople. If you choose to pay salespeople simply because they are persistent rather than helpful, it is a waste and is nobody's fault but your own. In short: Know who you are buying from, what you are paying him or her, and why.

Front-end loaded products are still prevalent in today's insurance industry. Expenses in the various products vary greatly, yet consumers and financial advisors still look at 10- and 20-year projections that distract them from what is really important—the *initial* expenses taken from funds that limit the amount of money that can go to work for them in the product. Avoid front-end loads to whatever extent possible, and by all means know how much of your money is going to be working for you in the product in the early years. If the company treats you fairly in the early years, it is more likely to treat you just as fairly in the later years. You can check performance by comparing results annually.

Financial journalists like to debate the need for intermediaries. They contend, "Read our magazine or column and you will not have to pay salespeople." Some in the industry suggest that you are best served by dealing directly with a company like USAA that markets by direct mail and referral in order to avoid the salesperson's commission. Alternatively, you have the choice of dealing with the no-load companies that market directly to the public, or in some cases to financial planners who then add an independent charge for acting as your intermediary. Do not be deceived. You pay marketing expenses whether they are incurred by paying commissions to salespeople or by direct mail, high advertising costs or fees to those who find you a product.

If you are going to hire a salesperson or other intermediary, that person should have the education, integrity, and expertise to be your staff employee—preferably someone who has special expertise in your area of need. Interview potential salespeople looking for those qualities. There are approximately 400,000 insurance agents eager to serve you, so you needn't give the business to the first one who knocks on your door. Keep in mind that fewer than one-third of those 400,000 are even properly licensed to sell you all the products mentioned in this book. If someone makes negative statements abouta particular product make sure it is actually because of the product, rather than just because the salesperson is not licensedto sell it.

Paying for the Product and Service

Understand that you will pay for the sales process. Even if a product is supposedly "no-load," there is a cost to bring that product to your attention, and you pay that cost. No-loads and low-loads typically have substantial marketing costs and can be expected to use advertising more than companies that employ a sales force. Companies that market to independent agents do so with good products and services and also with high commission promises and loss-leader interest rates that they do not intend to maintain. Which is your agent recommending to you—the superior product or the higher commission product?

Common wisdom used to suggest that you would be better served dealing with a "broker" or independent than you would be with a "captive" agent. The former would have access to all products available from all companies to choose from on your behalf, whereas the latter would have access only to those products provided by the company that employed him.

This theory never worked well because all insurance salespeople, captive or independent, are limited in their capacity to know everything about every product available. Now, more than ever, insureds must question the promises made by the product providers and limit their product search to companies they trust.

The distinction between the independent and captive insurance agent is irrelevant when you consider registered products, that is, those that are related to the securities market and sold with a prospectus. These stock- and bond-based products are provided to a salesperson through a "broker-dealer" or parent organization that screens the products before they are sold. Most broker-dealers insist that their salespeople sell only the securities-based products that the dealers have preapproved, which means that the salesperson's broker-dealer affiliation limits the products that the salesperson can offer.

The Shopping Process

The Intermediary

Your first cut is the agent or intermediary. Interview a number of them. Find out what products they are licensed to sell. Ask them questions about their background, their approach to the business, their present educational credentials, and those that they expect to attain in the future. If the agents that you are interviewing are relatively new in the business, find out what backup services are available to them. Ask to whom they go for help in a difficult case and, if you think you'll be needing them, ask to meet those individuals also.

Financial planners like to have quality insurance professionals available to them. Certified Financial Planners and Chartered Financial Consultants will look for insurance professionals with educational credentials comparable to their own in the insurance field. They will look for a Chartered Life Underwriter (CLU), who has received his or her designation from the American College in Bryn Mawr, Pennsylvania. CLUs must have completed 10 semester courses and 10 examinations over approximately a 5-year period in order to attain this designation. Certified Financial Planners and Chartered Financial Consultants also have had education in the personal risk management area. If the agent that you are interviewing has taken any of these advanced courses, it indicates two things that are advantageous to you. First, that the individual is committed and capable of taking and passing such exams; second, that the agent is committed to learning more in order to serve you better. The agent has, in effect, worked to become qualified to serve as your insurance consultant.

When you find a person that meets your requirements, with whom you can communicate and who can obtain the insurance products that you want, it will not matter how you pay that individual for the insurance services. Integrity is not purchased by paying an individual consultant fees rather than commissions. It's up to you to choose an individual to work with who has integrity and a professional approach to serve your best interest rather than his or her own. It will be up to you to sense the presence or the absence of such integrity. That is why the interview is so important.

Most of us need help in selecting and managing insurance products. We will pay for this help one way or the other. Seek the best qualified help you can find because poorly designed insurance is detrimental to your economic health, whereas properly owned, designed, funded, and managed insurance products are productive and valuable in enhancing your family's financial security.

If you decide to obtain your products without help by going directly to the company, you'll have to know what you are doing or it's liable to be more costly than hiring help will. Part of your evaluation of the intermediary will be the companies and the products that individual recommends to you. If they are not up to the standards you have studied in this book, you probably should find another intermediary.

CONCLUSION

Once you have found a company, product, line, and intermediary (or no intermediary), you are in an excellent position to compare costs and benefits. The objective at the outset of this book was to give you the tools to manage the products you purchase from insurance companies profitably and efficiently. By now, I hope you are able to do just that. With the tools provided herein, you are the new sophisticated consumer. You know the questions to ask and the benefits to demand. You know that when you are offered choices within the various insurance company products, your basic rule of thumb will be to:

- Know the costs built into the product, especially in the early years.

- Establish long-term relationships with quality insurance companies and quality intermediaries.

- Choose control over no control.

- Choose flexibility over inflexibility.

- Choose quality over current or future interest rate promises.

- Choose a survivor among insurance companies and intermediaries.

- Accept the fact that assets within insurance contracts require your management just as does every other asset on your balance sheet.

- Demand disclosure of the intermediary's compensation before purchase. Vigilance pays.

Life insurance and annuity contracts that are carefully purchased and well-managed are wonderful wealth-building and wealth-preserving vehicles. The basic truth is that you can do almost everything you can do with CDs, stocks, bonds, and mutual funds within life insurance and annuity products today and at the same time protect the return on those investments from being diminished by current income taxes.

♦♦♦♦♦

Insurance company selection involves using the same research techniques, tempered with good common sense, that you would use in making any other major purchase in your life. You cannot know everything about a company. Formulas don't always work and available information is not always current or reliable. This doesn't mean that you should despair. Many of the people who have been disappointed with product or company performance are the same people who demanded performance beyond what could reasonably be obtained. They bought from the first person or company who, in order to make a sale, told them what they wanted to hear. The results are inevitable—failure to perform.

Be a skeptic. If you are offered a product that sounds too good to be true, ask some of your knowledgeable friends or advisors about it. They may not be able to refute directly the claims of the salespeople; however, if it does not pass "the smell test" or if it defies "economic gravity," don't suppose you are getting a special deal because someone loves you.

Finally, when you are dealing with professional insurance intermediaries, your most effective questions are, "What would you do to solve this problem if you were in my shoes?," "Why?," "How have you handled this need for yourself?," and "Show me!" These questions put a good deal of pressure on the professional, and it is likely that the way in which they are answered will help you judge if the two all-important qualities—personal integrity and empathy—are present. If they are not, do not do business with that intermediary.

INDEX